museums and monuments XIV

Titles in this series:

preserving and restoring monuments and historic buildings

unesco paris 1972

1972 International
Book Year

Published in 1972 by the United Nations
Educational, Scientific and Cultural Organization
Place de Fontenoy, 75 Paris-7ᵉ
Printed by Arts graphiques Coop Suisse

LC No. 73–189463

Preface

Civilizations throughout the world have, over the centuries, raised monuments which express the ideals, aspirations and beliefs of peoples in material form. Many have survived to the present time and bear witness to the long span of human history and the varied contributions of the past to the present. Today, demographic and economic changes threaten, as never before, the survival of our cultural heritage. The growing interest in the conservation of sites and buildings of artistic importance was demonstrated by the adoption on 19 November 1968, at the fifteenth session of the Unesco General Conference, of an international Recommendation concerning the Preservation of Cultural Property endangered by Public and Private Works. Here is eloquent testimony of the concern felt about one of the most important threats to our cultural heritage.

Deliberate programmes for the conservation of sites and monuments are a relatively recent phenomenon. In several countries conservation services have existed for, at the most, about a hundred years. During this period, principles have evolved, and new techniques have developed. The results, however, are not widely known, and experience gained in solving the preservation problems of a given monument has rarely been profitably used in comparable situations elsewhere. The present manual could not hope to be so encyclopaedic as to describe all the results obtained in all countries, but an attempt has been made to cover typical problems and techniques and so help the reader to profit from the experience of a number of specialists.

The Conservation of Cultural Property (Number XI in this series) should be used in conjunction with this publication as it deals in detail with problems and solutions in the preservation of building materials such as stone, wood, brick and glass. A new manual on the preservation and development of historic municipalities or historic quarters, and the social and economic problems which affect the quality of the urban environment, will be published in 1972.

The preservation and restoration of monuments are frequently ensured through legislation and national services. On the other hand, rapid growth of urban populations and the rise in real estate values have resulted in the condemnation and replacement of many historically or artistically interesting buildings which are not considered to be valuable enough to warrant the protection of the State. Their replacement by parking lots or high-rise structures leads to increased population density and a banal city-scape. A counter-movement is taking place in which older buildings are being adapted to meet contemporary requirements and provide standards of comfort which will ensure a more varied city-scape and lower density of occupation. Principles and techniques described here may serve as a guide to individuals interested in such programmes.

The opinions expressed are those of the authors and do not necessarily reflect the views of Unesco.

Contents

List of illustrations

The authors

CONNALLY, Ernest Allen

B.Arch., University of Texas (1950); Ph.D., Harvard University (1955); Assistant Professor of Architecture, Miami University, Oxford, Ohio (1952–55); Associate Professor of Architecture, Washington University, St. Louis (1955–57); Associate Professor (1957–61) and Professor (1961–67); Associate Professor (1957–61) and Professor (1961–67), University of Illinois; Chief, Office of Archaeology and Historic Preservation, United States National Park Service, Washington, D.C. (1967–).

DAIFUKU, Hiroshi

B.A., University of Hawaii (1942); Ph.D., Harvard University (1951); Instructor, cultural anthropology, University of Wisconsin (1949–52); Assistant Curator, State Historical Society Museum, Madison, Wisconsin (1952–53); Unesco: Programme Specialist, Development of Museums (1954–62), Preservation of Cultural Property (1962–66), Chief, Section for the Development of the Cultural Heritage (1967–).

FORAMITTI, Hans

Eng./Arch., Technical University of Vienna (1952); Dr.Eng. (1958); Assistant, History of Architecture, Upper Technical School, Vienna (1953–54); Director for testing programmes and industry (1955–57); Librarian (1957–61); Curator, Department of Architecture, Federal Service for Historic Monuments (Bundesdenkmalamt) Austria (1961–); Director, Photogrammetry Department and Commissioner General for the application of The Hague Convention in Austria (1967–).

GAZZOLA, Piero

Doctorate in Architecture, Polytechnic of Milan (1932); D.es L., University of Milan (1934); Deputy Architect, Monuments and Galleries, Ministry of Education (1935–50); Superintendent for Monuments and Galleries (1950–55); Programme Specialist, Preservation of Monuments, Unesco (1953–54); Central Inspector, Ministry of Public Education (1955–); Representative of the Government of Italy, on the Council of the Rome Centre (1959–); President of the International Council of Monuments and Sites (1965–).

SANPAOLESI, Piero

D.Eng., University of Florence (1924); B.Arch., University of Florence (1931); Superintendent of Monuments and Galleries (1935–60); Professor of Architecture, Istanbul University (1958); Professor of Restoration, Faculty of Architecture, University of Florence (1960–); Director of the Institute for Restoration of Monumental Buildings, Florence (1960–).

13

SEKINO, Masaru

B.Eng., University of Tokyo (1933); Ph.D. in Architecture, University of Tokyo (1945); Professor of Architectural History, University of Tokyo (1946–69); Chief, Building Section, National Commission for the Protection of Cultural Properties (1950–57, 1961–66); Head, Department of Conservation Science, National Research Institute of Cultural Properties, Tokyo (1952–65); Director of the Institute (1965–).

Piero Gazzola

Restoring monuments: historical background

INTRODUCTION

Many factors contribute towards decisions leading to the restoration of a site or a building and its ultimate preservation as a 'monument'. These decisions, and the legal and administrative actions which follow (e.g. scheduling or classification), have little effect until the concept has seeped through to the general public. Scholarship, and its eventual influence on administrative programmes and on the people, are thus all-important in the preservation of our monuments. The act of restoring is thus a practical expression of judgement and is intimately bound up with the cognitive process it initiates and which in turn directly conditions it. This process, however, like any attempt to penetrate a work of art, is slow and laborious.

Some theorists think it beneath their dignity to explain the qualities of monuments in language which the man in the street can understand; hence his general tendency to ignore their recommendations. And, often, even the more educated are reluctant to give more than an occasional and cursory glance at the work of the historian, who should be their interpreter and guide. Most people imagine that they need only look in order to see; that, to be understood, a work of art does not require the same concentration and analysis as a work of literature; and that awareness and taste can be acquired without intellectual effort, constant application and the most careful

study. This prevailing attitude reduces informed artistic appreciation at all levels in society.

Only in the last hundred years or less has there been any serious research on artistic, as distinct from literary, monuments. A rule-of-thumb approach to restoration has lasted right down to the present day, and has gravely impaired the authenticity of many restored monuments.

Architectural restorations have invariably borne the imprint of their period and of the restorer's personality. From Roman times (e.g. the Teatro di Marcello) down to the first quarter of the present century, the restorer has relentlessly imposed his own idiom on whatever monument he was restoring, so that restoration throughout this period could be described as a sort of outer garment of varying transparency which gave a new appearance to the monument. Restoring a work meant, quite simply, adapting it to fulfil some new function and to satisfy the canons of contemporary taste.

From the Renaissance onwards the restorer, whether he was a Michelangelo or some anonymous engineer, often treated the monument he was working on as raw material to be fashioned into something more elaborate.

During the Renaissance, classical antiquity was regarded as an infallible teacher and a matchless source of inspiration, but almost unbounded admiration for celebrated monuments, its authentic witnesses, did not render them sacrosanct. However lofty their aspirations, however passionate their devotion to the humanities, it is difficult not to feel that, in extolling antiquity, these early classicists were really seeking the admiration of their contemporaries for their own elaboration of the original. Restorers entered into direct competition with the ancient artist whose work they were restoring; a monument challenged them to demonstrate their own creative abilities—even if they did not make additions and alterations to conform to the style of the original. Their work produced admirable proof of artistic skill and originality at various peak periods in the history of art, but is not really restoration though classified as such, but rather new creative activity.

Not all the arts use the same methods. Architecture ranks as an art in the same way as painting and sculpture, but unlike other works of art, buildings, its products, must in addition serve a specific purpose. This requirement conditions both the living significance of architectural monuments and their restoration.

When an architectural monument no longer serves the purpose for which it was built, its conservation ceases to be a practical necessity and becomes a purely cultural task, the importance attributed to which will depend on the cultural maturity of succeeding generations and their sense of the urgency of preserving their cultural heritage.

THE ARCHITECTURAL HERITAGE

The restoration of architectural monuments is particularly complicated. An appreciation of some external and certain unknown factors demands a profound knowledge of history, a true understanding of the present and an ability to anticipate the future.

A monument is more than just the construction itself. It affects and is affected by its setting, and its relations with that setting are intrinsic to its artistic value. Even when standing alone, with no other constructions near, it always forms part of a larger composition, natural or man-made. At the same time, architectural monuments are not merely works of art; they belong by right to a sphere of more complex values, and cannot be judged by aesthetic and historical criteria only. They alone, of all works of art, have to meet the practical test of utility which, in many cases, determines their artistic form. Architecture reflects man's needs in a way no other form of art does, and is thus the most complete and accurate witness to the material and spiritual conditions of an age. This in some ways is a privilege, but it also means that architecture is more exposed than other works of art to

the danger of disfiguring alterations; for it must continue to satisfy man's changing demands.

MAINTAINING ARCHITECTURAL VALUES

Architecture at its best represents a balanced, indissoluble symbiosis of the aesthetic values peculiar to works of art and the material requirements of practical utility.

All operations concerning architectural monuments, whether appraisal, conservation or restoration, must take account of this balance of spiritual and material factors, and to concentrate on the purely formal, artistic aspect to the detriment of the utility aspect, or *vice versa*, would be to reduce to a theoretical abstraction something that is essentially real and living. This is a fact that is only now beginning to be grasped in modern historical criticism and, so far, very few art historians have accepted it. In the past and, indeed, until a few years ago, this coexistence, in architecture, of opposing sets of values was not even suspected. There were two opposing schools of thought: those who regarded architecture as a reflection of the evolution of technology and society; and those for whom an architectural monument, like a picture or a piece of sculpture, was the expression of the feelings and culture of an individual artist. It is therefore not surprising that the foundations are only now being laid for the appraisal of architectural works as a whole, or for embarking upon the as yet unwritten history of architecture.

For lack of these foundations and of a general context within which to regard individual monuments, less progress has been made in ensuring their conservation and restoration than in the case of works of painting or sculpture. When it came to the point, rules laid down often proved to be based on a false and superficial conception of the nature of architectural works, and so remained a dead letter. Yet experience in painting and sculpture shows that principles and practical methods for the restoration of monuments, compatible with historical findings, are both feasible and desirable.

Painting and sculpture, unlike works of architecture, are usually produced wholly by the artist, who both conceives and executes his work in one operation. The greater the freedom a work of art is allowed to express the author's inspiration, the more important it is to respect its integrity. In order to reach this conclusion, aesthetics had first to be freed from its subservience to philosophy, and poetry given sovereign rights and declared independent of other manifestations of reason or sentiment. Poetry in form, like written poetry, is an end in itself even though conceived by its creator to serve an ethical or didactic purpose, or simply to tell a story, to delight the mind or, in some manner, to provoke particular reactions. Even the fact of being a part of another work (as in the case of reliefs, sculptures and mural paintings forming an integral part of an architectural monument) does not imply an aesthetic subordination. But this freedom, the freedom of art, is not to be confused with anarchy: a poetical work is the free expression of the imagination, the feelings and the knowledge of the author, and the relation of the work to the creative inspiration of the author is such as to preclude any interference from without. The ancients did not as a rule restore paintings or sculptures, though there were a few rare cases of frescoes being transferred in the fifteenth and sixteenth centuries.

The purpose of such operations, in fact, was to conserve certain images, not for their aesthetic value but on account of their subject matter and attributes they had acquired over the centuries, as objects of veneration or pilgrimage. This desire to preserve works not for themselves but for what they represented was also the reason for certain measures taken to prolong the life of monuments of particular renown but which, though classified as 'restoration', have absolutely nothing in common with what we today understand by the term.

The one and only purpose in restoring a damaged work was to make the image clear and whole again—essential in order that the particular work might continue to enjoy its traditional prestige and retain its religious and (no less important) its material value.

Such were the motives which both caused restoration to be undertaken, and determined the methods used. The sole consideration, in every case, was to ensure the clear and complete representation of the subject. 'Restoration' carried out on objects of special religious significance, at first extremely rare, became more frequent as time went on. The same criteria were adopted, by analogy, for other works in which the subject-matter was much less important, or not important at all.

This form of 'restoration' consisted merely of replacing what was missing: abraded paint was touched up with a brush, bare patches were painted in, missing pieces reconstructed and replaced by new ones. The age-old belief in progress in art is responsible for the practice of destroying the old to replace it by the new. Monuments of figurative art are condemned to destruction, to make place for new forms of artistic expression. This is particularly true of architecture, mural paintings and carvings, condemned not so much on account of damage as because tastes change. A piece of sculpture or a painting on canvas or wood can simply be transferred elsewhere and replaced by another; but a fixed monument has to be destroyed or obliterated in order to leave room for something more up to date. When it was impossible to use them elsewhere, monuments and their carved and pictorial ornamentation were plundered and destroyed to make way for others that reflected changed tastes. Irrational, shortsighted dislike, arising from ignorance, presumption and incompatibility of past and present feelings has led to the permanent defacement, ruin and falsification of many a monument whose loss was subsequently deplored. No less disastrous were what was perpetrated by barbarous or superstitious 'sympathizers'; by the amateurism of certain movements wanting to recover monuments and restore their value; by uncontrolled rationalist curiosity; and by the morbid love of ruins as a source of romantic inspiration. An attraction, compounded of subtle undertones, is undoubtedly exercised by ruined monuments (and has been responsible for the rescue of historical and artistic objects of great importance); but a kind of fascination is still exercised over all too many people by shapeless lumps, or fragments of almost obliterated painting . . . where nothing can be deciphered, the imagination has endless scope for play.

When the old came to be considered superior to the new there was at first little change. Ancient monuments still suffered, or were destroyed in a variety of ways. But a step had already been taken in the right direction: towards recognizing aesthetic values, shifting the emphasis from subject-matter to form, and discerning the logic of an evolving civilization. If a critical attitude to the present sometimes led to an over-valuing of the past, it at least had the advantage of creating a desire to protect monuments against the ravages of time and prolong their life by restoration. This desire to keep monuments 'alive' must not be confused with the return to antiquity that inspired every manifestation of the Renaissance. Conservation is a completely new phenomenon, involving technicians and laymen in what used to be the exclusive domain of the historian, and demonstrating that critical studies inevitably have practical repercussions on the treatment accorded to the objects which are their subject-matter.

Once the need for conservation is recognized, so also is the need for restoration, as a preliminary to saving monuments and restoring their rightful values.

PRINCIPLES GOVERNING RESTORATION

EARLY PRINCIPLES

For more than a century, restoration remained an experimental and wholly empirical activity. Using instruments and materials selected at random, it was pursued with little or no historical or critical understanding. In the great majority of cases, the cure was worse than the disease. Worst of all, the personality of the restorer was inevitably imprinted on the monument. Restoration was carried out by painters or sculptors who, having failed to make a name for themselves, used their limited talents to reproduce works of art. In the case of architecture, to respect the forms used by the original architect to express his ideas was regarded as equivalent to an admission of incapacity, a humiliating restriction which no self-respecting architect would accept. Until recently, all restorers, without exception, in every branch of the arts, considered it a pleasure and a duty as well as a right, to improve what they were asked to restore, to reinvigorate it by contributing something of their own in compensation for the deteriorations of time, to enhance the subject-matter and form, and to refashion the artist's own idiom in conformity with current taste (the restorer's in particular).

Restorers made little attempt to understand the complexities of the techniques used, the personality of the artist, or the form and spirit of the original, and failed to exercise proper care in the choice and use of the facilities afforded by science. Restorers of paintings were alchemists and would never divulge the professional secrets of the mixing of their pigments, so that the whole process was shrouded in obscurity, and every painting was a helpless guinea-pig. In ancient times, literary texts had also been restored, but only under the strict supervision of experts; and from the eighteenth century onwards it came to be considered unthinkable to touch manuscripts or inscriptions, or to attempt to fill in missing passages. Such scruples did not apply to the restoration of works of art, where reluctance to tamper depended mainly on economic considerations. The secrecy surrounding questions of composition, proportions and methods was so jealously guarded that master painters were never allowed to do the actual work. It was done by their assistants, who were not only not consulted about the preliminary research but never even allowed to examine the original, their job being simply to carry out the practical operations, blindfold, as it were. The purpose of this was to prevent the assistants who, from asserting their independence or becoming rivals, might challenge their master's prestige and steal their commissions.

Any assistant wishing to break away and assert his independence had to go back to the beginning and train as a restorer, in his turn using pictures as the raw material for his experiments. More damage was done in this way, directly to the pictures and in-directly to the detriment of a critical understanding of art, than was occasioned by the ravages of time and natural causes. Restoration badly done very soon necessitated further operations, likewise provisional. Art historians lost interest in the works concerned because they had been too modified, so that the way was paved for further dangerous experiments.

There are thus two categories of monuments which can fall into disrepair: those which deteriorate through age and weathering; and those which (often in addition) suffer from clumsy attempts at restoration that give an illusion of rehabilitation, but frequently accelerate decay because of the unforeseen reactions of some of the materials used.

What, then, are the results for a country's artistic heritage? There is a permanent loss in aesthetic and economic value; salvage operations become virtually impossible; the cost of rehabilitation increases in inverse proportion to the results obtained; philological and historical research is made extremely difficult; the educational value attaching to the works of art diminishes, and monuments are reduced to their documentary value only.

CURRENT PRINCIPLES

Even today, unfortunately, it cannot be said that restorers, in practice, always observe the strict principles that critical theory demands. The reasons why restoration is so often empirical remain: lack of proper training, professional jealousy, oversimplification, and the general view that, by a kind of aesthetic surgery, a monument can easily be touched up in fresh colours.

Practices inadmissible in literary texts and considered a falsification of the original by historians are still widely accepted in the case of visual art and even considered praiseworthy because of a widespread belief that the formal values of a work cannot be understood unless the work is complete.

19

Whereas scientific restoration ensures that the original is not tampered with, and is confined to eliminating excrescences and their causes, natural and artificial, empirical restorers try by meticulous faking to give back an appearance of completeness. Only a superficial and naïve observer can be taken in by a disguise of this kind, superimposed on the original; to say nothing of experts, any observant layman will find this kind of faking intolerable, and all the more so when the additions are supposed to blend imperceptibly with the original. The new parts never merge altogether, not only because it is impossible for the restorer to indentify himself completely with the creator of the original, but also because the new parts, after a short interval, begin to react independently. They are, in fact, subject to their own ageing process and, though initially accurately matched and integrated with the material and forms of the original, they gradually become detached, as time goes on, revealing their extraneous character. This is true of all forms of figurative art: even the filling in of gaps and missing parts presents pitfalls. The integrity of a monument cannot be restored simply by replacing the missing part. The gap itself constitutes an extraneous element in the same way as the graft designed to fill it.

But in most examples of restoration done in the past the restorer, in order to simplify and accelerate his work, has toned down the surviving parts the better to match with the added parts. Needless to say, the result of this is misleading and disastrous.

It is as misleading as the antihistorical methods from which it derives are illegitimate. The work of art, be it architecture, sculpture or painting, is degraded, its poetry is lost, and its documentary value hopelessly compromised.

This practice is now frowned upon but has not been abandoned; it still finds favour with the less expert and more ignorant sections of the public, and with art speculators. To leave a gap, however skilfully concealed, is regarded as a confession of failure on the part of the restorer and of scientific restoration methods, so that polishing patched-up pieces, making the monument look new and whole again and replacing battered parts by new ones are considered to be basic elements in restoration work.

Repairing damaged parts is, on the other hand, tedious, delicate, lengthy and costly; which, combined with the ignorance both of those responsible for commissioning the work and of those carrying it out, explains its unpopularity.

The problem is one of standards of culture, and so of education. The examples provided by museums, picture galleries and churches of panels, canvases, murals and sculpture restored in accordance with stringent criteria, and the examples—alas! all too few—of architectural monuments treated with proper care will gradually educate public taste and overcome age-old prejudice, superficiality and amateurishness and the general belief that a work of art is valuable only by reason of its external qualities.

If restoration is in addition to be a means of education, historians and technicians must pool their skills and experience. Results in the past were so deplorable mainly because the initiative came not so much from the historians as from opportunists. Every practical proposal for restoration should henceforth be subjected to the critical assessment of an historian who is capable of supplying the key to a proper understanding of the particular item. In addition to studying the aesthetic aspects of architectural monuments, experts must investigate the purpose of the original construction and of all subsequent additions, and the place it occupied in the development of art. To concentrate solely on the utilitarian function of architecture in relation to the passing requirements of a period would be a grievous mistake. But then again, it would be equally wrong to neglect the functional aspect and dwell solely on aesthetic values, ot to detach an architectural monument from its context and treat it in the same way as a self-sufficient work of art designed to stand on its own.

In other words, the restorer must make a detailed assessment, first, of the intrinsic elements (content and form) of the monument and, second, of its setting—seemingly less important; and base himself on a combination of the two. This course of action, dictated by the most recent advances in historical research, was not followed in the past, so that one of two things happened: either the desire to preserve the authenticity of the monument outweighed all other considerations (as in the case of the Colosseum); or else the monuments of past ages, representing completely different aesthetic values, were treated with neglectful contempt. Either way, the monument escaped falsification, so that less harm was done than by ill-conceived half measures.

Every architectural monument has an essential unity, and none can be detached from the setting for which it was conceived, and of which it forms an integral part. The setting, whether natural or man-made, is important, not only historically but also for the vitality it imparts to the monument. The width and layout of surrounding thoroughfares, the arrangement and form of the neighbouring buildings, the nature of the vegetation—all contribute to the general effect and must therefore be taken into account both in restoring and in conserving monuments.

The history of restoration effectively reflects the development of art criticism. Traces of restoration can be found even in the earliest monuments. Only in the case of small objects did the parts added match the original; with larger monuments the restorers became more ambitious, and decided to bring the original up to date.

SOME EXAMPLES

From the palaces at Knossos and Phaestus to the earliest architecture of Asia Minor, examples of restoration are as numerous as the monuments themselves.

ANCIENT EUROPE

Early historiographers describe minor operations, amounting in practice to restoration in which limitations were imposed not so much because of genuine respect for the monument as for what it was held to represent. Pausanias, for example (*Description of Greece*), writes about Olympia, where he had seen the last of the original wooden colums of the seventh-century Heraion Sanctuary before they were replaced by columns of marble—obviously because the ancient structures were disintegrating, and not simply because of changing tastes. On the contrary: people must have stood in religious awe of the ancient temple and been afraid to desecrate it by making changes. It is clear from the ruins that the new parts are not homogeneous. The columns differ from one another, and were erected one by one at different periods only when an old column could no longer be relied on. New elements were grafted, bit by bit, without impairing the spirit of the whole and without falsification, since every addition corresponded perfectly to the artistic taste of the period it belonged to. As a result, the temple at Olympia constitutes a model of architectural restoration which is valid to this day. Were it not for the religious associations, something quite different would certainly have happened: the natural deterioration of the archaic monument would have been accelerated so that it would be replaced by a new temple in the style of Mnesicles or Phidias. The religious aura of the sanctuary emanated in some measure from the ancient simplicity of the original construction—hence the care taken to retain the archaic columns which, as became structures dedicated to the gods

21

and imbued with profoundly devotional feelings, were fashioned of wood.

The case of the Heraion was a rare exception; but it is highly probable that, had modern techniques for conserving wooden structures been known at the time, the restorers working at Olympia would have used them for restoring this, the most precious of their temples.

We know of no other monuments to which posterity devoted such jealous care. The rule was that buildings, temples, shrines, porticos, palaces and theatres were not left to deteriorate with time, but simply pulled down and replaced by new buildings designed to outshine the old.

Architectural monuments were exposed not so much to natural decay as to sudden and violent destruction in time of war, and to the repercussions of economic upheavals. In brief but splendid flowerings of classical civilization, the monuments of the past were used solely as quarries for marble: constructions of the age of Peisistratus, destroyed by the Persian hordes, provided Themistocles with material for the fortification of the Acropolis, material in the form of dazzling, beautifully chiselled Pentelic marble.

The new constructions were in no way inferior to their predecessors: Phidias supervised the work of Letinus and Callicrates in the building of the Parthenon, which differed greatly from the original temple dedicated to Athena.

The practice of razing enemy cities to the ground was common in all ages; and all peoples continue to subject defeated enemies to *damnatio memoriae* in the crudest and most irrational form: the deliberate destruction of monuments which recall the past, or express certain ideals, or symbolize certain programmes. While claiming to be the standard-bearers of civilization, Persians and Egyptians, Assyrians and Greeks, Romans and barbarians alike, and other peoples too until recently, invariably struck at the enemy through his monuments, the tangible evidence left by his race and history. From ancient times to the present day, ruins have inspired the erection of more grandiose (or, very often, more pretentious) buildings.

The periods of greatest creative fervour, in all civilizations, have invariably coincided in time with the gravest losses to their artistic heritage. It is not until an age of civilized refinement is reached that the present regards the past as a source of inspiration, as a treasure to be defended against wanton mutilation and destruction. But even so, the monuments of the past are appreciated not in an absolute sense but as an expression of the elective affinities existing between past and present. This can hardly be described as conservation. The Pantheon is not a restoration of the temple of Agrippa but, so to speak, a specimen of neo-classical architecture, an intellectural reconstruction of a non-existent Greek model. That this 'restoration' produced something entirely different from the original, instead of a slavish or stylized imitation of it, is all to the good. We would not wish Hadrian's Pantheon or Antonino Pio's Propylaea at Elensis to be exact copies. The guiding principle was that antiquity, being admired and respected, should be imitated; but, though this was perhaps possible in the case of painters and sculptors (we have only to think of the art of Hadrian's time, inspired by classical and Hellenistic models, and of the Pompeian painters setting out deliberately and with consummate skill to transpose Hellenistic and Alexandrian models into a Latin idiom), the same was not true of the architects who, in reproducing the architecture of other countries and other ages, introduced considerable changes of form. Here we are concerned not with the reproduction of prototypes, but with the cultural influence exercised by the past over the present, and the development of art, chronologically and in different forms.

MEDIAEVAL EUROPE

In the Middle Age, building was slow. In addition to all the material and economic difficulties there were wars, rivalries and, in some cases, the untimely death of a patron.

If work extended over decades, the first parts of an edifice might need restoring before the whole was completed. To the builders there was no difference; they simply ignored the indications left by their predecessors, putting old and new side by side without any attempt to reconcile the differences. What they produced can in no wise be described as a restoration, but their methods have had a great influence on restorers down to our own day.

Few conservation operations were carried out in the Middle Ages, and their purpose derived less from historical respect than from a desire to save monuments which had become the object of veneration. Monuments were liable to damage from earthquakes, natural calamities and wars. They were usually not restored but rebuilt, the surviving parts being kept only in so far as they could contribute to the new structure. Cases of slight damage which could be repaired by ordinary building techniques, so that there was no alternative to restoration, were very rare.

The dome of Saint Sophia in Constantinople offers a good example. It collapsed for the first time while the Emperor Justinian, who had ordered it to be built, was still alive, and it was rebuilt immediately in a form only slightly different. Four centuries later part of it collapsed again, and it was again repaired. Only this second operation ranks as restoration. The first time, the plans were simply executed for the second time; the work done in the tenth century, on the contrary, consisted of replacing the damaged parts, without in any way altering the original design of the dome.

Actually there was no alternative. The ancient basilica was so renowned and imbued with majesty and magnificence that to modernize any part of it (even to the dome alone), was unthinkable. In the tenth century moreover, architectural styles were still virtually the same as in the early Christian period, particularly in western Asia, and not yet affected by the Romanesque elements which were beginning to transform church buildings in Europe. Saint Sophia was subjected to many other operations which were required to consolidate damaged parts. Other changes were made reflecting the change in religion from Christianity to Mohammadanism. The building survives today as a monument, bearing mute witness to the historic events it has experienced.

THE RENAISSANCE

The Renaissance and the humanist movements have claimed to be the heirs of the classical period. The passion for antiquity no doubt inspired philosophers, scholars and scientists, and the formal perfection of Roman monuments undoubtedly stimulated artists. Nevertheless, in so far as preservation is concerned, this period saw the marked alteration or destruction of many outstanding works. Architects, sculptors and painters wished to embellish the surviving ruins, giving to each building or fragment its assumed original sharpness of outline or luminosity which had been dimmed through the passage of time. This often resulted in wholesale destruction for the sake of a detail thought to be significant.

However, there were some notable exceptions. At the end of the fifteenth century, for example, it was decided to restore the famous basilicas of Ravenna. A number of reasons had made this urgently necessary. The ground level had risen as a result of sediments deposited by the tributaries of the River Po which flows into the Adriatic nearby. Monuments dating from the fifth to the seventh centuries were subsiding beneath a layer of alluvial silt (now over two metres deep) and immersed in water seeping up from the subsoil. The buildings were markedly affected: marble columns were shifting; pillars, faced with polychrome oriental marble were being twisted out of shape; arches were sagging and affecting the

23

spatial proportions inside. The mosaics, of which the earliest are dated to the fifth century and the latest to the seventh, were, however, still intact.

In order to preserve the basilicas the city undertook operations which were remarkably bold and enterprising. The colonnades were raised about two metres, together with the arches and the pillars, without demolishing the structures above them or damaging the precious wall paintings. This was an astounding achievement, not merely because of the technical mastery required, but also because it was devised at a time when, generally speaking, the original builders were held in such awe that the question of restoring their work never entered people's minds. There are, unfortunately, no records of this extraordinary operation. We can only suppose that the local craftsmen enclosed the arches with temporary walls, shored them up, and then raised the sunken columns and placed them on new foundations. In order to graft on the arcades, they had to demolish the pendentives at the level of the new emplacement of the columns; the arcades were thus put in place after the columns had been raised to the new level.

This complicated job unquestionably ranks as restoration in the modern sense for, as in restoration work today, it was inspired by a concern to conserve the originals and the artistic and historical character of the monument while at the same time carrying out essential repairs. The restoration at Ravenna was not perfect. The spatial proportions were to some extent affected. But, in the circumstances, it must be said that the maximum respect for the monuments compatible with effective restoration was certainly observed.

THE BAROQUE PERIOD
(SIXTEENTH-EIGHTEENTH CENTURIES)

The case of Ravenna remained unique, serving, for many centuries, as an example of what could be done. At the height of Renaissance fervour, classical models were regarded as an ideal which had never since been surpassed and an incentive to artists to emulate the work of their predecessors. Attempts to restore them were extremely rare. The monuments of the Middle Ages were summarily dismissed as barbarous, and fell into disrepair from neglect or even, in some cases, were deliberately damaged. This attitude was still more marked in the Baroque period, when Romanesque and Gothic monuments were altered out of all recognition by artists who fervently believed that the art of the past was inferior to that of the present and whose ambition, therefore, was to replace old buildings by new.

The fate of the most famous church in Christendom, the Vatican St. Peter's, offers an outstanding example. It was not for reasons of stability alone that alterations were made, but also because of changes of taste regarding form and magnificence. Thus, artists had no hesitation in demolishing imposing monuments which represented a successful combination of late mediaeval and early Christian elements, or even in sacrificing walls with frescoes painted by Giotto, Fra Angelico or Pisanello. The enthusiasm for modern art and the consequent lack of esteem for works belonging to what was considered an uncultivated and unenlightened age is shown by the readiness to let St. Peter's be rebuilt, despite the tradition which had grown up around it, and the renown in which it was held throughout the Christian world. The very fact that it was possible to disregard the veneration and religious devotion attaching to St. Peter's as the centre of the Christian faith is proof of the prevailing belief that modern art was so far superior to ancient art that the latter could be scrapped with impunity.

A glaring example of a different kind is afforded by the transformation of the mosque in Cordoba into a church. Irrational contempt for Arab civilization and Moorish philosophy and art, combined with religious fanaticism and the desire to mortify the vanquished enemy by destroying his works of art, led to the degradation of a stupendous edifice. Part of the mosque was transformed into an insipid imitation of late Gothic architecture, but the result was so ignoble that even Charles V, who had approved the idea, was indignant.

A compromise was sometimes reached between restoring monuments and building on to them. This what happened to the Pantheon in Rome. In the pronaos, Bernini replaced some of the capitals, inserting in the new ones the coats of arms of his patrons. It is quite clear that there was no architectural need for this. Bernini's aim was to 'improve' the strictly classical architecture and make it conform to the style of which he himself was so brilliant an exponent. There was perhaps a practical purpose in the subsequent addition of two bell towers at either end of the attic storey of the pronaos, and we need not endorse the condemnation of his contemporaries, who dubbed them 'ass's ears'. But there are sound reasons for criticizing Bernini's additions: they were designed by the great architect to make an opening in the existing, perfectly closed sphere. The addition, to a form of such complete unity, of absolutely extraneous parts intended to give it an effect it was never meant to achieve, could not but detract from the perfection of the whole.

The 'completion' of monuments was an operation frequently carried out in the seventeenth and eighteenth centuries, not so much because the state of the monuments required it as because the simplicity and severity of the Romanesque and classical styles conveyed, to artists of the Baroque and Rococo periods, a feeling of incompleteness. It was by chance that Gothic monuments were spared the substantial transformations made to Romanesque works (we have only to think of the fate of the famous churches of the 'Capitanata', in the north of Apulia). Although not recognized by the historians, there were real affinities between Gothic and Baroque, and the treatment of

linear and volumetric factors in sixteenth- and seventeenth-century architecture subtly recalled the dynamic external and internal forms and structural masses of the last period of the Middle Ages. Sixteenth- and seventeenth-century additions to Gothic monuments accordingly produced reasonably harmonious results.

The Sainte Chapelle at Vincennes is a good example of successful Baroque restoration. It cannot be said, here, that the restorer refrained from imposing his personal taste, as restorers nowadays are required to do—he was simply in natural harmony with the monument because of the close affinity that exists between these two civilizations, Gothic and Baroque, despite their wide separation in time.

At Vincennes, therefore, there was no need for the restorers to efface themselves. With Delorme or Mansart, restoring meant returning, through their genius, to the sources of their chosen idiom, which represented a veritable revolution against classicism.

Their work was in no sense an imitation or falsification of older monuments, but a genuine resurrection in new work of the spirit of the past.

Culturally and aesthetically, imitation merely degrades restoration. The cathedrals at Orvieto and Milan are notorious examples of Baroque additions to Gothic monuments. In building the additional storey on to the Gothic Sansedoni Palace on the Piazza del Campo in Siena, in the eighteenth century, the figures and style of the lower storeys were exactly copied. It is as though an ancient poem were considered too brief, and it was decided to add new verses, carrying on the subject and metre of the earlier ones. Could any literary historian or philologist tolerate such disrespect for the original?

THE NINETEENTH CENTURY

The end of the eighteenth century witnessed a mass indulgence of the artistic and intellectual taste for ruins which had first emerged

25

in the second half of the seventeenth. This did not as yet signify any real concern for the conservation of ruins: surviving fragments were valued not as historical documents but as poetic and evocative adornments for gardens and parks. Genuine monuments were confused with imitations, and old and new were combined to create architectural 'follies', in imitation of *capriccios* in painting and music. In both cases, such 're-creations' were purely decorative in purpose, inspired by romantic dreams of Arcadia.

As cultural attitudes differed from country to country, so also did the reconstruction of ruins. In Italy, moss-covered porches and ruined forums became associated with political servitude and incipient popular insurrection; but they also reflected the new enthusiasm for archaeological excavation, promoted by the English as a means of discovering the truth about a past that lay buried deep in the sub-soil and had so far surfaced only in legends.

Greece and Italy offered innumerable sites for archaeologists coming from France, Belgium, England, Germany and elsewhere, as well as locally. Their finds encouraged artists and architects to make closer and more detailed studies. The discovery of the cities of Pompeii and Herculaneum, almost perfectly preserved beneath volcanic ash, were a revelation, strongly influencing figurative art as well as the taste and culture of the public. Together with this expression of 'neo-classic' development, the foundations were laid for the genuine restoration of monuments.

Thus the end of the eighteenth and beginning of the nineteenth century saw restoration carried out for the first time on systematic lines. Rome was the testing ground for ambitious schemes and it was here that scholars gathered, impatient to reorganize the monumental remains of imperial days. The reign of Napoleon introduced a movement which was a resurgence in every sense of the term. The buildings of Trajan's great forum were identified, and a large part of the Basilica Ulpia was recovered from the surrounding mediaeval and renaissance edifices; Trajan's column was discovered, and the allegorical *volumen* separating off the area in front of the Greek and Latin libraries. This admirable work of restoration, which succesfully reconditioned monuments and sites without demolishing the surrounding Gothic and sixteenth-century palaces and houses—in themselves of great historical and artistic value—should have inspired the meticulous recovery and salvaging of monuments of every kind as essential factors contributing to the unity of the site; but the result was spoiled by the building—in our time, sad to say—of the Via dell'Impero, one of many creations which, for the sake of ostentatious effect, resulted in the wanton destruction of some of Rome's largest and most authentic groups of monuments.

Archaeological restoration in Rome in Napoleon's time was discreet and extremely sound. The campaign to save monuments and restore them to their original condition included Louis Valadier's work on the Arch of Titus. Eighteenth-century engravings show us what this splendid Roman monument then looked like. Originally it could have been described as 'monumental sculpture'. During the Middle Ages it was incorporated in a block of houses built by the Frangipane family, and substantially altered. The reliefs adorning the arch remained intact, but the portions added in order to graft it to the buildings behind deformed the original architectural structure, and altered its character as a triumphal arch.

Valadier's great merit was to discern the character of the monument accurately and restore it accordingly, a proceeding full of pitfalls even though almost the whole of the original was intact. His sense of proportions derived from a sound knowledge and understanding of the canons of classical art, as he proved in the case of the Arch of Titus by proceeding with great skill and circumspection, never seeking to make short cuts by adding new parts copied slavishly from the original: he knew that this would inevitably degrade the monument and compromise its authenticity.

He was the first to exhibit such caution. He in fact anticipated one of the basic and now generally accepted principles of restoration, namely, that a distinction must be made not so much in the material as in the treatment when new parts are substituted. To replace missing parts, he used architectural elements that were modelled on the original, but differed in the finish given to their surfaces; without either pedantry or artificiality, he reconciled a strictly scientific approach with an understanding of artistic requirements.

However, it should perhaps be remembered that his most famous venture in restoration concerned a monument that was purely artistic in character, and not designed to have any practical function. The Arch of Titus was erected to commemorate a triumph but, contrary to normal practice, the sculptured decorative elements were more important than the architectural factor. The principles which Valadier could apply in this particular case would have been inappropriate in restoring a mansion, palace, church or theatre where practical and aesthetic requirements would have rendered the restorer's task infinitely more complex.

The conflicting points of view of the neo-classical and romantic schools frequently resulted in restorers carrying out ambiguous compromises—which were not always successful—with practical considerations invariably prevailing. On the other hand, whether the restorer based his work on an exaggerated admiration for classicism or whether he was a romantic, the misleading belief that imitation was legitimate led to many blunders.

The classicists justified imitation in the name of certain rules for defining 'beauty'; the romantics maintained that their 'intuitive' restoration could not be assessed according to artistic canons. Neither produced satisfactory results, but led to a decline of standards in new building and restoration alike. On the one hand there was the triumph of 'style', on the other, uncontrolled empiricism and experiment. Replicas were made of ancient models. Objects were reconstructed to a far greater degree than their condition warranted, so that genuine fragments served merely as the starting point for complicated additions and clumsy completion. While romantic *Sturm und Drang* feelings prevailed, even ruins did not escape this unhappy fate.

Until the neo-classic epoch a ruin was treated as an entity in its own right, and made the centre of an artificial setting, but by the end of the eighteenth century ruins were no longer regarded with aesthetic curiosity. Each age reacts against the spirit and forms of its predecessor. Baroque and Rococo were succeeded by neo-humanism and a fervour for classical art and its artistic principles that was sometimes over-intellectualized and artificial. Restorers, in pursuit of the classical ideal of serenity and harmony, set out to give back to monuments the harmony and balance of which they had been robbed.

Busy venting their fury on Baroque and its works, the neo-classicist treated mediaeval art, Romanesque and Gothic, as if they did not exist and, following the old prejudices nurtured by Vasari, regarded them as proofs that—despite artists' desperate efforts to revive it—art had died in the Middle Ages. This explains why, during the neo-classical period, virtually nothing was done to conserve or restore monuments dating from the early Middle Ages to the end of the fourteenth century.

The Romantics reacted against their predecessors' neglect of Romanesque and Gothic art. Concentrating on them in the vain hope of reviving a period which, they believed, represented genuine freedom of imagination untramelled by academic conformism, they embarked on a series of pseudo-artistic restorations, imitations and wildly fanciful rehabilitations, inventing, by 'aesthetic surgery' a mediaeval and, above all, neo-Gothic oleograph form. They demolished Baroque structures with a view to recovering their hidden Romanesque elements, without stopping to think whether the damage done could ever be made good, or how any such elements recovered could be put together again. In a vain attempt to re-create the vanished form of the original they destroyed monuments whose every detail had its own proper artistic function, and broke up architectural units in order to throw into relief elements whose original purpose had never been other than purely practical.

This frenzied urge to recuperate, combined with the restorers' lack of skill and the uninformed impatience of their patrons, was responsible for much damage to works of art.

During the epidemics which for over two centuries swept through Europe, the interiors of buildings—particularly churches—were whitewashed, lime being at that time the best generally available disinfectant.

At the end of the sixteenth century, sanitary considerations prevailed over aesthetic, and many walls, external and internal, columns, pillars and vaults which had formerly been adorned with religious paintings and designs remained plain white until the lime peeled off, or perhaps accidental scraping with a penknife revealed traces of ancient murals underneath. Then the surface layer might be hurriedly scraped off, without any thought for the damage done. Nineteenth-century historiographers have described discoveries. More eloquent than their accounts, unfortunately, are the paintings themselves, with their streaks of soda, abrasions of distempered surfaces, and serious degradation of the paste, gold and silver adornments which highly skilled late Gothic masters used to impart splendour to their lovely miniatures.

All that remains of many murals are the general outline and surviving fragments of the original, now vitrified. Amateurish cleaning, which has done more damage to paintings than exposure to wind and weather, had its counterpart in the makeshift resto-ration carried out on architectural monuments, in which missing parts were replaced, completely artificially, by new.

FROM THE MID-NINETEENTH TO THE EARLY TWENTIETH CENTURY

A decisive turning point in restoration came in the second half of the nineteenth century, when a more serious attempt was made to provide a new kind of art history—something more than the traditional chronological sequence of artists and works. It was from then that insulation, remodelling, consolidation or other alterations to monuments were seen primarily and specifically as exercises in restoration.

What we rather condescendingly call 'nineteenth-century restoration' was in fact an expression, in practical terms, of a revolution which had occurred in historical and critical research.

The most distinguished exponent of the new concept and methods was Viollet-Le-Duc, author of a manual and several other works that set forth the fundamental principles of systematic restoration. He was responsible for various operations that put his theories into practice. His purpose—to give a new lease of life and restore the integrity of damaged monuments—was not in itself new. His great achievement was to provide a cultural basis and scientific authority for something which had hitherto depended on haphazard individual endeavour.

His defects (and they were considerable) detract nothing from his achievement; essentially, he transformed an unscientific, anarchic activity into the methodical discipline that restoration now is.

His methods reflect contemporary art criticism in France and the predominant importance, above all other historical or artistic values, it attached to form. Viollet-Le-Duc considered that restoration should give a monument back its original character (which necessarily included form), and should restore to the monument the appearance it had at the time of its greatest perfection. This was obviously mistaken. It is not legitimate to dismiss evidence and simply decide, on the basis of the personal views of the restorer, which one of the various aspects presented by a monument during the centuries is the most significant.

This practice, widely accepted, was neither realistic nor objective; it placed monuments wholly at the mercy of the restorer, and led to their being robbed of their authenticity. Many restorers—Viollet-Le-Duc was not the only one—were too convinced of their own genius and of their ability to identify with works of art, and lacked the critical sense to withstand the very strong temptation of making their own visible contribution to the monument they were restoring. Viollet-Le-Duc threw the weight of his strong personality behind the argument of the restorer's right to indulge in improvisations, his right and duty to ensure the artistic integrity of edifices left uncompleted or partially ruined. The restoration of monuments, in other words, was not a science but an art, in which the skill and inspiration of the restorer carried more weight, in the last analysis, than scrupulous respect for the monument.

A main weakness in Viollet-Le-Duc's work, revealing a certain amateurishness regarding historical perspective, is his failure to distinguish between creation, reproduction and imitation. In fact, he introduced the principle that any part of a monument can be replaced or reconstructed, provided only that the forms are accurately modelled on surviving parts of the original or on similar parts of different monuments. This is excused to some extent by the poverty of critical research on the history of architecture at the time, which made it difficult—as indeed it still is—to use yardsticks in architecture as effectively as in other arts. But it led in practice to much major restoration which, executed according to Viollet-Le-Duc's rules, obscured the essential character of the monuments concerned. The results were obviously inherent in the theoretical premises, for the completion of a building presents difficult problems that cannot be solved by the addition of copied parts, still less of substitutes 'in the same style' borrowed from similar monuments and for that reason considered suitable. The final result was no longer restoration, but imitative adaptations on a theme.

Despite these inherent defects, Viollet-Le-Duc's methods were widely acclaimed, and influenced the development of historical research in France; this was due to his outstanding personality, and also to the fact that he was one of the country's leading exponents of historical positivism. The support he enlisted was infinitely more powerful than the hostility he aroused: in fact, political opposition to his work was provoked mainly by envy of the esteem in which he was held by Napoleon III and the leading patrons of the period. Thanks to the flourishing state of the French economy around the middle of the nineteenth century, Viollet-Le-Duc was able to carry out a large number of projects that greatly influenced the appearance of many French cities. And his theories gained ground also abroad owing to the spread of positivism, from whose sources he drew his inspiration. Mention may be made of the following operations carried out under his influence in Italy: the so-called restoration of the Church of San Paolo Fuori le Mura, rebuilt by Poletti on the orders of Pius IX after the fire in 1837; the almost total reconstruction of the theatre at Ostia and—a last misguided example—the stylistic remodelling of the castle on Rhodes in 1934, when the island was under Italian mandate.

DEVELOPMENT OF
CONTEMPORARY STANDARDS

If Viollet-Le-Duc could claim to have invented the science of restoration, it fell to others to discover the restorer's conscience.

29

Critical study and the development of taste led to a more sensitive appreciation of what constitutes the authenticity of monuments; and this found an enthusiastic advocate in the Italian Camillo Boito, who laid down certain principles that are still regarded as forming the basis of restoration theory. To Boito, a monument in its entirety is significant as a document of history and art, and every historical and artistic aspect expressed and attested by the monument contributes to that significance. This is the exact opposite of Viollet-Le-Duc's view of the supreme importance of harmony, and the need for taking measures to restore it when lost or impaired, or establish it if non-existent. Boito shared the modern idea of the importance attaching to all evidence of a monument's historical and artistic significance and the modern view that restoration should conserve and recover, as far as possible, all figurative and documentary elements that go to make up the significance of the monument as a whole.

This would require restorers to be far-sighted and learned, rational and impartial.

In practice, these strict principles were not always scrupulously observed; and respect for the authenticity of a monument did not always prevent even Boito and his followers from indulging in additions and reconstructions, or committing the same errors and excesses (stylistic imitations, extensive remodelling) that vitiated the work of Viollet-Le-Duc.

It is important to remember, however, that the technical facilities for the study of monuments available to Viollet-Le-Duc and subsequently to Boito were very imperfect. Research and analyses were still carried out empirically, and the restorer's training in art history was inadequate.

Specialists of our own times have tried to avoid the same pitfalls, but they cannot be said to have been entirely successful. The work done at Knossos shows that, even as recently as fifty years ago, and under the supervision of scholars of world renown, monuments could be subjected to inexcusable arrangement and that there was still a tendency to reconstruct, even when the damage was such that reconstruction served no purpose other than to enable the restorer to offer a gratuitous display of his skill.

The problem of restoration has been particularly acute since the end of the Second World War. First-aid treatment had to be provided for monuments which were badly damaged and ruined, leaving no time to revise out-of-date methods or to work out measures commensurate with the gravity of the situation. Solutions were varied. For example, Coventry Cathedral which was destroyed by bombing was not restored but the surviving elements were consolidated as a monument. A similar solution was adopted by the Germans in the case of the Kolumba-Kapelle in Cologne.

Reconstituting a monument as far as the state of remaining fragments allow is one of the responsibilities of the scientific restorer. The original pieces are reassembled as they were in the original building. This anastylosis method was first worked out long ago in dealing with the Propylaea of the Acropolis at Athens, the Temple of Athena Nike, and the side of the Parthenon which was destroyed by explosions in 1687.

The past few decades have seen a turning point in the theory and practice of restoration. The charters drafted and adopted in Athens in 1931 and in Venice in 1964 do more than codify general principles.

Their originality lies in recognizing that, as result of continuous research, materials and techniques evolve. Restoration is thus always amenable to improvement, and is not static. The concept of 'monuments' is being replaced by that of 'cultural property'; and active preservation programmes, concentrating on careful and continuous maintenance which avoids the need for more drastic measures, are producing a new phase in the history of preservation.

Hiroshi Daifuku

Monument conservation programmes 2

From early times, man has attached importance to particular places or buildings. Among many peoples, such as the ancient Polynesians, these were considered to have intangible power (*mana*). Others associated a particular nature spirit or deity with them, and such associations were continued for centuries by successive cultures. Grottoes or springs in many European sites believed to have curative powers, for example, have yielded *ex voto* offerings to various deities dating from the Bronze Age to the present. The same kind of continuity is found in many places throughout the world. In Latin America churches were built on pre-Hispanic monuments resulting in the continuity of religious associations in a given place. By contrast, shrines, communities and even empires disappeared and were forgotten until their remains were found and excavated by archaeologists later.

Sites and buildings with no such religious associations may also be preserved for their intrinsic beauty or their association with historic events.

However, much as one might like to, there could be no question of saving all the structures of the past. New requirements, more growth and change, inevitably condemn and discard much of the past. The loss, aesthetic or historical, may be minimal. Items which would merit saving under ordinary circumstances are condemned because of the greater economic or social claims or importance of what replaces them. However, the decision can be extremely difficult. At times, sites and monuments are sacrificed despite their intrinsic value because of the magnitude of the task or of the budget required to save them. The danger is frequently compounded by the lack of any planned, coherent programme. In too many parts of the world people realize what they have lost only after the slow, almost unnoticed disappearance of one structure after another, until finally hardly any survive. Again, conservation may be piecemeal, depending on the interest of an individual or a small association in a particular monument; should the individual lose interest or die, the group dissolve, or high prices tempt its owners to sell, an historically or artistically interesting building will be abandoned or destroyed.

Rapid social and economic change during the twentieth century, particularly in urban centres, has usually proved too much for such individuals or groups, although there have been the happy exceptions. Hence nearly all countries have found it necessary to introduce legislation, and set up institutions or organizations which are either governmental or operate under governmental auspices, to ensure that adequate, long-term measures are taken nationally to guarantee the preservation of the cultural heritage.

NATIONAL LEGISLATION

Many countries enacted legislation during the early nineteenth century when interest first began to be taken in the conservation of buildings dating from earlier periods. Subsequent laws took more elaborate account of different requirements and traditions.

FRANCE

Under the *classement* system in France, monuments are defined as structures whose conservation in whole or in part is a matter of public interest from the point of view of history or art. They are classified, i.e. registered on the official list established by the Ministry of Fine Arts, and protected by a series of measures which, for example, forbid modifications or work affecting appearance or structure without prior authorization from the ministry; repairs may be carried out to privately owned monuments with the consent of the owner, or if such consent is not forthcoming, may be imposed.

In addition to classified monuments, a second category exists: edifices or parts of edifices of archaeological interest, or buildings adjoining a classified monument are registered in the *inventaire supplémentaire*; the State is empowered to take appropriate measures to prevent the disappearance or regulate the modification of such buildings or sites.

No work is then allowed, and no changes can be made without prior authorization of the Historic Monuments Architectural Service. The owner may receive a grant (up to 40 per cent of the total cost) to help pay for conservation of the monument; if the monument is deemed of sufficient importance, the State may ensure conservation at its own expense even if the monument is in private hands.

Law 62–902 (1962) legislates for historic quarters and modern conservation requirements. Buildings which the State acquires in order to ensure their restoration may subsequently be ceded (sold or leased) for private use. Within a defined historic quarter, the types of commercial, artisanal, or industrial enterprises which may continue to make use of ancient buildings are specified. New construction is subject to the proviso that it does not disturb the general style of the quarter.

The Marais quarter in Paris offers a good example of the practical effects of this legislation. It is recovering its status as a residential quarter, with public gardens, where only small shops and artisanal industries are allowed. Such famous classified monuments of Renaissance architecture as the hotels Carnavalet, Sully, Soubisse and the Place de Vosges will lose surroundings that had become dingy and inappropriate and find their former glory again. Thus one of the historic centres of Paris that had greatly deteriorated will be restored, and preserved for posterity.

UNITED KINGDOM

The Ancient Monuments Acts of 1913 and 1931 and the Historic Buildungs and Ancient Monuments Acts of 1953 constitute the basic legislation. The term ancient monument is widely interpreted but, for the most part, applies only to unoccupied buildings or structures. Thus buildings which are ecclesiastical property in ecclesiastical use, inhabited buildings, are excluded. The Minister of Public Works may, however, with Treasury consent, accept as a gift or make a purchase of any ancient monument.

Important monuments may be protected by a scheduled preservation order. As in France, a scheduled monument cannot be altered and no work may be carried out on it without express approval. In some instances the ministry may give subventions to aid the proprietor in the conservation of a monument. The National Trust for Places of Historic Interest or Natural Beauty was set up also by Parliament (National Trust Acts 1907–53), with similar bodies in Scotland and the Isle of Man. Country houses, town houses and other major examples of English architecture have been presented to the National Trust. Usually the Trust insists on an endowment to maintain the building or scenic beauty. The former owners and their families are usually allowed to remain in residence, and the public are admitted at stated times. Certain tax concessions can also be obtained in respect of houses made over to the Trust. Private agencies concerned with conservation exist but lack the statutory authority of the National Trust.

The Local Authorities (Historic Buildings) Act of 1962 authorizes local authorities in England and Wales to contribute to the repair or maintenance of buildings adjoining scheduled buildings, and other buildings of architectural or historic interest, by low-interest, or even interest-free, loans as well as by grants. It is then usually agreed that the owner will allow the public to visit the premises at stated times.

The Civic Amenities Act (1967) empowers local authorities to schedule areas of special architectural or historic interest, which then become 'conservation areas' in which repairs, alterations and new construction are controlled. Loans are authorized to assist proprietors to undertake appropriate conservation measures. Proprietors may be ordered to undertake necessary repairs, and failure to comply may result in fines, imprisonment, or both. Local authorities are thus given the means of preventing a proprietor who wants to profit from a sale for development or other purposes from deliberately ruining or neglecting his property; they may futhermore expropriate such property to ensure its conservation.

UNITED STATES OF AMERICA

In the United States, federal legislation covers federal property, supplemented by state legislation and programmes which vary in the individual states from excellent to inadequate or wholly inexistent.

The main federal agency for sites and monuments is the National Park Service, which is responsible for the 'scenery and the natural and historic objects and the wild life' of the areas under its administration. In addition, a National Trust for Historic Preservation was set up by Congress (Public Law 160 of 1953) to 'facilitate public participation in the preservation of sites, buildings and objects significant in American history and culture . . .'. The Trust operates as a tax-exempt educational agency and accepts property, usually on condition that an endowment is also provided to cover maintenance.

Under a number of other Acts which also have a bearing on preservation, the primary initiative rests with local authorities. These include the Housing Acts of 1954 and 1961, under which Urban Renewal Funds can be used for preservation purposes, and the Highways Act, which allows funds to be used for salvage programmes. From time to time, the Federal Government has disposed of nationally owned historically important structures as surplus property, with the proviso that they must be used as public parks, monuments, or as public recreation facilities.

Far-reaching legislation (Public Law 89–665) was recently adopted authorizing the Secretary of the Interior to:

1. Maintain a national register of districts, sites, buildings, structures and objects which are significant in history, archaeology and culture; grant funds to States to prepare surveys and plans for the preservation, acquisition and for development of such properties.
2. Establish a programme of matching grants-in-aid to states for the preservation,

33

acquisition and development of such properties.

3. Establish a programme of matching grants-in-aid to the National Trust for Historic Preservation in the United States to carry out the responsibilities of the Trust in the preservation and conservation of historic monuments and sites.

An Office of Archaeology and Historic Preservation was established as part of the National Park Service, and an Advisory Council was set up to advise the President and Congress on administrative and legislative measures.

POLAND

All prior legislation was superseded by the 1962 law on the protection of cultural property and on museums, entitled Protection of Historical Monuments in the Polish People's Republic with Special Consideration to the Reconstruction of Towns (Documentation Centre for Historical Monuments, Warsaw, 1965). Cultural property is defined as 'movable or immovable, ancient or contemporary, having historical, scientific or artistic value to the cultural inheritance and cultural development'. Article 3.1 is worth quoting in full, in view of certain 'applied' aspects which are a distinguishing feature of the Polish legislation:

'The purpose of the protection of cultural property is to preserve, maintain and make use of such property for the purpose of social, scientific, didactic and educational goals so that they should serve science and that such property may be used to spread knowledge and arts and become a stable factor in the development of national culture and an active component of the contemporary life of socialist society.'

'Historic monuments' include those entered in the register of historic monuments. They also include objects in museums, libraries and public archives, so that the 'monuments' also covers works of art, historic material, archaeological finds as well as documents and publications, although the latter are not registered.

The rights of private owners of historic monuments are protected if the monument is registered, subject to controls exercised by the Provincial Department of Culture ('voivodship' conservator). Such registered monuments may be repaired at the expense and under the supervision of the provincial authorities, who may also order the owner of an historic monument which is not registered to maintain it in satisfactory condition at his own expense. Property of exceptional value can be expropriated by the State under the right of eminent domain, in which case the owner is compensated at market value.

Under Article 20, the Minister of Culture and Arts and the Conservation Service have specific powers in regard to historic quarters or urban sites declared to be of historic value:

'In order to protect historically valid plans of old urban quarters and groups of historic buildings entered into the register of historic monuments the (national) conservation service with the understanding of the architectural supervision service of the provincial authorities (voivodship unit) may define the conditions of building activities in such areas, or they may order the removal of certain buildings, or the renovation or reconstruction of buildings, and issue other appropriate regulations.'

JAPAN

Law 214 (1950) superseded previous legislation and concerns the preservation and use of 'cultural properties, so that the culture of the Japanese people may be furthered and a contribution be made to world cultural understanding'.

The Japanese legislation[1] is extremely

---

1. National Commission for Protection of Cultural Properties, *Administration for Protection of Cultural Properties in Japan*, Tokyo, 1962.

comprehensive. The definition of 'cultural properties' has four subdivisions:

Tangible: buildings, works of art, ancient documents, and so on.

Intangible: music, drama and arts which 'possess a high historic or artistic value' and which the State is therefore justified in subsidizing and maintaining, e.g. *No* drama.

Folk culture: manners and customs related to the culinary arts, clothing, religious festivals and other distinctive features of Japanese life.

Monuments: including sites of historic or scientific significance such as historic urban quarters, castles and their grounds, scenic landscapes, protected species of animals, plants, geological features, and so on.

Tangible cultural properties can be desig-nated either as 'important' or as 'national treasures'. The owner of an 'important' property may undertake repairs and receive a subsidy covering part of the expenses. In the case of 'national treasures', the National Commission for Cultural Proper-ties may instruct or advise a private agency which is the proprietor and also pay part or all of the costs involved. To encourage proper care, inheritance taxes may be re-duced when title is transferred upon the death of a proprietor to his heir or heirs. 'National treasures' and, in principle, 'im-portant cultural property' cannot be ex-ported. In the latter case the National Com-mission may make exception if there is a 'special necessity from the viewpoint of international exchange of culture or other considerations'.

INTERNATIONAL AGREEMENTS

The increase in the rapidity and ease of communications, the distribution of indus-trial products and the spread of techniques have not taken place without upsets; since the nineteenth century, they have placed considerable strains on social and economic organization and involved serious dangers for cultural property. There has also been a marked increase in the destructive capacity of armed conflicts. As a result, international agreements have been worked out to safe-guard the cultural heritage of mankind.

The Hague Conventions concerning the Laws and Customs of War on Land and on Naval Bombardment in Time of War (29 July 1899 and 18 October 1907) provided for the protection of historic monuments. Analogous provisions were included in the Washington Pact of 15 April 1935 for the Protection of Artistic and Scientific Institu-tions and of Historic Monuments (Roerich Pact).

THE HAGUE CONVENTION

On 14 May 1954, at The Hague, forty-three States and the Holy See signed the Conven-tion and annexed instruments on the Protec-tion of Cultural Property in the Event of Armed Conflicts which was sponsored by Unesco. The Convention provides for: (a) preventive measures (shelters, special in-structions to military authorities, and so on) to safeguard cultural property; (b) the nega-tive obligation not to destroy or damage such property; (c) arbitration mechanisms when cultural property is affected by armed conflict; and so on.

The following are among the measures which ensure application of the Convention: (a) the establishment and maintenance of an international register for cultural property under special protection; (b) the establish-ment in the event of armed conflict of a controlling body to ensure the protection of cultural property under a Commissioner-

General nominated from an international list of persons by joint agreement between the Party to which he will be accredited and the Protecting Powers; (c) means and controls to be used in the transport of movable cultural property to ensure its preservation.

A special Protocol is intended to prevent the export of cultural property from territory occupied during an armed conflict, and deals with the custody of such property and its return at the close of hostilities. By the end of 1966, fifty-four States had ratified or adhered to the Convention and Protocol.

INTERNATIONAL
RECOMMENDATIONS

Unesco has also prepared a number of International Recommendations setting out various principles and norms adopted by the General Conference. Member States are invited to take whatever legislative or other steps may be necessary to apply such standards. Two are pertinent here.

Recommendation concerning the Safeguarding of the Beauty and Character of Landscapes and Sites, adopted by the General Conference at its twelfth session (Paris, 11 December 1962).

Among the general principles, the Recommendation states that 'Protection should not be limited to natural landscape and sites, but should also extend to landscapes and sites whose formation is due wholly or in part to the work of man. Thus, special provisions should be made to ensure the safeguarding of certain urban landscapes and sites which are, in general, the most threatened, especially by building operations and land speculation. Special protection should be accorded to the approaches to monuments.' Supervisory measures are suggested in the case of works and activities likely to damage landscapes and sites, and corrective measures are proposed with a view to repairing any damage caused and, as far as possible, restoring them to their original condition.

Recommendation concerning the Preservation of Cultural Property endangered by Public and Private Works, adopted by the General Conference at its fifteenth session (19 November 1968).

Apart from natural cataclysms, war and vandalism, man's own activities represent the next major threat to cultural property. Two categories of measures are recommended in order to ensure: (a) the preservation of an entire site, structure, or other forms of immovable cultural property from the effects of private or public works; (b) salvage or rescue if the area in which it, the cultural property—all or part of which is to be preserved and removed—is found to be transformed by public or private works.

The following are considered to be the major threats: (a) urban expansion and renewal projects; (b) injudicious modifications and repair of individual historical buildings; (c) the construction or alteration of highways; (d) the construction of dams; (e) the construction of pipelines and of electricity power and transmission lines; (f) farming operations, including deep ploughing, drainage and irrigation operations, the clearing and levelling of land, and afforestation; (g) works required by the growth of industry and the technological progress of industrialized societies.

Paragraph 9 recommends: 'Member States should give due priority to measures required for the preservation *in situ* of cultural property. . . . When overriding economic or social conditions require that cultural property be transferred, abandoned or destroyed, the salvage or rescue operations should always include careful study of the cultural property involved and the preparation of detailed records.'

In view of the manifold threats to cultural property, conservation and salvage programmes must be based on adequate legislation and budgets, and trained and dedicated personnel.

ADMINISTRATION

National services for the preservation of sites and monuments vary considerably. They come under various ministries, e.g. education, interior, fine arts, public works, tourist development. For protection and conservation purposes, scheduled or classified monuments may come under one ministry, historic quarters under a second, privately owned monuments under a third. In federal States, national services may be concerned only with national monuments or, on the other hand, may leave practically all responsibility to local authorities.

Highways, urban renewal projects, control of the building of dams, airports, pipelines, and other threats to cultural property may also come under different ministries, with the unfortunate result that, if liaison and co-operation are defective, an historic monument or site may be destroyed or so adversely affected that it loses much of its historic and artistic importance. These dangers are aggravated if a country's economy is expanding: plans and actual construction may get so rapidly under way that modification or changes are ruled out on the grounds of cost, and would cause much ill-will among the different services and the public.

The best remedy would seem to be an advisory committee and secretariat to review all proposed new projects on the lines just mentioned, and secure the co-operation of the various services responsible for public and private works with a view to ensuring that due priority is accorded to the claims of historic quarters, sites and monuments. It would review all programmes before their ultimate submission to the responsible ministry and make its recommendations accordingly. These recommendations would be communicated to all of the various agencies or authorities concerned.

The committee members should include the ministers or their representatives; representatives of the different administrations responsible for projects which may in one way or another affect cultural property; the director of the national conservation service (*ex officio*); selected members of parliament; local authority representatives; art historians, architects, university professors and other individual specialists. The committee would normally meet at least once a year; *ad hoc* sub-committees could meet more frequently as required. Provision would have to be made to cover secretariat costs, and members' travel and *per diem*.

STAFFING

Most countries with a long-established tradition of conservation have national services. Federal States frequently have local services also, to which they accord considerable autonomy.

A proposed scheme for a national monument and museums service in Malta[1]—a small country with a large number of historic monuments and sites—is shown in diagrammatic form, page 38.

Larger countries would, in addition, need extra administrative staff, a library and archives, and a laboratory to serve the protection and museum services.

Coremans suggests that the key to successful administration is to have a director of high standing, capable of dealing with '. . . a very complex function in a working group requiring the co-operation of specialists in widely differing fields such as archaeologists, art historians, physicists and chemists, architects and engineers, technicians in conservation and photography'.[2] In a country rich in monuments (in the limited sense used by Coremans), the following services would be necessary.

Architects. The architect should be a specialist in the conservation and restoration

1. Davey and Plenderleith, 1965.
2. Coremans, 1967.

Scheme for the establishment of a museums and monuments service in Malta

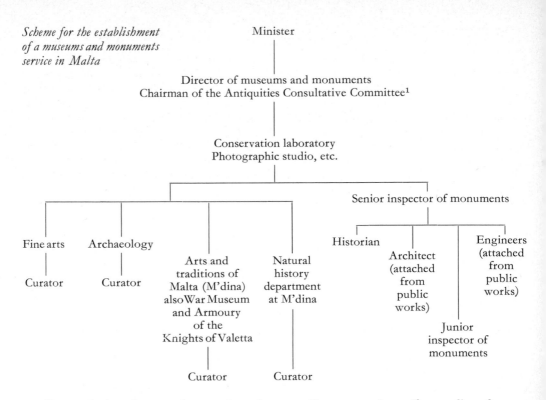

Ancillary staff: draughtsmen, photographers, documentalists; restoration staff; custodians, foremen and labourers

----

1. It is suggested that the Antiquities Consultative Committee might be of great service to the director and staff if it numbered among its members a leading architect and engineer.

of buildings, with a good background in history, and an intimate knowledge of ancient and contemporary building materials and techniques. He should know of the objections to past methods of restoration, the charges of careless execution, lack of respect for historical and aesthetic factors, incompatibilities, etc., and be acquainted with the international standards that are gradually being developed.[1]

Engineers. Problems of structure, soil and fundations may be matters for the engineer, but an architect specialized in conservation might also have the required qualifications.

Art historians or architect historians. Large services may need such specialists, with a master or doctor's degree, and a specialization in architecture, qualified to deal with questions of design, cultural affili-

----

1. The International Centre for the Study of the Preservation and the Restoration of Cultural Property, in co-operation with the Faculty of Architecture, University of Rome, now gives a graduate course in conservation. Visiting lecturers from several countries review methods, standards and techniques to be used in the conservation and restoration of historic buildings.

ations, history, furniture, and other considerations that enter into restoration work.

Archaeologists. Specializations may range from pre-history to urban cultures and the recent past. Pre-historic sites may also have 'monumental qualities', either by reason of their size or of special importance (e.g. Paleolithic cave paintings) which should be preserved. Larger sites of later periods are frequently preserved as well. Excavations in historical sites often yield information that supplements the knowledge of the historian, by establishing foundations, investigating brick sizes, clays, the shape of nails and so on, as well as recovering items for museums.

Conservation laboratory. Here the chemist has a key role, investigating factors which contribute to weathering and other causes of disintegration, identifying materials, pigments and so on. He must be qualified in both physical and analytical chemistry and should have a doctor's or, at the least, a master's degree. The main conservation laboratories frequently accept trainees from abroad; some have regular training programmes and accept a limited number of students annually.

Inspector. Inspectors should be qualified as restoration architects or art historians. It is they who survey the state of monuments, check on restoration work (particularly in countries where the architect is normally engaged from the private sector), plan projects, advise local authorities or private owners on procedures to be followed, and where necessary initiate legal action to safeguard monuments.

Photographic staff. The staff should include a photographer, and dark room and other technicians. Photography is important in recording cultural property, the condition of monuments if reconstruction is required, and the different stages of the work decided upon so that parts removed, treated, or restored can readily be identified later.

Technical and maintenance staff. Draughtsmen, electricians, maintenance staff and craftsmen are essential. The type of craftsmen required will depend very much on the nature of the monuments—mason or carpenters according as they are predominantly of stone, brick, or wood, and so on. The standards of workmanship must be high. In countries where craftsmen can use only the standardized products and tools of an industrial civilization, staff may have to be specially trained to reproduce ancient forms of workmanship, usually under the direction of the architect.

DOCUMENTATION, LABORATORIES, WORKSHOPS

Library

The library of a conservation service may also hold the photo-collections, archives and records. A small service library may contain reference works only, a larger service may need a specialized library with thousands of volumes, including folio-sized books, a public reading room and facilities for students and specialists. Card catalogues, shelving, and other arrangements generally follow standard library practice.

Photo and other illustrative material

Photographic equipment. A widely used format is the 9×12 cm view camera, with all of the tilts required. It is portable, and has a wide range of lenses which meet most architectural photography requirements. Enlargers, developing tanks, and other dark-room equipment are mass produced and reasonable in cost.

Larger format cameras were necessary before the development of fine-grained film and the marked improvements that have been made in equipment for enlarging and printing; they gradually lost their popularity because of the relatively high cost of accessories, lenses, enlargers, and other equipment needed.

The 6×6 cm camera, single- or twin-lens reflex, is also widely used for detail shots. There are obvious economies in film and developing costs, and fine-grain film permit good-sized enlargements. The 35 mm camera, particularly the single-lens reflex, which may have a large number of accessory lenses, is now also widely used, particularly for colour work.

Photogrammetry (see Chapter 5) needs specialized apparatus but uses ordinary dark-room equipment for developing and printing.

Negatives can be filed in standard drawers and indexed, each being stored in a separate envelope marked with the file number in indian ink. Colour films should be kept in transparent plastic sleeves to prevent scratching. The index should record the name of the photographer, date, place, and circumstances under which the photograph was taken, and the occasions on which it was used in publications.

A contact print may be kept with the negative. Enlargements are usually stored separately.

Maps, prints, line drawings are usually catalogued and stored in special drawers and cabinets.

Inventory

A most useful, but frequently neglected record is provided by a national inventory of scheduled or classified monuments (including important historically or artistically interesting monuments and sites).

SUMMARY AND DISCUSSION

Since the nineteenth century, the interest in conservation has developed steadily. Sites and monuments, like all material things, are subject to change and degradation. Changes in temperature and the natural degeneration

Inventories are essential to the proper organization of a comprehensive conservation programme. Many countries have their own forms (see Fig. 1); the Council of Europe has produced standard forms which are to be used by all its Member States (see Fig. 2).

Computerized inventories should eventually be possible; they would facilitate the keeping of records, the forecasting of budget and staff requirements, and allow a more prompt response when safeguarding, maintenance or reconstruction is needed.

Laboratories and workshops

Where museums, and sites and monuments, come under a single ministry, a common laboratory can serve both, since both have the same interest in carved or painted wooden beams, sculptural elements, frescoes and so on, which need the same kinds of treatment and restoration. Certain other kinds of work (e.g. compression tests, tests of concrete aggregates) could be handled by an appropriate ministry (e.g. public works, highways, schools of engineering and so on). If not, a centralized conservation and testing laboratory might be set up to meet the manifold requirements involved in new construction and in restoration and conservation.

Specialized workshops are frequently required for carpentry, metal work, and brick or stone masonry, especially in industrialized countries were machinery has largely supplanted the artisanal skills that, during the eighteenth and nineteenth centuries, used to be acquired through long apprenticeship under skilled masters, as in the United States, for example.

of stone or wood through the action of moulds, bacteria, lichens, mosses and so on help to destroy objects made of mineral or organic matter.

Again, a building that is in daily use needs

7. DESCRIPTION

CONDITION	Excellent ☐	Good ☒	Fair ☐	Deteriorated ☐	Ruins ☐	Unexposed ☐
	(Check One)			(Check One)		
INTEGRITY	Altered ☐	Unaltered ☒		Moved ☐		Original Site ☒

DESCRIBE THE PRESENT AND ORIGINAL (If known) PHYSICAL APPEARANCE

Outstanding external features are the unbroken horizontal lines of walls and roof (the cantilevers of which, placed at disparate levels and opposite angles, produce a tiered effect); a central chimney, the form of which is repeated by brick piers at both ends of the facade; the continuation of interior walls to the porch sections, thus uniting the house with its surroundings; and the elevation of the main floor over a raised basement. Building material is brick with sandstone caps and sills, and the windows are matching strips of leaded glass. Interior trim is oak. Original floors and the main inside stairway are concrete.

At the present time some repair is needed, although the house is structurally sound. Principally, this would involve restoration of the interior in accordance with the original plans, new tuckpointing, and rebuilding of the red clay tile roof.

1 b

Form 10-300
(Dec. 1968)

UNITED STATES DEPARTMENT OF THE INTERIOR
NATIONAL PARK SERVICE

NATIONAL REGISTER OF HISTORIC PLACES
INVENTORY – NOMINATION FORM

(Type all entries — complete applicable sections)

STATE:
Illinois
COUNTY:
Cook
FOR NPS USE ONLY
ENTRY NUMBER	DATE

1. NAME

COMMON:

AND/OR HISTORIC:
Robie (Frederick C.) House

2. LOCATION

STREET AND NUMBER:
5757 South Woodlawn Avenue

CITY OR TOWN:
Chicago

STATE	CODE	COUNTY:	CODE
Illinois	12	Cook	C31

3. CLASSIFICATION

CATEGORY (Check One)	OWNERSHIP	STATUS	ACCESSIBLE TO THE PUBLIC
District ☐ Building ☐	Public ☐	Occupied ☒	Yes: Restricted ☐
Site ☒ Structure ☐	Private ☒	Unoccupied ☐	Unrestricted ☒
Object ☐	Both ☐	Preservation work in progress ☐	No: ☐
	Public Acquisition:		
	In Process ☐		
	Being Considered ☐		

PRESENT USE (Check One or More as Appropriate)

Agricultural ☐	Government ☐	Park ☐	Transportation ☐	Comments · ☐
Commercial ☐	Industrial ☐	Private Residence ☐	Other (Specify) ☐
Educational ☒	Military ☐	Religious ☐	
Entertainment ☐	Museum ☐	Scientific ☐	

4. OWNER OF PROPERTY

OWNER'S NAME:
University of Chicago

STREET AND NUMBER:
5801 Ellis Avenue

CITY OR TOWN:
Chicago

STATE	CODE
Illinois	12

5. LOCATION OF LEGAL DESCRIPTION

COURTHOUSE, REGISTRY OF DEEDS, ETC:
Cook County Recorder's Office

STREET AND NUMBER:

CITY OR TOWN:
Chicago

STATE	CODE
Illinois	12

6. REPRESENTATION IN EXISTING SURVEYS

TITLE OF SURVEY:
National Survey of Historic Sites and Buildings

DATE OF SURVEY: December 1963	Federal ☒	State ☐	County ☐	Local ☐

DEPOSITORY FOR SURVEY RECORDS:
Office of Archeology and Historic Preservation, National Park Service

STREET AND NUMBER:
Department of the Interior

CITY OR TOWN:
Washington

STATE:	CODE
District of Columbia	08

APPROXIMATE ACREAGE OF NOMINATED PROPERTY: .3

STATE:	COUNTY:
Illinois	Cook

FOR NPS USE ONLY
ENTRY NUMBER	DATE

CODE	CODE
12	12

1 a

41

Significance Form

8. SIGNIFICANCE

PERIOD (Check One or More as Appropriate)

| Pre-Columbian ☐ | 16th Century ☐ | 18th Century ☐ | 20th Century ☒ |
| 15th Century ☐ | 17th Century ☐ | 19th Century ☐ | |

SPECIFIC DATE(S) (If Applicable and Known) 1908-1909

AREAS OF SIGNIFICANCE (Check One or More as Appropriate)

Aboriginal ☐	Education ☐	Political ☐
Prehistoric ☐	Engineering ☐	Religion/Phi- losophy ☐
Historic ☐	Industry ☐	Science ☐
Agriculture ☐	Invention ☐	Sculpture ☐
Art ☒	Landscape Architecture ☐	Social/Human- itarian ☐
Commerce ☐	Literature ☐	Theater ☐
Communications ☐	Military ☐	Transportation ☐
Conservation ☐	Music ☐	Urban Planning ☐
		Other (Specify) ☐

STATEMENT OF SIGNIFICANCE (Include Personages, Dates, Events, Etc.)

Frank Lloyd Wright has been the foremost American architect of the 20th century, and the Robie House is the embodiment of his Prairie Style architecture. Built between 1908 and 1909, the house set precedents which influenced national and international domestic architecture for the next sixty years as it represented a radical break with traditional form and style. The house is highlighted generally by the strong horizontal planes of the exterior, the open and fluid organization of interior space, and specifically by the introduction of indirect electric lighting and concealed heating, the integration of garage with dwelling, and the central placement of the fireplace.

Wright's Prairie Style was an attempt to eliminate the boxlike home. It was a new interpretation of space which emphasized beauty in function and joined interior to exterior in a single, continuous unit. Overall architectural form was to be dictated by function and the individual lines and planes, by environment. Wright's radical break with traditional architecture was exemplified by a simplicity of style and innovation in the design of necessary elements such as windows, stairways, and lighting.

SEE INSTRUCTIONS

Continuation Sheet

Form 10-300a
(Dec. 1968)

UNITED STATES DEPARTMENT OF THE INTERIOR
NATIONAL PARK SERVICE

NATIONAL REGISTER OF HISTORIC PLACES
INVENTORY - NOMINATION FORM

(Continuation Sheet)

STATE
Illinois
COUNTY
Cook
FOR NPS USE ONLY
ENTRY NUMBER	DATE

ROBIE HOUSE

(Number all entries)

6. Historic American Buildings Survey

        Code: 08

1963

Library of Congress

Washington, D. C.

FIG. 1 (pages 41 to 43)

Forms nominating important cultural property for inclusion in the national register. Note that much of the data can be transferred to IBM sorter cards (United States National Park Service).

SEE INSTRUCTIONS

9. MAJOR BIBLIOGRAPHICAL REFERENCES

Ashbee, Charles Robert, Frank Lloyd Wright, (ine Studie zu seiner Wuerdigung. (Berlin: Ernst Wasmuth, 1911), pp. 112-13.

_____, Ausgeuchrte Bauten und Entwuerfe. (Berlin: Ernst Wasmuth, 1910).

Farr, Finis, Frank Lloyd Wright: A Biography. (New York: Charles Scribners' Sons, 1961), pp. 100-4, 225.

Hitchcock, Henry Russell, In the Nature of Materials. (New York: Duell, Sloan, and Pearce, 1942), pp. 40, 79, 102.

Manson, Grant C., Frank Lloyd Wright to 1910. (New York: Reinhold Publishing Corporation, 1958), pp. 35, 79, 154n., 171, 187, 198, 201.

10. GEOGRAPHICAL DATA

LATITUDE AND LONGITUDE COORDINATES DEFINING A RECTANGLE LOCATING THE PROPERTY

CORNER	LATITUDE			LONGITUDE			CODE
	Degrees	Minutes	Seconds	Degrees	Minutes	Seconds	
NW	°	'	"	°	'	"	
NE	°	'	"	°	'	"	
SE	°	'	"	°	'	"	
SW	°	'	"	°	'	"	

O R — LATITUDE AND LONGITUDE COORDINATES DEFINING THE CENTER POINT A PROPERTY OF LESS THAN ONE ACRE

	LATITUDE			LONGITUDE			CODE
	Degrees	Minutes	Seconds	Degrees	Minutes	Seconds	
	N 41	47	23	W 87	35	45	

LIST ALL STATES AND COUNTIES FOR PROPERTIES OVERLAPPING STATE OR COUNTY BOUNDARIES

STATE:		CODE	COUNTY:		CODE
STATE:		CODE	COUNTY:		CODE
STATE:		CODE	COUNTY:		CODE
STATE:		CODE	COUNTY:		CODE

11. FORM PREPARED BY

NAME AND TITLE: Elizabeth A. Dippel

ORGANIZATION: National Register

DATE

STREET AND NUMBER: 801 19th Street, N.W.

CITY OR TOWN: Washington STATE: D.C. 20006 CODE 08

12. STATE LIAISON OFFICER CERTIFICATION

As the designated State Liaison Officer for the National Historic Preservation Act of 1966 (Public Law 89-665), I hereby nominate this property for inclusion in the National Register and certify that it has been evaluated according to the criteria and procedures set forth by the National Park Service. The recommended level of significance of this nomination is:

National ☐ State ☐ Local ☐

Name _____

Title _____

Date _____

NATIONAL REGISTER VERIFICATION

I hereby certify that this property is included in the National Register.

Chief, Office of Archeology and Historic Preservation

Date ___January 25, 1969___

ATTEST:

Keeper of The National Register

Date ___January 25, 1969___

I e

COUNCIL OF EUROPE	Protective Inventory of the European Cultural Heritage	I.E.C.H.	MONUMENT	I.E.C.H. Number :	
(Country)	(Ministry)			(Department responsible)	
Region :	Province or County :		Municipality :		Town District or Rural Locality :
Location :	Name :		Registration particulars :		

Situation, surroundings and contents :

Period :   Present utilisation :

Description :

| State of Preservation | A Satisfactory / B Poor / C Bad | Main fabric | A B C | Subsidiary portions | A B C | Roof | A B C | Interior | A B C | Damp | A B C | Degree of Protection : I.E.C.H. : |

Existing Protection :   Protection proposed :

Plans and photographs for identification

Comments		Compiled by :	Date :
		Checked by :	Date :
		Revised by :	Date :

The information on the front constitutes the basic index card and is essential to any protective action – The data given on the back are supplementary.

2 a

constant maintenance. Cumulative repairs (which may be badly carried out or introduce unsuitable material) can affect appearance and structural resistance. Additions in different styles can sometimes add up to a harmonious whole; more likely, they will be poorly executed (e.g. a once noble structure that now serves as a tenement, or a workshop), and the only alternative to demolition and replacement is radical restoration. It may be easy to get rid of shoddy additions, but is not always simple to decide which of the frequently well-built additions should be retained or sacrificed. If the monument is important, the advice of an art historian or a group of specialists may be sought with profit.

During the nineteenth century architects, when reconstructing a monument, frequently replaced missing elements which may have been present in original desings, but some of which never seem to have been built. Sometimes they were inserted by the architect to suit his own sense of design. The amount of new elements introduced frequently produced a building which spuriously matched the old.

A counter movement inspired by the English Romantic movement wanted to preserve, if not to enhance, the look of age. Subsequently (during the first half of the twentieth century) there was a tendency to indicate what had been restored by using different materials or colours, so that any restoration—fresco, statue, pottery, building—looked patched.

A compromise is now usually sought. The restored sections blend in with the old

SUPPLEMENTARY CARD		
Typological data	Chronological data	Technical data
	Architectural history	Materials
	Proposed utilisation	Restoration operations
Special characteristics	Possible utilisation	Prospects of restoration
Additional reference material (graphic, photographic, etc...)		

Basic bibliography	Comments and potential dangers	
	Compiled by :	Date :
Legal data (form of ownership and address of owner)	Checked by :	Date :
	Revised by :	Date :

2 b

but can be noticed on closer inspection—an attempt to reconcile aesthetics with authenticity.

What has been said above might give the impression that the principles governing reconstruction and conservation are widely known and understood, and put into practice by trained people. This is not necessarily the case, and this is one reason why legislation and some form of central control are called for; it also explains the concern about training (see Chapter 12), laboratory facilities, and so on. Apart from the means to carry out a successful conservation and restoration programme, the desire and determination to do so must also be present, and it is influenced by a multitude of other factors, including the growth in urban populations, the spread of industriali-

zation, and an improvement, actual or expected, in living standards.

Widespread economic and demographic changes affect conservation programmes. The motor car and greater public transport facilities, for example, have produced an urban sprawl which engulfs small, local communities. Functioning social units (extended families, villages, old neighbourhoods) lose their cohesion and, together with it, the local church or temple, buildings in the 'old' style, local social or cultural centres, which tend to be replaced by garages, shops, multi-unit dwellings. Urban redevelopment projects drastically change the urban landscape. Although an important monument may be spared, the square it once graced is given over to new construction or used as a car park, and neighbouring

COUNCIL OF EUROPE		Protective Inventory of the European Cultural Heritage	I.E.C.H.	SITE	I.E.C.H. number :	
(Country)	(Ministry)				(Department responsible)	
Location	Administrative :					
	Topographical :					
Denomination :						
Description :						
Present utilisation :						
Prospects of revival :						
Existing protection	Nature :					Degree of Protection I.E.C.H.
	Extent :					
Potential dangers :						
Protection proposed :						
Basic bibliography :						
Comments :				Compiled by :	Date :	
				Checked by :	Date :	
				Revised by :	Date :	

1 S549

2 C

buildings of the same scale and period, unless scheduled or classified, are razed. The monument becomes an anachronistic survival, diminished by the new buildings, and all sense of spatial, historic and aesthetic relations is lost.

In most countries, there is a lamentable lack of cohesion as between national services, municipal and provincial authorities, and commercial or private interests. Scheduled buildings and groups have been destroyed to make way for highways or for profit—the increased revenues to be obtained by the construction of multi-storey buildings. The ground-floor frontage of nineteenth- and early twentieth-century buildings has been scrapped, and replaced in contemporary styles which clash with the storeys above and adversely affect the feeling of a street. Laws may impose fines or penalties, or require special permission before alterations can be made. But such laws are frequently ignored. The owner does not worry about the penalty if it represents a mere fraction of the anticipated profit. He may refuse to maintain a scheduled building, deliberately expose it to vandalism or rapid deterioration in other ways so as to have it condemned as usafe and then have it legally destroyed. Zoning laws which many municipalities enact to preserve a residential or historic quarter have frequently been so laxly administered that little if any trace remains of what was once a charming and interesting town or locality.

Some rapidly developing countries embark on programmes for the conservation of sites and monuments and the protection

GRAPHIC, CARTOGRAPHIC AND PHOTOGRAPHIC REFERENCE MATERIAL

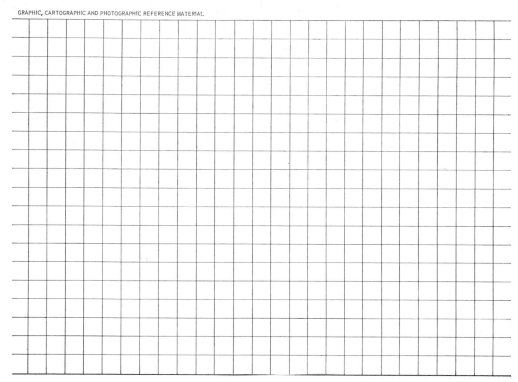

2 d

of historically or artistically interesting communities in order to establish focal points for an incipient tourist industry. New airports, motorways, accommodation, and related industries (such as catering) help to produce a general improvement in the standard of living. Paradoxically, the more a country develops, the more difficult conservation may become as economic development comes to depend more and more upon expanding commerce and industry. Conservation receives little priority and, all too frequently, attention is given to the need for it after much of what is valuable has been destroyed. Unfortunately the process is irreversible: the new can hardly be destroyed again in order to make way for the building of replicas, in an attempt to restore a way of life based on a population

FIG. 2 (pages 44 to 47)

Council of Europe forms for an inventory of major sites and monuments in its Member States. Detailed scientific data can be added as annexes.

which has disappeared. On the other hand, even in industrially advanced countries, a city can both preserve its character and play a constructive economic role (Amsterdam in the Netherlands is a good example): the tourists its character continues to attract add to the funds it can earmark for further municipal projects.

Apart from these economic considerations, a major question is at last receiving greater attention: what constitutes a suitable environment for man ? It has many facets—pollution from industrial development and ever-increasing motor traffic, green or open spaces in cities and so on—that demand the services of biologists, economists, designers, sociologists and a host of other specialists. Those working on conservation must join forces with them, in an effort to meet one of man's most important challenges in the latter part of the twentieth century: upgrading the quality of the environment.

Administrative and technical competence in ensuring the conservation of cultural property are thus only the basic requirements. A new outlook—interdisciplinary and international—calls for dedicated and determined leadership. As, day by day, newspapers record the disappearance of one landmark after another, the pressures increase and the challenge must be met, or our heritage will be irremediably lost.

General principles

3

The architect restorer can benefit from recent research on traditional building materials. Reports are available on the deterioration of various materials in different climates: wood, stone, metals, mortar, plaster, paint, cement, varnish, baked and unbaked bricks, terra-cotta, and so on.[1] Techniques should be worked out on the basis of experiments which have shown good results; practical, traditional materials and methods should be combined with procedures based on precise scientific experiments—though the restorer, who is an architect by training and must remain one, will still need to exercise his acute, critical faculties.

New products are continually being developed. Provided they have been thoroughly studied under laboratory conditions and practically tested, they can be employed with new techniques or in combination with existing materials.

The fact that material form, content and intrinsic beauty are all equally important makes it imperative to apply a wide variety of techniques. Different materials will demand different methods, subject perhaps to change with the fluctuation of artistic values. This makes it extremely difficult to lay down any hard-and-fast rules. It is nevertheless essential to work out practical methods and collate specific technical information regarding the behaviour and use of various materials (suitability, durability, resistance, colour, dimension, volume, and so on).

A work of art is expressed through some kind of material, and must be conserved by restoring the material in which it is embodied. This has not always been the purpose of architects. Bramante, for instance, destroyed the original St. Peter's—which, by our standards, could probably have been restored fairly easily—on the orders of the Pope, because the construction of the greatest Christian monument the world has ever known on the very spot where the tomb of the first Apostle was located symbolized the resuscitation of the greatness of the Christian ideal. This would not have occurred in present times, for the idea of conserving works of art as such has since gradually won acceptance.

Conservation implies a scale of values which may differ widely from that of laymen; conserving an historic quarter or community may imperiously demand in addition the conservation of some very ordinary buildings.

WHAT IS RESTORATION?

How does restoration differ from conservation? All those concerned with conservation will agree that, in principle, it means maintaining edifices to prevent them from falling into disrepair, and repairing previously disfigured parts. In practice, when dealing with important buildings, an economic factor is almost always involved.

---

1. See also *The Conservation of Cultural Property*, Paris, Unesco, 1968 (Vol. XI of this series).

These buildings are to be used—indeed, this is often a condition of their survival—and certain concessions have to be made accordingly. Thus conservation pure and simple is seldom possible; some changes usually have to be made, either to modernize or to adapt the edifice. Rules are thus needed to govern the partial reconstruction of buildings intended for everyday use. In dealing with edifices which are already in ruins and not serving any practical purpose, on the other hand, the natural form of restoration is conservation pure and simple.

A distinction must therefore be made, not between restoration and conservation, but between the conservation methods and the reconstruction methods. Restoration is partly justified when it adapts for new purposes edifices that had ceased to have any, but only the condition that the restorer has creative and artistic ability can ensure that the reconstructed or new elements are in harmony with what remains of the original.

Architects working on restoration need precisely the same qualities as any other architects. A mediocre architect will be mediocre at restoration, which demands an artistic and historic sense in addition to an ability to apply technological formulae.

Unlike an architect starting on a new building, the restorer has to deal with an existing building circumscribed by legal, financial and many other conditions which may depend in part on the origins of the proposal to restore the building, and the motives for doing so. In most cases, however, he will be given a free hand. Before making any plans, he must consider the character and aims of the original builders, the purpose for which they intended the edifice, and its relation to its setting; which no longer exist or are hidden as a result of transformations; now considered to be detrimental to the appearance of the whole; and its physical condition.

DOCUMENTATION AND SURVEYING

The need for careful historical, technological and structural research is evident. Even after the work has begun, further research will frequently be necessary, so that plans for restoration are nearly always provisional. For major edifices it should be made a general rule not to embark on restoration without first making an exhaustive study that includes the exterior, the individual sections, the roof, the foundations and even the most remote and inaccessible parts where deterioration may have occurred; a survey alone is not sufficient. For example, all the beams of a truss roof must be examined to make sure that the supports are sound, since anyone with experience of such work knows that wooden beams usually do not have rot on the outer surfaces but mainly at the mortise joints; and it may often be necessary to take precautionary measures immediately, without waiting until the complete plan of work has passed through all the cogs of the bureaucratic machine.

In principle, restoration should not be influenced by financial or other extraneous considerations. The architect in charge should have every facility to carry out surveys and collect data on past history. He must be in a position to carry out further research in the course of operations, and make any adjustments necessary to the original plans.

A detailed log-book of work in progress must be kept, complete with black-and-white and colour photographs, to serve as a guide subsequently; full details of tests, work done, results and explanations of measures taken, will help to save future generations of experts from misunderstandings and faulty 'corrections'. Such mistakes are particularly liable to occur in classical and Gothic architecture, when restorers insert 'corrections' based on more 'purist' canons than those which in fact applied at the time of the original construction. Unfortunately, such 'corrections' are often irreparable. The final report should give full details of all the work done, describing the initial condition, with plans and photographs; the various operations; and the results, illustrated by surveys, plans of work done, and photographs.

SOCIAL, ECONOMIC AND OTHER FACTORS

All buildings are subject to a natural process of deterioration, and so require maintenance. Even ordinary houses need adapting—we only have to think of the utilities and amenities introduced over the past fifty years (e.g. heating, plumbing, electricity, lifts, and so on).

With changes in population patterns and shifts in belief, churches, for example, have been transformed for other purposes. Mansions have been subdivided into smaller units when their original owners became too impoverished to keep them up. In such cases, the artistic value must be weighed against the immediate needs. The decision will be affected by cultural policy, general cultural level, the location of the building, and the various purposes for which it could be used. In principle transformations should produce the least possible change in the building's general appearance—care being taken, for instance, to conserve gardens, general layout, staircases, entrances, ceilings, vaults; to use the original materials when floors have to be repaired, to replace wood by the same kind of wood, stone by stone, brick of the same dimensions; and so on.

Apart from changes in use, deterioration may result from economic factors. Impoverished owners may allow dilapidation, wealthy ones may ruin a building by tasteless ostentation—there are numerous examples of both processes.

Buildings in complete disrepair may have to be abandoned—as when part of the roof or ceilings have fallen in, and restoration would be too difficult and costly. This often happens after wars, when damaged buildings are less valuable than the sites they occupy. Sometimes monuments in poor areas are adopted for habitation (e.g. the Marcellus Theatre in Rome, the Diocletian Palace in Split), or used as warehouses. In the former case, the building, particularly the interior, may be radically transformed, but at least it is maintained and to some extent salvaged. In the latter case the result may be its gradual demolition.

Buildings still in excellent condition are sometimes demolished to make way for a new building, motorway, and so on. This rarely occurs if they are sufficiently important to be scheduled or classified, but can all too frequently happen to buildings unprotected by legislations.

WHY RESTORE?

Restoration is seldom undertaken until deterioration has reached an advanced stage. At this point, the need for it cannot be questioned, whereas the need for preventive measures earlier can always be questioned and work deferred for financial reasons. Such being the case, the problem is almost invariably to restore a monument in a more or less advanced stage of degradation, caused by all kinds of factors—the passage of time, weathering, infiltration of water, and so on.

In industrialized countries in the temperate zones, car and factory fumes cause great damage to plaster, paint, and the actual building materials. Buildings in Egypt suffer on the outside from abrasion by windblown sand, while delicate mural paintings inside, either on plaster or on the stone itself, are perfectly conserved because of the constant low rate of humidity.

Thus the state of conservation of a monument can depend on both climate and location. If cold north winds occur, the windward sides of buildings suffer more than the sheltered sides. In the case of marble carvings, the disintegration of calcium carbonate is brought about by the combined action of wind, frost and rain. Building stones may be cracked by frost action; the stone absorbs humidity from the atmosphere which forms into ice crystals, and the resultant increase in volume causes ruptures. This is particularly important in the case of sandstone and calcareous stones but is less serious in porous stones (most stones of volcanic origin such as trachytes) which have greater resistance to traction, although it may occur in any stone where fissures that admit moisture exist. In areas with marked diurnal ranges in temperature, the interior of stones (whose heat conductivity is low) remains cool while the surface heats up to 50°–60° C. As a result of the expansion of the surface layer, the spalling which occurs is more difficult to remedy than cracking caused by frost.

Frost can be counteracted by treatment with waterproof waxes. Water soluble microcrystalline wax has been used to good effect, but silicones have not always been successful—the moisture retained within may form ice-crystals in times of prolonged cold.

MATERIALS

In stone buildings, most (if not all) of the bearing structures, are usually also stone. Buildings may be made mainly of brick, wood or metals, or may combine a variety of materials, so that a close analysis is necessary before they can be assigned to a particular classification. They may be in reinforced concrete or steel. Monuments may incorporate modern elements that can now be regarded as an integral part of the whole or may be safely replaced. In the early part of the last century, certain extremely elaborate parts of Gothic buildings were replaced by cast-iron elements (e.g. the spire of Rouen Cathedral, which caused an outcry at the time, still exists). Upon deterioration should they be replaced by the kind of stone used originally or should cast-iron be used again? It would not be permissible, for instance, to remove Vasari's altars from the Church of Santa Croce in Florence, since they are beautiful in themselves—we must not be guilty of the mistake made by Vasari himself in destroying those already in existence (a characteristic example of a lack of critical sense in the man who was in fact the founder of modern criticism). In the case of later substitutions, we are nearly always justified in replacing the substituted element by another more adequate one. But each case must be considered on its merits. The only general rule is that a thorough preliminary investigation which takes account not only of the original forms but of all subsequent changes must always be made before embarking on any restoration whatever.

Should the prime consideration be to restore a work of art to its original form, or should it be approached first and foremost as a part of a cultural heritage? In pursuit of an imaginary 'ideal of beauty' having no historical or critical justification, some architects, again, want to correct 'errors' committed by the original builders. Others, on the contrary, believe that the best form of restoration is none at all, but it is difficult to justify simply leaving a monument in ruins, even if reconstruction inevitably entails certain alterations.

The Parthenon can serve as an example. Most of its constituent materials were left in a heap after it had been partially destroyed by bombardment during one of the wars between Venetians and Turks. After Lord Elgin had purchased the Parthenon marbles from the Turkish Governor, the dismantling of both the inner frieze and of the pediments continued, with the result that part of the architrave which still stood was destroyed. When the colonnade was eventually reconstructed, cement replicas had to be used to replace the missing pieces. Replacing the whole frieze would have involved too much restoration, but one side was entirely reconstructed. The hardness of the marble was a saving factor and thus the monument was fairly well preserved despite the violence of the explosion, so that the position of the columns was still discernible. In any case, the situation is better now than when the columns of the right façade lay strewn on the ground; at the same time, the ruined walls of the inner sanctuary still bear witness to what has happened.

A monument can be a striking token of continuity. If its main significance is to recall a person, an event, a stage of civilization, any modification introduced lessens this evocative value and should be avoided.

In deciding whether or not restoration is justified, it is not only the degree of deterioration that counts, but the purpose, and the methods that can be used. It is better to maintain a monument in its existing condition until its value can be more properly appraised than to subject it to ill-considered changes, however well-intentioned.

SOME GENERAL CONSIDERATIONS

The first step is to decide the amount of work required to restore a specific edifice, and then ascertain if the funds available are sufficient to cover all or only part of the work.

Over the years a building will have undergone changes in the course of normal upkeep—repair of floors, roofs, fixtures, chimneys, kitchens, paintwork, and so on. Generations of owners of a private residence, successive dynasties inhabiting royal palaces, different creeds or forms of worship practised in churches, medical progress made in old established hospitals and the changes in the life of ancient cities all have their effects. Buildings acquire in the process a new historical significance as witnesses of past events and the stream of human life which supplements their formal beauty. These additions may have their own aesthetic value, in which case they warrant conservation even though they are superimposed on a structure belonging to a different epoch and a different style. This prin-

ciple becomes doubly valid if the added elements harmonize with the old, or replace ancient parts long since completely gone.

A monument may thus be mainly a work of art, or mainly an historical document. The second criterion is easily weighed by anyone familiar with local history; the first implies expert knowledge, considerable experience, acute critical ability, and familiarity with restoration problems. The case may have to be studied both in absolute terms and in terms of the relative value of constituent parts. When the decision lies between two equally fine works, the factor of uniqueness will obviously tip the scale, for a work which is unique and irreplaceable must be conserved at all costs.

A case in point is that of the seventeenth-century baroque church of S. Urbano alla Caffarella, on the Via Appia outside Rome which, quite by chance, was found to be constructed on top of a Roman tomb in a good state of preservation. Which of the two is more worth conserving, since restoring the Roman tomb, though not difficult, would involve destroying the church? There are plenty of similar Roman tombs, but S. Urbano is unique and also serves a specific purpose; moreover, the Roman tomb need not be destroyed and can even be rendered visible despite the seventeenth-century walls.

In any case, it is a sound rule never to destroy anything which might cause the loss of a work of art or an outstanding local and historical monument, except to recuperate something of quite exceptional value and importance (Plate 1).

As regards the possibility of removing a later edifice in order to uncover a more ancient one, no general principles can be laid down. There may of course be other reasons for deciding to remove a particular monument e.g. the Abu Simbel temples in Upper Egypt which were removed to save them from being sumerged after the construction of the High Dam at Aswan (Plate 2).

53

Plate 1

Peru. During the early colonial period the Spanish frequently built European style structure on the foundations of Inca buildings in Cuzco. The polygonal blocks of stone, laid without mortar, provide a striking contrast to the masonry structure above.

Plate 2

One of the many temples in Nubia (Arab
Republic of Egypt) which were saved from
being flooded by the construction of the High
Dam. The temple of Kalabsha was dismantled
and reassembled on higher ground during 1962
(Photo: Unesco/Gerster.)

It is similarly difficult to say when ana-stylosis is justified—the rebuilding of a fragmented monument by reassembling its elements, or the reconstruction of buildings or colonnades by piecing together again in their original position the fragments of the original, found lying strewn around. This may appear, at first sight, to be justified in the case of collapsed buildings without columns, where the original materials still exist; but since collapse may be tantamount to dismantling, the analogy does not hold except in cases where the stones used for construction were originally joined without mortar. If any of the walls of a building contain irregular stones or plaster, the reconstruction method will have to be used, the difference between the two methods being that the latter involves the use of new materials and even new techniques.

The fact that, in anastylosis, missing pieces of a column may have to be replaced does not alter the nature of the process, since such pieces constitute only a very small proportion of the whole and second, they are easily identifiable by the difference of surface. Following the example of the columns and frieze of the Parthenon, anastylosis has taken its place among modern restoration methods, and it appears to be justified when we consider some of the offences committed in the last century, particularly by archaeologists. The visitor to the Archaeological Museum in Istanbul sees a whole room full of pieces of famous classical architecture (e.g. a typical section of the temple of Artemis Leucophryéne at Magnesia, in Asia Minor). At Magnesia itself, all that remains are the ruins of the temple, strewn around in appalling confusion following the 'digs' made by excavators who were obviously concerned less with the original building than with measuring and classifying the separate parts in order to reconstruct it in the museum. In this instance, anastylosis would constitute the sole means of properly reassembling one of the monuments of this great Hellenistic city in the bend of the Meander. It should be undertaken to avoid loss of the original materials, which at present lie exposed to the rigours of the Anatolian climate *(Plate 3)*.

This raises two very ticklish questions. The first is whether, in operations involving archaeological excavations we are justified, even when all proper precautions are taken, in exploring or extracting part of an edifice without first surveying the whole. The answer is no; all excavations should be preceded by a general survey of the group as a whole. Moreover, agreement must be reached regarding the amount of conservation and restoration that will be indispensable since, otherwise, structures may be destroyed and finds dispersed (e.g. Pompeii, Persepolis, the pre-Hispanic cities of Peru, Pergamum, Nineveh, Priene, Tlemcen and, recently, the extremely interesting and instructive example of Barcelona).

Pompeii gives to the visitor today the impression of being transferred straight back into the life of 2,000 years ago, as though the last desperate cries of the inhabitants of the doomed city lingered on in the frescoed halls and peristyles. But this cannot be maintained much longer for difficult as it is to keep a living city in repair, it is more difficult still when most of the buildings are roofless and exposed to the ravages of the elements. This would appear to suggest that archaeological excavations should never be undertaken in Pompeii, since the ruins now there are at least well preserved. An economic factor exists, however, for it is essential—before starting any excavations of sites of this magnitude—to ascertain what the cost of the conservation of a monumental site would be, as it is now technologically possible to carry out measures to ensure its survival.

The second question to be settled at the outset concerns the transfer of objects and entire architectural units to museums for display and conservation. This is all right with small objects (sculptures, paintings, domestic articles), but not for large archi-

3 a

Plate 3

The temple of Apollo in Didyma, a Greco-Roman site located on the south-western coast of the Anatolian peninsula.
(a) The drums of a column preserved *in situ*.
(b) Columns which have been reassembled through anastylosis to give visitors an impression of the scale of the original building.
(Photos: Sanpaolesi/Unesco.)

3 b

tectural units—the gates of the market at Miletus, as reconstructed in the Berlin museum have been stripped of all poetry—and it is clear that all such units lose their artistic value when removed from their natural setting *(Plate 4)*. It is always preferable to reconstruct them on the spot, providing adequate protection, as has been done at Gela in Sicily, at Sabrata and at Leptis Magna in Libya, rather than reconstitute a monument in museums. During the First World War, especially when the first military planes began bombing towns remote from the scene of fighting, the problems of protecting cultural property were seriously considered. Lists of cultural treasures in enemy territory were drawn up, and the military commands were given orders to spare them; and since looting causes as much loss as destruction, movable objects were removed to safety and placed under protection *(Plate 5)*.

Nevertheless, the destruction was immense. It was not only individual works of art that had to be restored, but entire cities, presenting governments with a financial problem and architects and restorers with the artistic one of deciding whether to restore or to reconstruct.

If practically nothing is left standing, there are two possible solutions: (a) to construct a copy of the original on the same site (as in Warsaw); or (b) to construct something quite different (Rotterdam, Yokohama). Neither is restoration; in (b) the main emphasis is on practical needs and contemporary patterns of living.

There have been many successful restorations of war-damaged monuments. The first step must be the immediate recovery of all materials which can be re-employed—including stones or bricks which must be set aside and protected from further damage by demolition, fire or vandalism; taken early, these precautions can save a great deal of trouble and expense later.

Plate 4

The capitol of a column of the Temple of Artemis Leucoprene, Magnesia, preserved in the Archeological Museum of Istanbul.

5 a

5 b

5 c

Plate 5

Many monuments suffered severely during wars. The Hermitage in Leningrad was badly damaged during the Second World War and has since been carefully restored:
(a) Detail of the façade of the palace in 1944.
(b) Reconstruction and its appearance in 1964.
(c) One of the rooms of the Petershof Palace (1944) located near Leningrad.
(d) The same room after restoration. The work necessitated the establishment of schools to train carpenters, moulders, stone cutters, etc., in order to restore the buildings and the various rooms in accordance with the techniques used during the seventeenth and eighteenth centuries.
(Photos: Ministry of Culture, U.S.S.R.)

5 d

Preliminary surveys

4

Restoration should be based upon documentation which is as complete as possible: original plans, their execution, contemporary building practices, types of materials used and subsequent history. Books may provide records, plans may have been conserved in national, regional or municipal archives. If such documentation is inadequate or absent, archaeological excavation may furnish considerable information—it was, for example, able to reveal several stages in the construction of the Basilica of St. Denis (Seine, France) of which no records had survived. Old newspapers and journals are excellent sources of information on more recent constructions. The familiarity thus gained will suggest the best methods of restoration to follow.

MAKING A SURVEY

A preliminary architectural and photographic survey of the building in its present state is necessary to obtain data on its general design, structural details, and general condition. It will also help to throw light on obscure features of the monument and of its past. This survey requires the utmost care and precision. Photographic documentation should be followed by measured drawings or by photogrammetry (described in Chapter 5) to determine dimensions, structural features, concealed parts not visible on the surface and other details.

The monument and its parts should be drawn to scale, with conventional signs to indicate their type, composition and position. The most convenient scales are 1:500 for mapping; 1:100 and 1:50 for general plans, isometric drawings and isometric projections; and 1:10 and 1:5 for details.

As a general rule, one plan should be drawn up for each horizontal plane, adopting the convention of the horizontal section 1 metre above floor level. This need not be done if inappropriate in relation to the configuration of the monument. In such cases, the horizontal section or sections should be indicated and marked, if necessary, on the sectional drawings.

A broken line is used to mark in the vertical projection of any parts not included in the horizontal section that may facilitate an understanding of the monument. The intersection points of vaulted surfaces should likewise be marked on the diagram by a dotted line.

The same method can be used to indicate the soffit profile of barrel or circular vaults, swung around to form an angle of 90 degrees with the vertical walls against which they are outlined. This procedure may also be useful for cross vaults to prevent them from being confused with cloister vaults.

All the façades should be drawn in orthogonal projection from a point in infinity in relation to the plane, and to non-right-angle faces.

Sections should be taken through the most significant parts of the building so as to reveal the concealed architectural features. All plans should of course indicate the trace of the predetermined vertical planes through which the ideal sections have been taken. Surveyors should accurately check curve and thickness at the crown of arches, the nature of successive taperings in the thickness of bearing walls, and all the significant details, structural and decorative (the latter being drawn large scale or even full size).

Geometric plans should indicate the basic dimensions provided by the metric survey, including elevations. The heights of the various floors must be given when a building—because of its particular volumetric characteristics, its surroundings or its special architectural features—necessitates a detailed graphic analysis. The survey may be supplemented by recapitulatory plans, explanatory diagrams or isometric projection drawings.

MARKING DATES

Modern monuments do not require date indications, as their dates can be established fairly accurately. However, older structures should have their parts built during different periods clearly marked. Regular, glazed or incised plastic markers (the latter made in cemented, two-colour sheets so that the incised letters and numerals show up clearly) which are available commercially can be used to indicate the dates of additions or changes, or the points of demarcation between two or more sections. Abbreviations may be used: e.g. Built between 1272 and 1320 (1272-1320); First stone laid on 15 February 1245 (1st stone 15/2/1245); Monument restored in the fifteenth century (rest. 15th C.); Enlarged in 1528 (enl. 1528); Part demolished about the year 1677 (demol. c. 1677).

Indirect data obtained from historical, topographical, iconographical, literary or other sources may provide indications of dates. For example, a diary written in 1812 might recall a dedication of a section of the church which was repaired after the fire of 1798. This section could then be dated as 'before 1812' or 'between 1798 and 1812'.

PHOTOGRAPHS

Surveys should be supplemented by clear photographs (black and white or colour) giving a view, details and the setting. Drawings cannot always show ornamental details, and may fail to convey shapes, colours, general appearance, perspective, surroundings, and the beauty of the landscape. Irregularities of shape and outline, and damaged parts, can be shown more clearly by photographs than by any other means; hence their vital importance for this purpose.

A combination of graphic surveys and photographs should provide a clear and exact picture of the monument.

MODELS

Surveys and photographs give a two-dimensional picture; models and casts can be used to obtain a three-dimensional representation.

Models made of wood, wood derivatives, metal, plaster, cardboard or transparent or non-transparent plastic substances can be prepared to illustrate the volumetric and spatial arrangement of urban units or groups of monuments, or a general view of ruins and site topography in the case of archaeological excavations. They are useful in visualizing missing parts and deciding how to reconstruct them, for skilfully illuminated photographs can be used to bring the past to life with amazing vividness. Models can be used for calculating and testing the resistance of existing or projected structures.

CASTS

A cast gives an exact reproduction. Into a matrix taken from the original a fluid substance (plaster, wax or a compound of plaster and synthetic rubber) is poured and removed after it has solidified. This method, excellent as it is, may present serious difficulties when it comes to complicated pieces of sculpture necessitating a number of carefully made matrices. Another drawback is that making the matrix involves coating the surface with various substances which may harm the colour, the polish or the surface itself. The surface can, however, be protected by covering it with a thin sheet of aluminium foil or similar material, taking care to avoid folds before making the cast. The foil can easily be removed afterwards.

Casts can also be taken to reproduce the shape, position and surface of mosaics, frescoes, epigraphs or of any section whose surface and structure is to be studied. Papier mâché gives good results; when dampened it adheres to the surface and carries the imprint when removed after drying. In some cases, rubbing is convenient: a small cotton bag containing powdered graphite or some other powdered dye is rubbed on a thin sheet of white paper placed on the surface of which a tracing is required (for copying epigraphs, it is enough to rub a soft pencil gently over a sheet of paper laid on the engraved surface).

ANALYTICAL STUDIES

A wide variety of other problems must be considered once the surveys have been completed. A complete schedule, which can be adapted to cover a wide range of monuments, is set out below.

Historical. Who commissioned the monument; circumstances in which it originated; details of how it was made; changes which occurred during the life of the building.

Artistic. Aesthetic principles; composition and proportions; artistic value. Particular attention should be paid to the style and characteristic work of the artists, even when they cannot be identified by name.

Structural. Purpose; building methods, materials used (form and arrangement, as bonding styles of brick or stone); ultimate result.

The analytical studies detailed below are necessary to ascertain all the features of the edifice concerned, including those which were not executed or left unfinished.

Data displayed on the edifice itself. Epigraphs, signatures, initials, monograms, dates or special signs marked more or less visibly; escutcheons and emblems, mural decorations (stuccoes, frescoes, revetments, etc.); graffiti, often accompanied by dates and signatures, which may have been executed casually or even hastily.

Data discovered in the structure. Stonemasons' marks and stamp marks on tiles; coins and medals, and documentation concealed in the masonry and foundations; information (as to form, chronology, etc.) obtained from specimens taken.

Data deduced by study of surveys. Metrological information about the units of measurement used for building; geometric diagrams indicating modules or space proportions; preparatory composition diagrams, etc. Besides this, there exists a large quantity of accessory material to be scrupulously assembled and subjected to critical examination.

The whole of the literature so far published about the monument, its history and its builders.

Existing graphic and photographic documentation. Old drawings and photographs, models, plans and sketches relating to the edifice; geographical charts, maps, plans of cities, general views, including those in the background of pictures, bas-reliefs and illuminated manuscripts; cadastral plans; library and archival sources.

Ancient manuscripts and documents relating to the foundation of the monument, any modifications and enlargements made, its original purpose, and subsequent uses of it; administrative documents; orders, contracts, sales, receipts, wills, donations and other deeds; old descriptions; documents; censuses; accounts of pastoral visits, etc.

Archaeological excavation. It will sometimes be necessary, especially when dealing with very ancient monuments as well as archaeological sites, to undertake exploratory excavations in order to get down to the original level and uncover the buried parts of the structure, or to discover earlier versions and thus establish more surely the sequence of building operations. In either case the excavations must be made by personnel qualified in the investigation and dating of archaeological evidence and finds.

Laboratory analyses of pigments, materials used (identification of wood, chemical composition of metals, quarry from which stones were obtained, etc.).

Comparative studies of contemporary or similar monuments in order to define general patterns and determine which features are unique.

The list includes all possible factual data and documentation which must be sought out, even though it may be difficult to trace.

In addition, research must cover various other aspects of the monument which, though not easy to define, are of equal if not greater importance—the whole world of ideas, civilization and culture pertaining to and finding clear expression in the monument concerned; the personalities, aspirations and ideals of the artists who created it; the features which raise a masterpiece above the general level of artistic production.

We consider it unnecessary to give examples illustrating the points to be covered under the various sections, but should like to make one final recommendation, namely, that the scrupulously minute, comprehensive study of a monument is intended not merely as a record, but as a means to full and complete understanding and knowledge of it. It is to be hoped that such studies will form the basis for serious publications.

The changes which have taken place in a work of art, or an historically important structure traced from the moment of its creation in the distant past down to recent times, give an intimation of its essential significance, of the artistic and human message it conveys.

Hans Foramitti

Classical and photogrammetric methods used in surveying architectural monuments

5

FORMS OF BUILDINGS

A certain duality is implicit in the concept of form, for a distinction must be made between apparent form (the monument as seen by an observer) and real or measured form. Only the latter can be the basis of a proper survey. Sketches, perspective drawings and photographs yield apparent forms, while real forms can be determined only from data giving the exact dimensions of the object through orthogonal projections, elevations, sections and so on which are drawn to scale and accompanied by measurements. In addition theoretical form, the idealization of the object which represents it as it should be, must be distinguished from the real form.

The precision with which the real form can be determined is in practice limited by the size of the drawing (in which, for the sake of legibility, the smaller the scale, the more details have to be omitted). The ideal procedure is to show the real form in its entirety and then execute the plans, sections and elevations required, together with the relevant information. Only isolated points can be determined by classical and topographical methods, and since an endless number of such points are required if the real form is to be determined, these methods are time-consuming and very expensive. In order to minimize these two factors, the number of points is usually kept low, and they are joined by arbitrary lines which are derived from the theoretical form, and may well differ from reality.

Photogrammetry, in which special cameras are used, can determine the lines of the real form. A single exposure produces up to 200,000 points, whose position in space may be accurately defined by means of plotting devices. This process not only produces more accurate results but also requires much less time. Increasing use will therefore obviously be made of this technique, older methods only in cases when photogrammetry would no longer be worth while, e.g. the preparation of plans of small intricate objects.

CLASSICAL METHODS OF SURVEYING

In undertaking a survey by the classical methods, the first step is to make a sketch, more or less to scale, keeping as close as possible to the orthogonal projection desired. Measurements are then added. They may be determined either by direct measurement or by using a topographical instrument.

DIRECT MEASUREMENT

The methods used may vary widely—from the most primitive (if need be, even 'human' measurements such as a pace, a stride, a hand's span and an arm's span can be used) to the most sophisticated. This is not the place to list them all; it will suffice to point out certain ways in which they can be used.

Whatever the methods employed in drawing plans to scale from the measurements on the sketch, it is essential to follow strictly a system of determining the position of the different points in relation to each other, i.e. to determine a system of co-ordinates. The co-ordinates must be used in selecting the points and lengths measured and, of course, in adopting a particular method of measuring. Various systems may be followed.

Triangulation

The triangle has long been used as the basis of surveying (Fig. 3(a)). Its main advantage is that it can be determined from length alone, and that many surfaces can be divided into triangles (Fig. 3(b)).

Another very old method consists of using a single-leg compass (e.g. a rope attached to a pole) to find the apices of squares, hexagons, octagons, pentagons, etc., on the circumference of a circle; these in turn can then be divided into triangles. The plan can be drawn very quickly, both on the ground and on paper, using the same process to construct a circle within the figure obtained. This method is called 'triangulation' or 'quadrature', according to the figures used; with it, more or less accurate right angles, large axes, and so on, may be drawn for large areas, using nothing but a rope.

Cartesian co-ordinates

By determining axes intersecting at right angles, we can obtain the data needed to establish Cartesian co-ordinates, i.e. to fix the position of each point in relation to directions perpendicular or parallel to the axes of rectangular co-ordinates (Fig. 3(c)). It then becomes possible to calculate a length, even if it is not directly measurable, by determining the position of its extremities in the system of co-ordinates.

Let us take an actual example (Fig. 4(a) bottom right). The length AD cannot be directly measured because of obstacles (houses). Points A and D are plotted on the ground; we now want to determine the position, also on the ground, of intermediate points (e.g. where AD is crossed by a drainpipe). Another line A′D′ is then drawn on both ground and paper, and points are taken on this straight line, from which, on paper, perpendiculars are drawn to AD. By means of the co-ordinates, the points where these perpendiculars cut AD can be accurately plotted on paper. The position of the points to be found in the line AD can then be determined by simply measuring on the paper the lengths thus obtained.

The axes of the co-ordinates can be represented in the building (inside a church, for example), by cords or steel ropes with chalk marks on the ground, or something similar (Fig. 4(b)).

The points may also be plotted perpendicularly on these axes by means of a small instrument such as a cross staff or a prism. Measurements can be taken by fixing to a pole a horizontal measuring-rod placed against the object which would otherwise be inaccessible (Fig. 4(c)).

In order to avoid serious errors which irregularities in the objects might give rise to, a level of reference should be marked and transferred to the wall by means of a horizontal chalk line, which can easily be effaced after the work is completed. This line will be the 'zero' of the vertical co-ordinates. The figures indicating the distance from this line to the ground will be negative values.

The same method can be used to determine the outline of the base of a column or the details of a capital (Fig. 5(a)). One measuring-rod held vertically will give the abscisses, and another, placed in a horizontal position by means of a plumb-level held in the same hand and pushed forward until it

FIG. 3

Simple use of triangulation:
(a) Use of triangulation to obtain the measurements of a room.
(b) Dividing a polygonal room into triangular units.
(c) Obtaining Cartesian co-ordinates.

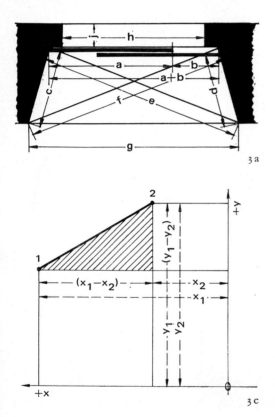

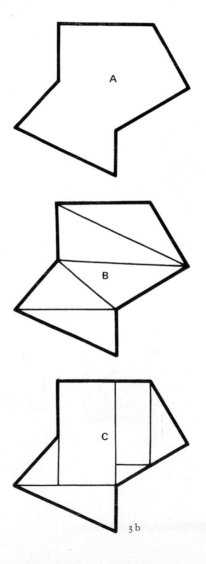

3 a

3 c

3 b

meets the object, will give the ordinates. The co-ordinates can be read off at the intersection of the two measuring-rods.

Speaking of columns, it should be noted that in determining the diameter of solids of revolution it is advisable to use a stone-cutter's compass or, failing that, an ordinary folding rule (Fig. 5 (b)).

In practice, if the object is not directly accessible, the Xs or Ys can often be determined only in successive sections,

which are subsequently added together or substracted from known lengths. Let us take a few examples.

The height of a gallery and the heights above the floor of the gallery $(-c+a)$ and $(-c+b)$ of a level corresponding respectively to the lower and upper ridges of a cornice opposite the gallery are known (Fig. 4(a), lower left). From these data we can find the height above the ground of the lower ridge: $b_1 = d - c + a$, and of the

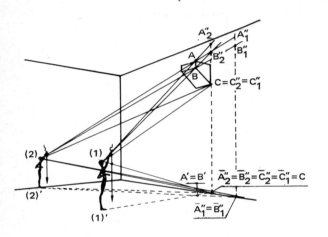

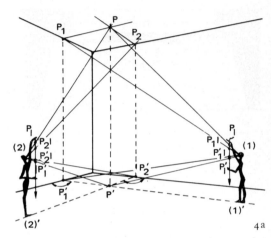

4a

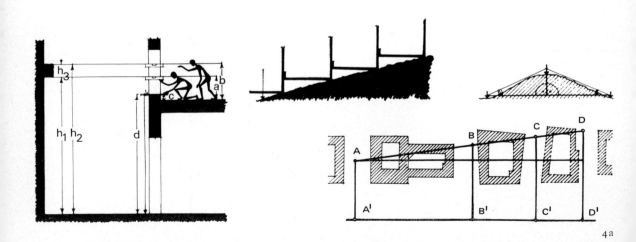

4a

upper ridge: $h_2 = d - c + b$. The thickness of the cornice is found by substraction: $h = h_2 - h_1$.

Another example (Fig. 6(a)): differences in the level of a tract of ground can easily be measured by taking intermediate points, and adding several differences of level found by successive observations on absolutely vertical laths (using a surveyor's level). When the instrument is moved, the last lath sighted should be left in position so as

to provide one of the data for the next observation.

Figure 6(b) shows how simply measurements obtained by means of a plumb-line or a steel measuring tape can be added to a levelling when the difference in level cannot be directly measured by observation (because of a wall).

If no surveyor's level is available to place on the laths, the latter can easily be placed in an approximately vertical position

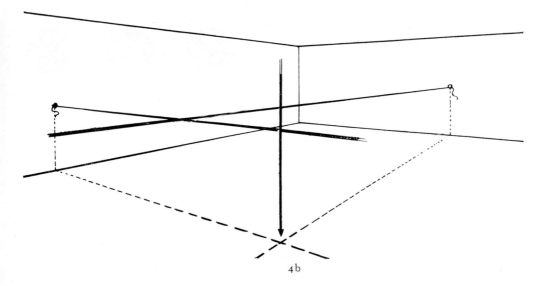

4b

FIG. 4

Triangulation, application of principles.
(a) Measuring verticals and objects covered with obstructions.
(b) Measuring the axes of co-ordinates within a building.
(c) Measuring verticals.

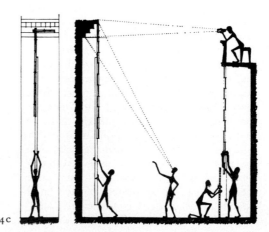

4c

by using the reticle of the levelling telescope; while an assistant increasingly inclines the lath, a note is made of the time when the lowest graduation of the lath appears on the horizontal wire of the telescope Fig. 7(a)).

Right angles on the ground can be determined by means of measuring-rods or cords. Some such methods are shown in Figure 7 (b), (c) and (d). Others are illustrated in Figures 8 and 9 (a) and (b).

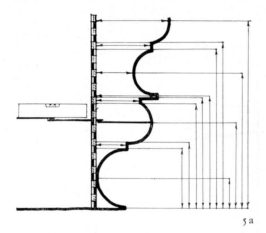

5 a

Polar co-ordinates

Polar co-ordinates determine the position of points by means of a pole and a straight line 'O' which passes through the pole (Fig. 9(c)). Other directions are determined from the angle they form with the direction 'O'. Starting from two poles whose distance— that is, whose base—is known, each of the points can be found from the angles formed by the base and the straight line connecting the point with the pole, and also from the two distances from the point to the poles which form a triangle with the base. Since the position of this base in the system of co-ordinates is known, all the points measured can be accurately plotted in the system. This method is particularly useful in determining irregular parts of an object.

Geodetic traverses

If instruments for taking exact measurements of angles (theodolites and dioptric compasses) are available, geodetic traverses can be made consisting of a succession of straight lines marked out on the ground, whose lengths, and the corresponding angles of the polygon, have been accurately

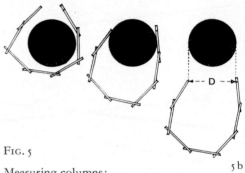

Fig. 5

5 b

Measuring columns:
(a) Measuring the capitals.
(b) Measuring the diameter of a column using a folding rule.

determined. These lines can serve as a basis for measurements such as those described above, and more especially where the points of intersection are inaccessible.

It may be noted that approximate traverses can be made without topographical intruments (Fig. 11). For this purpose, we must consider (Fig. 10(b)) the horizontal triangle formed by two theodolites a_1 and a_2 and the projection Z' of the point marked Z on a horizontal plane of reference. If we know the base $S_1 S_2$ of the triangle and the two angles $Z_1 S_1 S_2$ (which can be found from the observations made at each position of the theodolite towards point Z and towards the position of the other theodolite), we can deduce from these data the length of the other two sides $S_1 Z_1$ and $S_2 Z_1$ of the horizontal triangle. Each of these, together

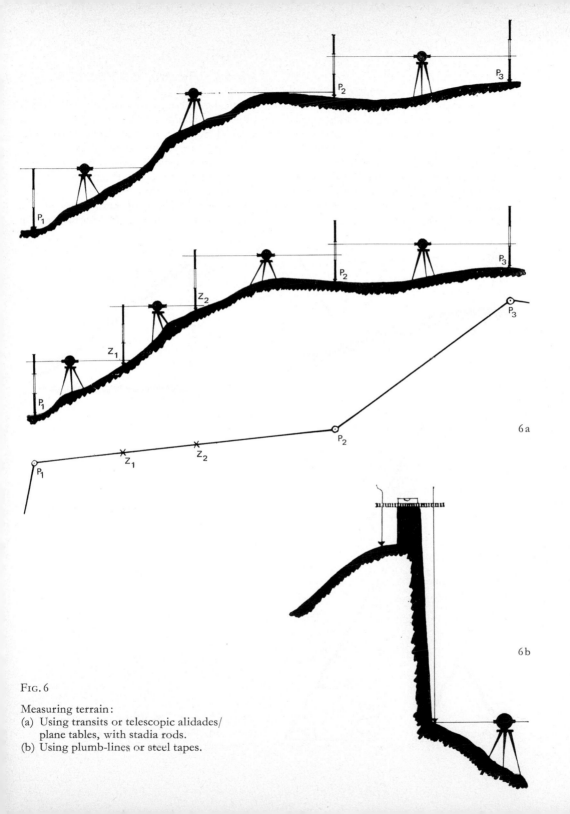

6 a

6 b

Fig. 6

Measuring terrain:
(a) Using transits or telescopic alidades/
     plane tables, with stadia rods.
(b) Using plumb-lines or steel tapes.

73

with the line ZZ_1, forms a right-angled triangle, two angles of which we already know (the right angle and the angle formed by the theodolite sighting, α_1 and α_2 respectively) and one side S_1Z_1 and S_2Z_1 respectively). It is therefore a simple matter to calculate the side Z_1, or the height of the point observed above the level of the instruments. By adding the height of the instruments we can find the height of point Z above the ground.

Vertical planes. Plotting of points on the ground

Vertical planes can be established visually by means of plumb-lines or, better still, the vertical hair-line of a theodolite view-finder moving in a strictly vertical plane.

After two or more vertical planes passing through the same point P have been established, the projection P' of this point can be established from the intersection of the plane on the ground. By repeating this

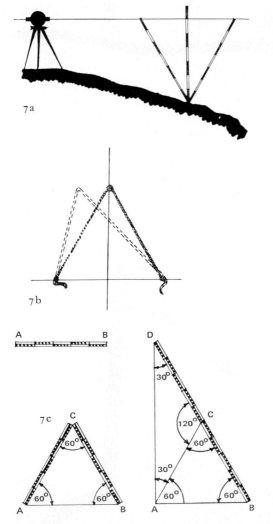

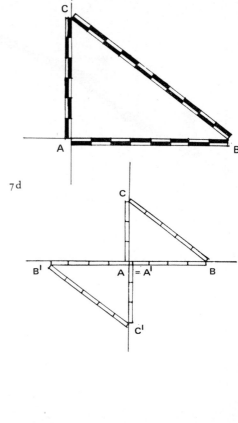

FIG. 7

(a) Improvisation by tilting the stadia rod.
(b), (c), (d) Determining right angles using measuring-rods or cords.

procedure for several points, it is possible to plot, on the ground, the whole outline of the inaccessible object or detail.

An example is given in the top left-hand drawing in Figure 4(a). The object of the exercise is to take the measurements of a façade, of which all the higher parts are inaccessible. We take up a position facing the parts to be measured and, using a small theodolite, a diopter or, failing these, a plumb-line, we line up the instrument whose level or levels have previously been clamped. Without altering the position of the sighting horizontally, the view-finder or diopter is then pointed towards the ground, and an assistant is asked to put a chalk mark at the point of intersection.

If the two sights—towards the point and towards the chalk mark—are in a plane perpendicular to the plane of reference of the orthogonal projection, hence in this case to the surface of the façade (sight one), it

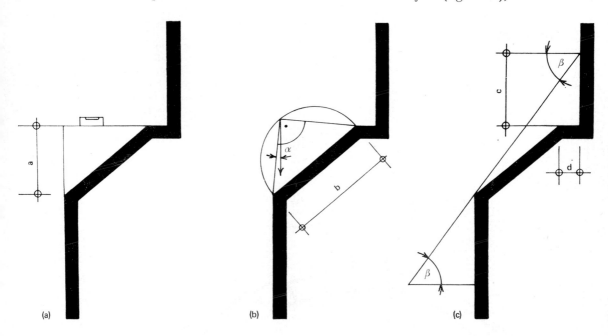

(a)   (b)   (c)

FIG. 8

(a) Measuring the recess of a high opening of a window using a spirit level and vertical measurement.
(b) Using a builder's level.
(c) Using a clinometer and sightings.

does not make much difference whether the point being observed is in front of or behind the plane of reference; it will still be plotted at the desired point on the ground.

If, on the other hand, the line of sight forms an angle other than a right angle (sight two) with the plane of reference, any point not in the plane of reference will, when plotted on the ground, be shifted forward or back by a distance which in-

creases with any increase in the deviation from the right angle and with any increase in the distance of the object from the plane of reference. This is a very serious potential source of error.

It is a good idea to use different-coloured chalks to mark the points plotted on the ground for each storey. The distance of each of these marks from one end of the building selected as the starting point for all measurements (to avoid the addition of

Fig. 9

(a) Measuring an inaccessible point by using a tape, a tape with an attached plumb-line, and tape and plumb-line mounted on a rod.
(b) Establishing a horizontal plane with a level which is out of order by averaging two successive measurements.
(c) Measuring polar co-ordinates.

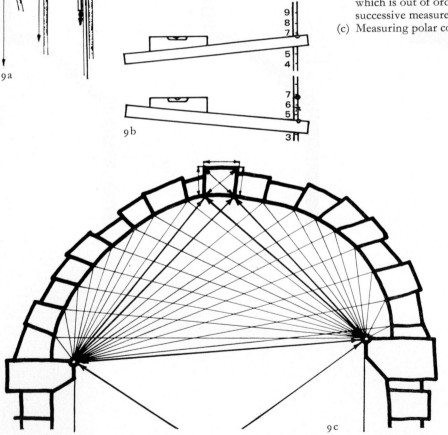

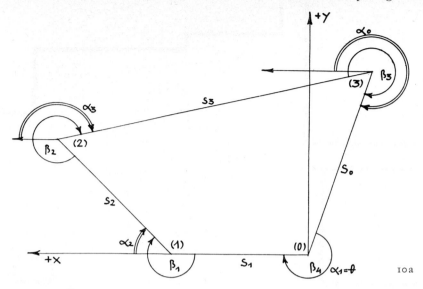

10a

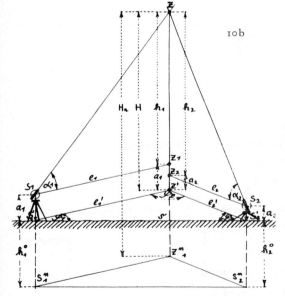

10b

FIG. 10

(a) Polygonal trace.
(b) Contour lines using a builder's level.
(c) Polar co-ordinates, measurement by
    intersections from the apices of a traverse.

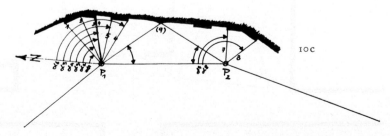

10c

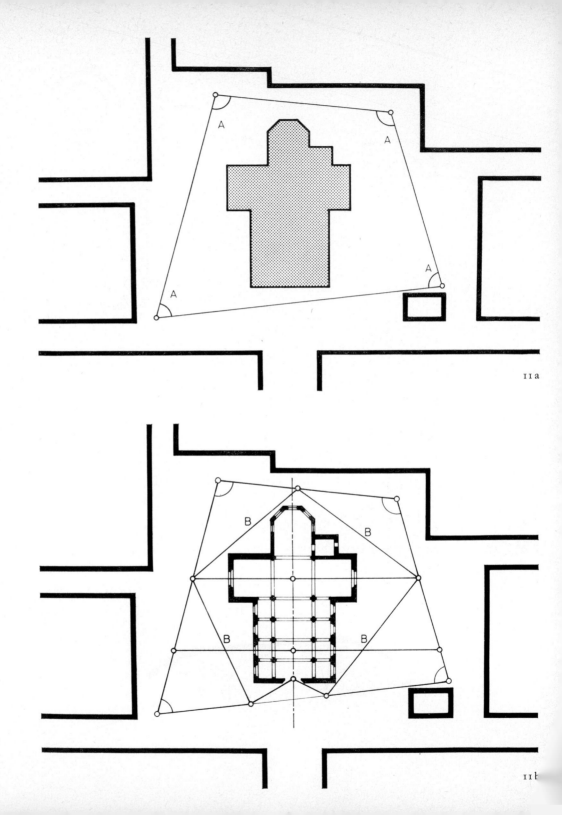

11a

11b

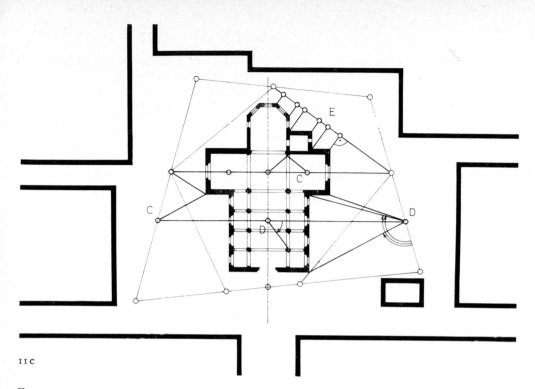

11c

FIG. 11

Geodetic traverse:
(a) Building surrounded by a geodetic traverse
    showing measurement of angles and sides.
(b) Traverse in which the measurement of
    angles are replaced by triangles. These can
    be constructed simply by using steel
    measuring tape.
(c) Different uses of the traverse. From the
    apices or intermediate points of the traverse,
    points can be plotted in different ways:
    from C—using lengths only (triangles);
    D—polar co-ordinates (angles and lengths
    of intersections); E—rabatting point per-
    pendicularly to a line which is part of the
    traverse.

partial measurements, which is another source of error) is then calculated with a steel measuring-tape (Figs. 10, 12). Vertical measuring rods will then be placed wherever possible to reach up to the points concerned at the various levels; all that need then be done is to read off the heights, whilst the distance between the points can be measured directly by measuring the distance on the ground between one rod and another.

These points will then be incorporated into the system of co-ordinates.

Optical plummets are useful for this purpose; these are instruments which direct the *coudé* radius from a view-finder vertically upwards and make it possible, by means of a plumb-line, to project on the ground such features as a keystone or a plaster ornament, the plan of which can thus be traced on a sheet of paper placed on the ground and

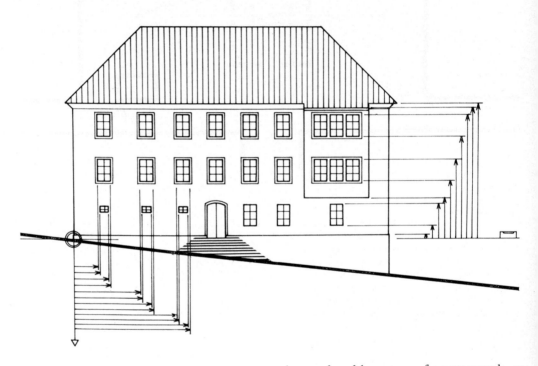

Fig. 12

Measurement of a façade by using Cartesian co-ordinates.

later reduced by means of a pantograph, or photographically.

SELECTION OF POINTS AND OF THE PLANE OF REFERENCE

All of these measurements require a great deal of care, experience and time. There is therefore a temptation to plot the theoretical rather than the actual form so as to reduce the number of points to be measured. The selection of these points may be guided by technical considerations: which measurements, for example, did a Gothic builder take in order to give a vault its particular shape and dimensions? Such measurements, in any case, must be recorded accurately. Hence the importance of knowing about ancient building methods, how plans used to be drawn, and so on.

Once the main points have been established, intermediate measurements may be taken to check roughly in what way the actual shape differs from the theoretical one, either through incompetent execution, deliberate aesthetic choice, subsequent damage, warping, or settling.

Objects in a surface which is not parallel to the plane of reference, such as the walls of a polygonal apse, must be plotted by means of a parallel plane of reference, and the orthogonal projection transformed into an affine image by means of the plane or of a transformation equation.

There is no need to go into all the details at this point, or to dwell too long on the opportunities offered by various instruments in combination. It is enough to mention them and indicate what an enormous amount of work is involved if they are to be used to make the survey as complete and accurate as possible. Such surveys are accordingly difficult. They are growing more and more so because specialists are becoming rare and the pressure of work becomes correspondingly greater. The solution lies in simplifying the photogrammetric method and adapting it for conservation purposes.

PHOTOGRAMMETRIC METHOD OF SURVEYING

On the basis of experience, suggestions were made regarding the design and manufacture of instruments which enable people without special qualifications in geodesy, architecture, art history or ancient building techniques to carry out far more accurate surveys, meet contemporaty preservation criteria and take much less time.

Photogrammetric methods have been used with satisfactory results for surveying historic monuments since the middle of this century, but not on a very wide scale as not enough surveyors trained in the older methods were available.

At one time, moreover, restorers did not consider it necessary to record the real form of buildings, as they were much more concerned with the theoretical form . . . and hence accurate measurements were not as necessary. However, as the interest in scientific accuracy and in scientifically recording the history of monuments developed, standardized methods were worked out to meet this need and the growing shortage of people capable of using the older methods.

PHOTOGRAMMETRIC PRINCIPLES

Intersection photogrammetry (Fig. 13), aerial photogrammetry and photo-interpretation will not be discussed in detail here. However, mention must be made of large-scale procedures that require elaborate equipment and a large staff, and of a simplified form of terrestrial stereophotogrammetry that can be used in most preservation problems.

Essentially, photogrammetry consists in fixing on two photographic plates—the exposures being taken from two different positions with special cameras under set conditions—all the elements likely to be of use in preparing plans and determining lengths, distances, etc. Only the elements which are visible on both plates can be seen stereoscopically, i.e. in relief, in a stereo-plotting device which gives the viewer a three-dimensional picture from the pair of photographs.

The stereoscopic view of the subject has a reference mark, a small black dot which the operator, by means of two fly-wheels

81

and a pedal disc, can direct at will within the image space from right to left, downward and upward, backward and forward. These three dimensions correspond, in the stereo-plotting instrument, to the Cartesian co-ordinates.

The reference mark can be brought to any point on an object visible in the stereoscopic vision, and can easily be made to follow the lines and contours in the model space. The movements of the reference mark are trans-

system is entirely free from distortion, having a fixed, accurate focal length. It is equipped with a support and mechanically adjustable reference marks which fix the horizontal line and nodal point of the central projection on the exposure. It can be clamped with screws and levels. The distance between the two viewpoints (i.e. the base) must be accurately known, together with the orientations of the two cameras, i.e. the disposition of the lines of sight in relation to the base.

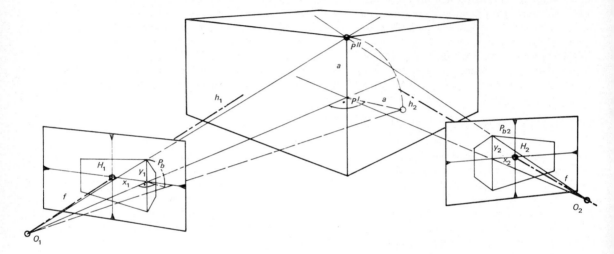

mitted to three co-ordinates. Two of these operate a drawing device which traces the elevation, plan, sections etc. and the third operates a counter which gives the third co-ordinate in figures. Two drawing tables can be controlled at the same time for the simultaneous drawing of two orthogonal projections (plan and elevation for instance). In the same way, by means of cutters operated by the stereoplotting instrument and by following the contours, it is possible to make a relief model directly on a block of plaster.

REDUCTION TO 'NORMAL' USE

The photographic apparatus used differs from the ordinary camera in that the optical

FIG. 13

Intersection photogrammetry.
O_1 and O_2 are nodal points of the lens of the eye. Since the plane of the negative is in front of the eye an image (contact print) is obtained whose sides are not inverted. By plotting points O_1 and O_2 on a plane of the plotting scale and the focal length, according to the direction of the lines of sight, and also a perpendicular correspondence to the traces of the image, the project centre O_1 can be joined to a point corresponding to the ordinate of a point P_b. The operation is repeated from position O_2. The lines $O_1 P_b$ and $O_2 Pb_2$ intersect at P'. This intersection corresponds to the plane of P. By rabatting the abscisses of the image Y on the plan, the line $O_1 H_2$ may be drawn, which gives in the plane, on the perpendicular a, the height of P'' over P'.

Different orientations are possible. The special knowledge needed by the operator can be reduced to a minimum if he has to deal only with the most simple case of terrestrial photogrammetry, the 'normal', which is distinguished by (normal) lines of sight, perpendicular to the base (Fig. 14). However, this involves a rigidity which precluded its application in the cramped situations frequently encountered in preservation and inventory work.

technical capacity of the average historical department—and could not in any case be carried out by their staff without interfering with their normal work. In such cases, the curator must decide precisely what he wants, invite estimates, and award a contract.

Instruments and procedures are described below which should enable curators to handle their own day-to-day photogrammetric tasks.

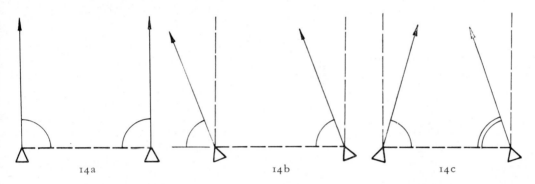

14a   14b   14c

Fig. 14

(a) Normal line of sight, perpendicular to the base.
(b) Oblique axes.
(c) Convergent axes.

An attempt has now been made to deduce the principles, and produce equipment in collaboration with a firm of optical-instrument makers which would enable a curator to use photogrammetric methods without having to depend on specialized agencies, expensive equipment and highly qualified engineers. The latter find it difficult to free themselves to act immediately whenever an urgent case arises, nor are they organized for relatively small jobs. And, of course, their charges are of necessity relatively high.

However, the services of specialized agencies, such as that which forms part of the National Geographical Institute in Paris, are indispensable for large-scale projects which demand resources beyond the

TAKING THE PICTURE

Two photogrammetric cameras are mounted at the ends of a metal tube 120 centimetres long. Normally their orientation is based on the lines of sight being perpendicular to the tube which constitutes the base (see *Plate 6* and Fig. 14). This double camera is equipped with a high-precision spherical level, and is mounted on a tripod, so that it can easily be levelled by means of adjusting screws. The tripod is fitted with batteries and a small control panel which enables the shutters of both cameras to be released simultaneously. The latter have fixed diaphragm stops. Since the depth of field runs from 5 metres to infinity, only the exposure time has to be adjusted.

The system of co-ordinates, on which the stereoplotting will later be based, is given by the direction of the lines of sight and by the choice of the plane in which the photographic plates are arranged. This plane will constitute the plane of reference for the stereoplotting orthogonal projections.

After various tests, 9 × 12 centimetres was selected as the size most universally applicable.[1]

However, with other sizes (6 × 9 centimetres and 13 × 18 centimetres, pictures can very easily be taken, also with a fixed base of 120 centimetres and horizontal axes.

Thanks to a counterpoise bar, the camera can be used to take pictures through narrow openings and windows, while still standing on a tripod inside the room (Plate 7). In designing this instrument, flexibility was the main consideration.

Passing at will from vertical to horizontal format

So that the object will appear as large as possible in photographs, it was deemed necessary to be able to pass at will from the vertical to the horizontal format. The small sides of the photographic plate being arranged parallel to the base tube, horizontal exposures can be obtained by rotating the base vertically (Plate 10 (a)).

In this way unnecessary background (sky, ground) can be eliminated. This is particularly important in the case of stereophotogrammetric exposures. With the lengthwise format, the left-hand side of the left-hand print and the right-hand side of the right-hand print may register elements which do not appear on the other print and are consequently unusable for stereoscopic plotting. By making it possible to take a wide exposure, the vertical position of the base increases the area of overlapping of the two exposures in that direction and so, in many cases, the number of details which can be plotted.

Orienting at angles of 27, 63, or 90 degrees

The wide angle of the lens and the possibility of orienting the cameras to angles which

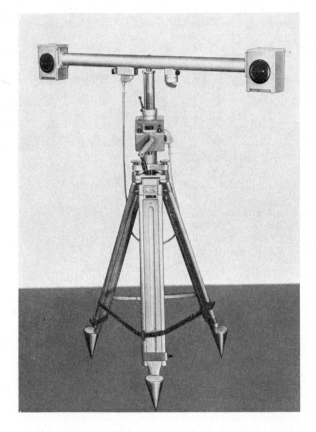

Plate 6

Zeiss SMK 120 set in normal position with the base and the lines of sight in the horizontal plane (photo: Carl Zeiss).

1. cf. H. Foramitti, Die praktische Arbeit der Bildmessung bei der Bestandesaufnahme historischer Bauwerke, *Geodätisches Kolloquium der Rheinisch-Westfälischen Technischen Hochschule Aachen*, 11 November–9 December 1966, and 10 February 1967.

7a

can be adjusted from the horizontal base provide exposures which considerably over-lap and can easily be plotted by assembling sections.

For simplicity of handling, all measures of angles and dials have been omitted; instead, an orientation cube is placed either on the base tube or on one of the two cam-eras (preferably the latter). Regardless of whether the base is horizontal or vertical, one side of the cube will be horizontal. A spherical level can then be magnetically fixed to that side. Depending on how it is set, the lines of sight will vary from 0 de-grees to 90 degrees *(Plate 8)*.

For an angle of 27 or 63 degrees, all that need be done is to place a 27-degree wedge

7b

Plate 7

(a) Coupled cameras mounted on a tripod, equipped with a counterpoised rail.
(b) Cameras protruding from the window.

Plate 8

Stereo cameras set at 90 degrees with lines of sight directed vertically.

between the front or rear side of the cube and the base of the level. An adapter, set on the tripod and taking the camera, roughly determines the angle; it then merely remains to fix the level with the foot screw.

The angles of 0, 27, 63 and 90 degrees have been found from experience to be sufficient for architectural purposes, and can be obtained by simply setting a spherical level *(Plate 9)* which at the same time ensures that the base is horizontal.

These angles are often necessary in order to photograph lofty objects which are not sufficiently distant, e.g. outdoors (lanes a few metres wide and 4- or 5-storey frontages, gables, towers, etc.), and indoors (the high and narrow naves of Gothic churches, cupolas, etc.). They make it possible to include in a single view (from the gallery of a church, for example) practically the whole interior (Fig. 15). This also applies to surveying archaeological excavations by taking photographs downwards.

With focusing thus simplified and reduced, photogrammetry can thus be used by persons without specialized training, including those concerned with art history, archaeology, conservation and architecture.

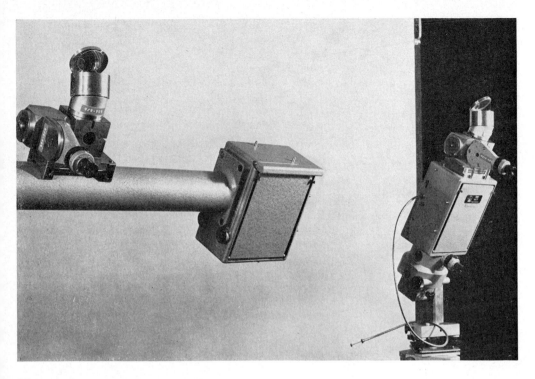

Plate 9

SMK 120 and TMK arranged as a single unit with an added device for inclined sighting and alignment of the base. Notice the insertion of a wedge, shown in the photograph, to the right.

Oblique photography

The range of application becomes still greater if a further device is added (Fig. 16 (a–g)). It is often necessary to photograph an object from the side because it is hidden by something else and a frontal shot is impossible. The cameras are placed in position on a vertical base, with a side view. A reference plane parallel to the main surface of the object (façade) is chosen and a view-finder with a magnetic base which delimits the reference plane is attached perpendicularly to the orientation cube. An assistant marks this direction as far away as possible (e.g. on a façade on the other side of the street) by a sighting mark or chalk mark which will appear in the centre of the cross-wire of the view-finder. The latter is then removed, the 27-degree wedge placed on the cube and the view-finder on the wedge. The adapter is then swung round at the point of entry into the tripod until the chalk mark or sighting mark again appears in the centre of the cross-wire of the view-finder, duly deflected by the 27-degree wedge. The horizontality of the lines of sight and the verticality of the base are assured by the

87

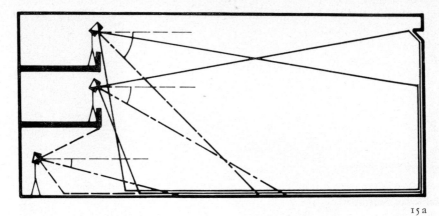

15 a

FIG. 15

(a) Photographing an interior, taking elevations and sections.
(b) Photographing a castle wall from a moat.
(c) Surveying a façade from the other side of a
narrow street lined with tall buildings.
(d) Photographing a high, narrow room.

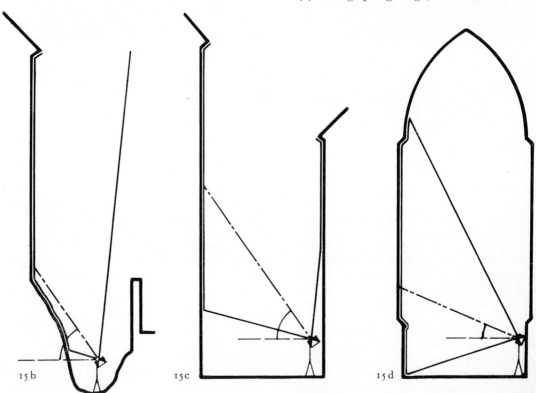

15 b   15 c   15 d

spherical level placed on the upper side of the cube. The lines of sight are deflected 27 degrees in relation to the reference plane.

By getting round obstacles which obstruct the view and by using the restricted space of a narrow lane, quite bulky objects can be photographed on two prints which form a plotting pair.

Once again, handling is simple and there is no danger of error.

For various orientations (which are of course also possible with the counterpoise bar shown in Figure 16), a normal view-finder is used which is more practical than the elbow view-finding sight usually delivered with the SMK or TMK apparatus; and it also allows the observer to adopt a more comfortable position. The elbow view-finder has been designed for various applications which are discussed below and renders these instruments suitable for dealing with practically any problem.

Enlarging the base by two successive positions of the same camera

For accurate stereoplotting, the distance between the object and the camera must be from five to twenty times the length of the base. Only for very flat objects can the distance-base ratio be lower than 1:5 (1:4, even 1:3). Theoretically therefore, the 120-centimetre base permits distances from 3.5–25 metres and in practice, for distances of up to 30 metres and a little over.

Single camera

For greater distances, the solution is a single camera *(Plate 10 (b))* placed successively in two positions and oriented by means of an elbow view-finder aimed at a mark inserted in the tripod at the opposite position.

With the base in a vertical position, the same orientations can be obtained with adapters as are possible with the double camera.

This method is frequently useful and the field of application is thus enlarged, since it is not always feasible to work with a single 120-centimetre base.

When the viewpoints are in the splays of upper-storey windows, orientation by sighting from one position to the other would be impossible. In such cases, therefore, the camera is mounted on a platform which projects beyond the window-ledge and is fixed inside the room by means of a telescopic support (Fig. 17).

Double camera—single-unit arrangement

If a single camera is not available, but only a double camera with a 120-centimetre base, the following method is used. To enlarge the base, the tube must then be set in a single direction in two successive positions (Fig. 18). If two tripods are available, a mark should be placed on one of them, and used as a sighting point for an elbow view-finder fitted to the orientation cube of the camera mounted on the other tripod. Once the picture is taken, the position of the mark and of the camera can be reversed and the operation repeated from the other position.

The four plates corresponding to the two successive positions of the double camera are consequently on a horizontal straight line, and all the lines of sight are perpendicular to that base. Any obstacles to visibility which might have hidden certain details on one stereoscopic pair will not hide them on the second. Thanks to this single-unit arrangement, with the plates kept parallel to the reference plane, most obstacles of this kind (chandeliers, furniture and so on) can be eliminated.

For the survey of a large structural feature (Fig. 19), such as the nave of a church, or in photographing a very lofty cupola from ground level (60 metres is not unusual for a nave 15 metres high), a single length of base would not be enough, since a base of 120 centimetres is suitable for a distance up to 25 metres only. After that, by using the

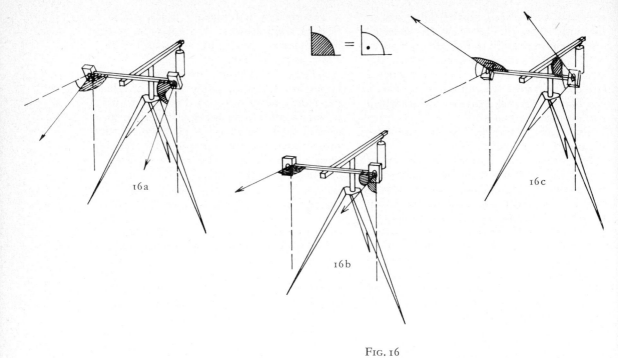

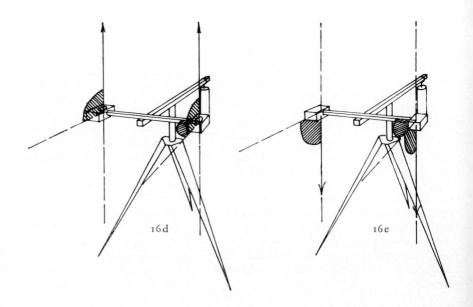

FIG. 16

Stereocameras set with counterpoise rail in various positions.

single-unit device of two double cameras it is possible—by selecting the pair offering the least number of obstacles to visibility—to join the right-hand print of the left-hand double camera to the right-hand print of the right-hand double camera or, on the contrary, to two left-hand prints, or finally, for long distances, to the two outermost prints of the unit. Or again, in the same way, a stereoscopic pair can be formed from two inside prints.

specially made, together with a platform for placing the camera close to ground level (*Plate 11*).

Thanks to the cube which acts as a base for the elbow view-finder, it is possible, depending on the side selected, to intercalate or not intercalate the wedge and the adapter so as to form single units with cameras having vertical or oblique lines of sight on a horizontal or vertical base, in alignment or on parallel tubular bases which

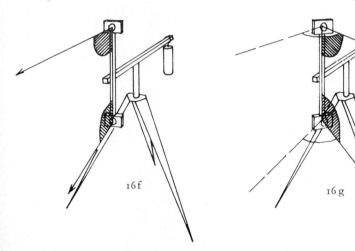

16f

16g

In what is perhaps the most usual case of only one tripod being available, the elbow view-finder set on the cube and oriented successively to the right and to the left makes it possible, by sighting, to find a straight line parallel to the base which can easily be materialized by positioning two sighting marks or surveyors' staffs. After photographing with the double camera, the latter is moved further away with its tripod in the alignment earlier represented by the sighting marks. A sliding and adjustable triangle, or a wooden triangle with bosses enabling it to slide to the ground, facilitates this alignment, as does an eccentric device for fixing the camera to the tripod. These devices are not at present available from the manufacturers. However, they have been

are themselves perpendicular to that alignment.

Hence, different base lengths and varied combinations are feasible.

Single camera and double camera

In addition to this single-unit apparatus, a unit can easily be formed with a 120-centimetre double camera and a single camera.

The single camera is set in alignment with the elbow view-finder placed on the orientation cube of the double camera, or *vice versa*. Parallel lines of sight are obtained when the centre of the lens of the elbow view-finder on the single camera appears in the centre of the cross-wire of the elbow view-finder

91

set on the double camera, and *vice versa*. As the tripod of the double camera is fitted with a racked rod and a handle by which it can be hoisted 2.5 metres from the ground, the double camera can easily be placed at the level of the single camera. Once again, only a few movements are required to obtain a quite complex orientation.

Surveying rounded solids

All single-unit orientations can also be used for surveys of rounded solids (Fig. 19), particularly those having a considerable volume, such as the drums of cupolas. The use of photographs to survey such bodies can easily involve errors (of which architects are often unaware). The photograph has a central projection. The radii all converge towards a centre, which is the nodal point of the lens. The radii corresponding to the contour registered on the image are tangents, that is, they touch the solid at the extremity of two separate radii and not at the extremities of a single diameter, the two extremities of a single diameter not being visible from a single viewpoint. In the case of the elevation, which is an orthogonal projection, the contour represented corresponds to two radii of the parallel projection, these touching the solid at the extremities of a diameter, the diameter which is in fact perpendicular to the radii. The drum of a cupola, the cupola itself, and the apse will appear on the photograph narrower than on the orthogonal projection. A stereo-

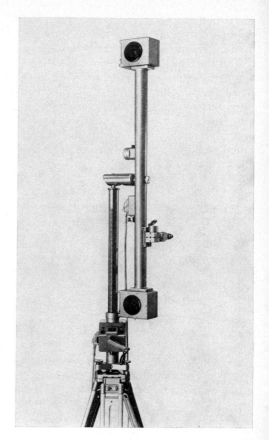

10a

Plate 10

(a) Stereoscopic cameras mounted vertically with an adapter.
(b) Zeiss single camera unit, TMK.

scopic pair corresponding to a front shot will not permit plotting of the entire half of the plane and will not go beyond the contour visible in the central projection.

If the plane and the elevation are plotted simultaneously, it is easy to complete the plane where the forms are regular—as in the case of circles, for example—and to deduce from them the contours in the orthogonal projection of the elevation.

If that is neither convenient nor possible, recourse must be had to at least three shooting positions, aligned on one straight line, which will make it possible to process the prints in two pairs, each pair representing, in stereoscopic overlapping, the centre of the object and one of the parts corresponding to the contour of the orthogonal elev-

because it is not necessarily controllable, lies in measuring the distance between the cameras with a steel tape.

Close-ups

A double camera also exists with a 40-centimetre tubular base with fixed focus lens, allowing from 2- to 10-metre close-ups *(Plate 11)*.

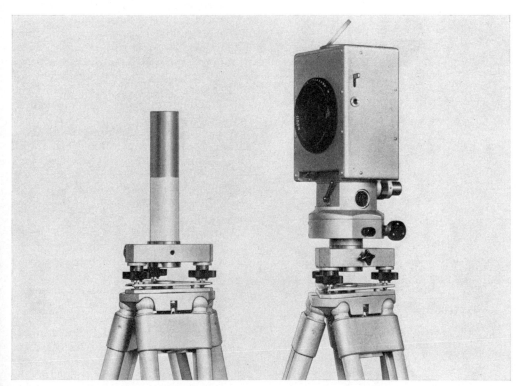

10b

ation. These surveys of rounded solids, which are not easy if traditional methods are used and sometimes call for rather delicate handling of normal photogrammetric equipment, become simple with the single-unit device, either a single stereoscopic camera and one or two tripods, or a stereoscopic camera and a single camera. The only possible error,

ELIMINATION OF ERRORS—CONTROL POINTS

All the methods discussed above are simple in operation. With such a degree of simplification, can the accuracy of the results be absolutely guaranteed? The accuracy of the equipment described is, generally speaking, ten times greater than with the older types but, as with any other mechanism, accuracy may be impaired by the slight alterations to the settings caused when the apparatus is moved or knocked.

By reducing the choice of setting devices to a single standard case, the set of instruments as described gives rise in practice to only three errors, none of them of any magnitude. Knowing this, it has been pos-

sible to allow for them by three simple devices which the operator has on his apparatus for eliminating setting errors that may occur at the time of exposure. After the correction, the results will be as accurate as if the errors had never occurred.

To hunt out possible errors, the operator determines the exact location of at least four well-defined points visible in each frame. These are known as control points (Fig. 20). They must be plotted with the greatest care and accuracy. This may be very difficult because of the inaccessibility and poor definition of features (rounded cornices, thick plasterwork, etc.) and frequently because of their poor definition in the photograph. The placing of sighting marks is not always possible. Under some working conditions, the job is enough to scare even experienced surveyors.

A safe and simple solution is therefore advanced which seems to offer justification for reducing this system to a 'standard case'. The position of the right-hand camera, or position B, is the basis for the system of co-ordinates. The base line and the line of sight provide the two directions.

A theodolite, or more simply, a pantometer (Fig. 21) is placed in front of the object, perpendicular to the base formed by the line of sight of camera B (determined by the centre of the reticle in the magnetic view-finder on top of the camera). The pantometer is a small surveyor's square to which two diopters are attached perpendicularly to each other; the first is trained on the magnetic view-finder affixed to the chamber B, the other defines a plane parallel to the plane of the plates of the double camera (plane of reference). A line can easily be drawn in this plane by aligning two sighting marks with the aid of the diopter of the pantometer. A strip of board or plumb-line can also be placed immediately in front of the object to establish the vertical. The position of the control points (sighting marks) can be calculated accurately by measuring the distance between the camera and the

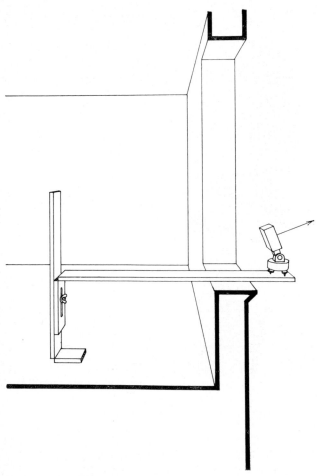

FIG. 17

Single camera set on a board projecting from a window.

Fig. 18

Using coupled cameras as a single unit.

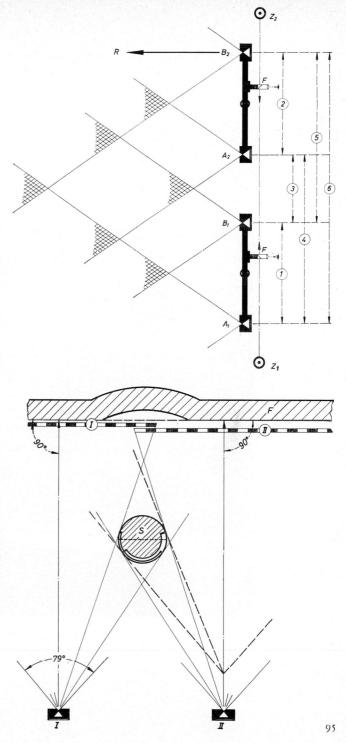

pantometer and then the distance between the pantometer and the sighting marks.

If it not possible to measure the distance between the camera and the pantometer directly, an invar steel bar can be used in place of the latter. A theodolite placed beneath camera B can then be used to measure the angle formed by the two sighting marks at each end of this bar. The required distance, reduced to the horizontal, can then be read off directly from a scale. An invar bar can easily be used instead of a pantometer if forced-adjustment theodolite tripods are used to draw the control line.

Let us now see how this easily and rapidly assembled apparatus is used. Before restitution begins, the reference points are drawn in, following the system of co-ordinates described above and using the measurements which have been obtained directly. Only then are the photographs focused in the restitution apparatus and a comparison made between the control points which have already been drawn in and the corresponding points as they appear in the restitution. These should coincide unless there has been some error.

Fig. 19

Two stereoscopic cameras (I and II) set in the vertical base position covering more than half of the obstacle 'S'. The two units thus photograph the whole of the object 'F' as the obstacle appears in front of a different part of 'F' in the photographs taken from the two positions.

If there have been errors in the setting at the moment of exposure, it will be immediately obvious. As already pointed out, the error may be of three types:

The extremities of the line obtained by plotting are situated on the straight lines joining camera B to the extremities of the control line, but both lines suffer parallel displacement.

The line plotted appears as a curve whose extremities coincide with the control points and whose point of greatest distance falls within the line of sight of camera B.

While the line plotted passes through the point at which the line of sight of camera B and the control line intersect one another, its extremities are out of alignment—one protruding and the other receding—with respect to the lines joining camera B to the extremities of the control line.

Plate 11

Cameras mounted on a 40-centimetre base. They may be mounted in turn on a tripod. Here they are shown on a platform so as to photograph low structures.

The last two errors occur only if the cameras have been ill-treated and are out of adjustment. The vertical photograph (plumb-line or lath) allows a check on the level at the moment of exposure. Moreover, level control is rendered easier by the fact that the twin cameras are equipped with a built-in level and a magnetically attached level which can be compared from time to time.

If any of these three errors should occur, it would immediately be detected thanks to

Plate 12

Establishing a stereoscopic model in the Bundesdenkmalamt (Vienna). The plotter is equipped with a 'calculator-corrector' attached to the left of the operator's hand for inclined-axis shots, and in turn it drives the mechanism on the drawing board.

the control points and can be corrected by adjusting the special focusing screw provided for each type of error until the plotted line and the control line coincide perfectly.

PLOTTING

As indicated at the outset, the aim is to set up as stereoscopic 'model' inside the plotter *(Plate 12)*. The operator follows all the contours with an adjusting mark moving in

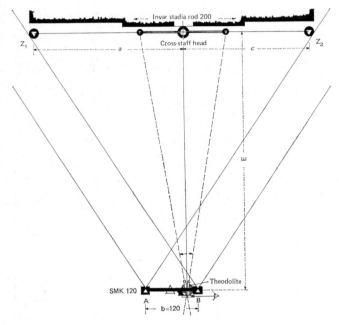

FIG. 20

Setting up control points.

virtual space, and this activates a drawing appliance which traces the movements in orthogonal projection.

The prints must, of course, first be placed in the plotter and adjusted. With a large apparatus this can take several hours. It does not matter in the case of aerial prints which subsequently remain in position for a very long time and provide a great deal of information, all of which will normally be

of use. The problem is different in the case of conservation and architecture, where the prints are often filed away in case they may one day be needed, or are only partially plotted in order to settle a single detail (width of a bay, height of a cornice, etc.). The positioning process has therefore been simplified so as to take only a few minutes. Once this has been completed and possible errors eliminated by reference to the control points, the operator follows the lines he wishes to plot with the adjusting mark, and the movements are automatically transmitted to either one or two drawing appliances, one of which traces the plan, and the other, an elevation, a section, contour lines, etc., as required. Moreover, gears and base corrections provide a very wide choice of scales.

In practice, for an experienced plotter, the work corresponds to free-hand tracing for a draughtsman. While there are limits to the speed at which the operation can be performed, it is much faster than the traditional methods used to prepare scale drawings.

FIG. 21

A pantometer.

Calculator-corrector for plotting inclined-axis shots

To plot this type of print, a calculator-corrector is interposed between the plotter and the appliance driving the plotting mechanism on the drawing-board. This adjusts the number of revolutions so that the operator gets the orthogonal projection he wants, rather than an affined image distorted (according to the orientation) in its ordinates or abscisses. Here, too, the apparatus reduces correction to a matter of simple manipulation.

Rectification

The problem is different if the rectification method can be used, and a few words must be said about this (Fig. 22).

Although reasonably complete and accurate rectification-plotting of flat or nearly flat objects—such as many simple façades, frescoes, graffiti and so on—is possible with amateur equipment, precise work can be carried out only with horizontalized cameras. As it is impossible to position them in such a way that they are strictly parallel to the reference plane, which would be the only way of obtaining a central projection resembling the orthogonal projection, lines which are actually horizontal will appear in the photograph (the exposure-axis of which was not rigorously perpendicular to the reference plane) to converge towards a vanishing point. To rectify these frames, an apparatus resembling a photographic enlarger must be used to create the following conditions.

Newton's condition for the distances between the negative, the objective and the projection plane, in order to obtain a clear image.

Scheimpflug's condition: the planes of the negative, the objective and the projection overlap on a single straight line, which means that a clear picture is obtained for the whole of the inclined projection plane

without the necessity of reducing the opening of the diaphragm.

The perspective condition, which consists in translating the negative into the negative plane, eliminates the occurrence of an affined transformation in cases where there is a difference between the focal lengths of the exposure and projection optics.

At present, one instrument is commercially available, the Carl Zeiss SEG V *(Plate 13)*,

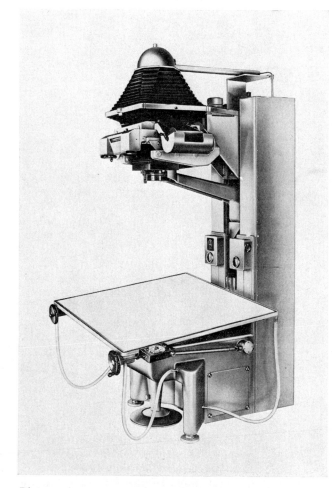

Plate 13

Rectification: Carl Zeiss SEG V.

which automatically satisfies these three conditions. The operator tilts the platen and adjusts the enlargement until the control points (at least four) fixed by stereoplotting or by the use of direct methods, or simply by assuming that certain lines of the building can be regarded as horizontal, coincide with the projected image. Copying on nonshrink paper with a photographic emulsion surface then produces a photograph which

obtained. When the plotting is copied in ink, these two elements are combined in a single picture on an original which can be reproduced by the ferrogallic process.

For greater clarity, see the examples, in the form of figures and their captions (Figs. 23–30).

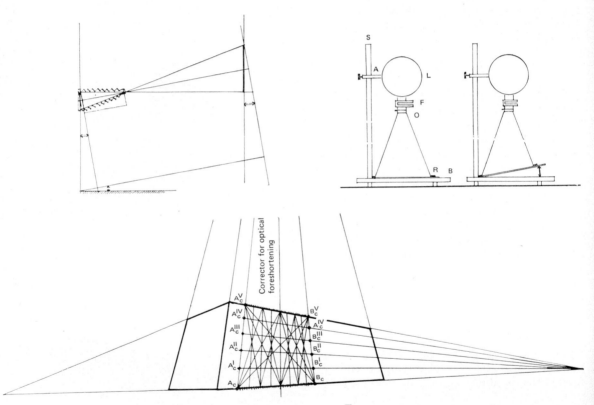

is at the same time a plan. This is referred to as the 'photo-plan' or 'photographicmap'.

Practically speaking, it is possible to plot by stereophotogrammetry whatever parts and details stand out in relief, as well as outer contours of the flat parts; the flat parts themselves can then be rectified by fitting them into the partial plotting thus

FIG. 22

Rectification: diagrams showing the use of amateur photograph enlargers. Scale is determined by perspective graphic division.

FIG. 23

Geometrical construction for determining orthogonal projections from a photograph and some data. It is too slow, and not accurate enough a method to be of practical use.

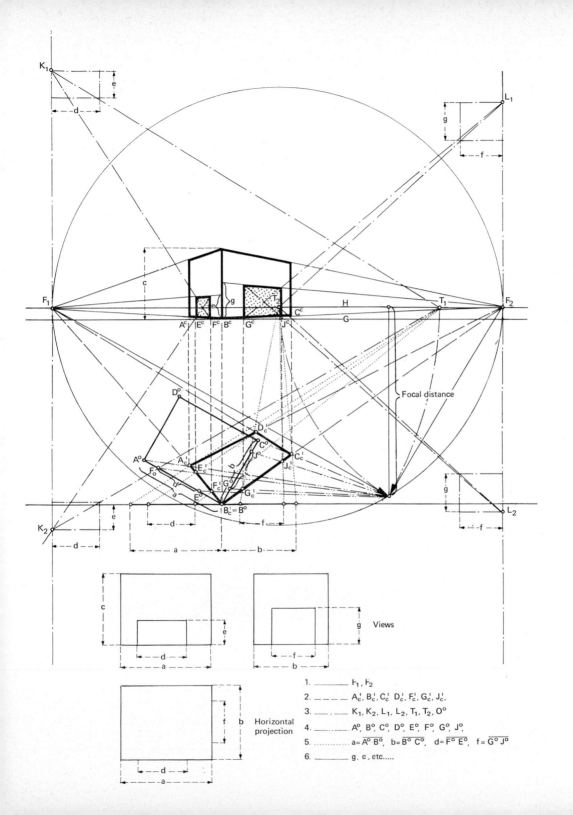

Focal distance

Views

Horizontal
projection

1. ——— F₁, F₂

2. – – – A'c, B'c, C'c D'c, F'c, G'c, J'c,

3. –·–·– K₁, K₂, L₁, L₂, T₁, T₂, O°

4. ——— A°, B°, C°, D°, E°, F°, G°, J°

5. ········· a= A̅°B̅°, b= B̅°C̅°, d= F̅°E̅°, f= G̅°J̅°

6. ——— g, e, etc.....

Fig. 24

Survey of Maulpertsch fresco in the main hall
of the Imperial Castle, Innsbruck. Hollow-
sounding parts and cracks caused by an earthquake are plotted and marked with chalk. Chalk
marks were effaced after the weak parts had
been reinforced. A check will be made in a few
years' time on the basis of this survey.

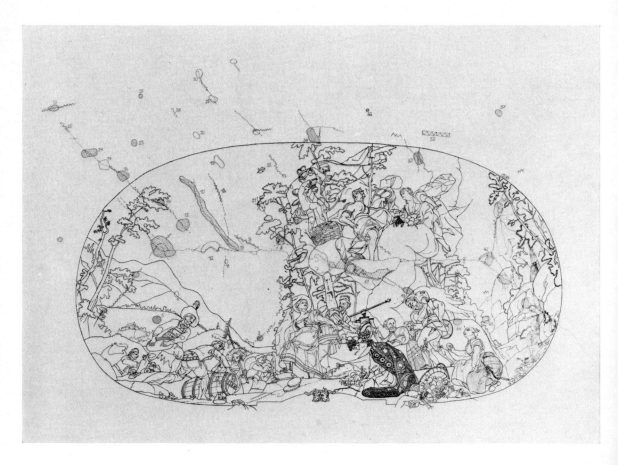

FIG. 25

An item over 26 metres high was photographed
at a distance of 5.5 metres with inclined sight-
lines, and the whole plotted (corner tower in
Schallaburg, southern Austria).

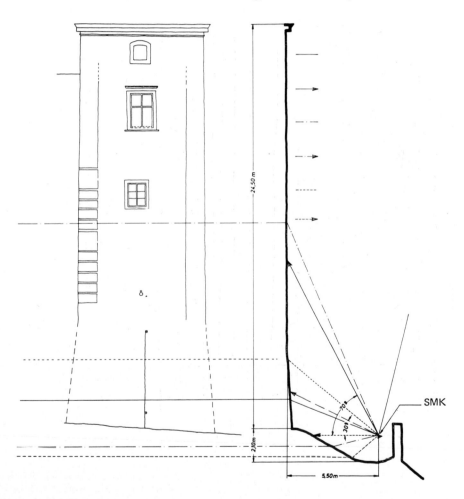

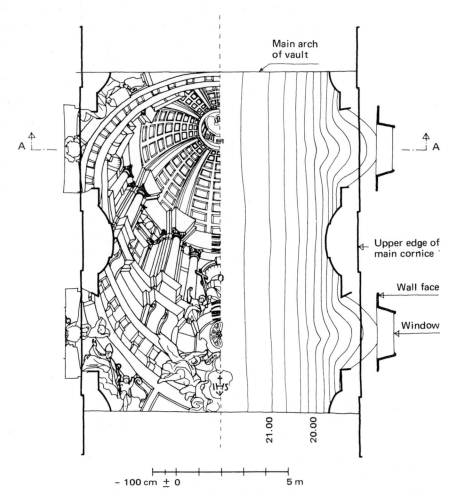

Main arch
of vault

A

A

Upper edge of
main cornice

Wall face

Window

21.00

20.00

- 100 cm ± 0   5 m

Fig. 26

Survey of vault and *trompe-l'œil* fresco by
A. Pozzo in the Jesuit church in Vienna. Note
the reversed curve contours near the actual
ovoid recesses which give the effect of a cupola
on the circular plane.

FIG. 27

The structural weakness (above the doorway) was revealed by the survey, and the building consolidated.

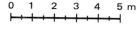

FIG. 28

A series of façades in the town of Eggenburg, southern Austria.

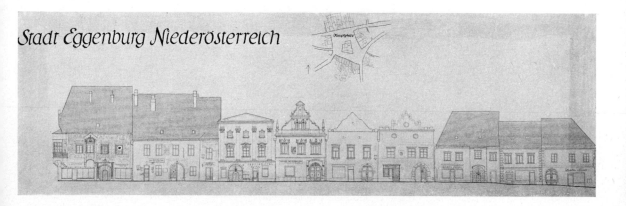

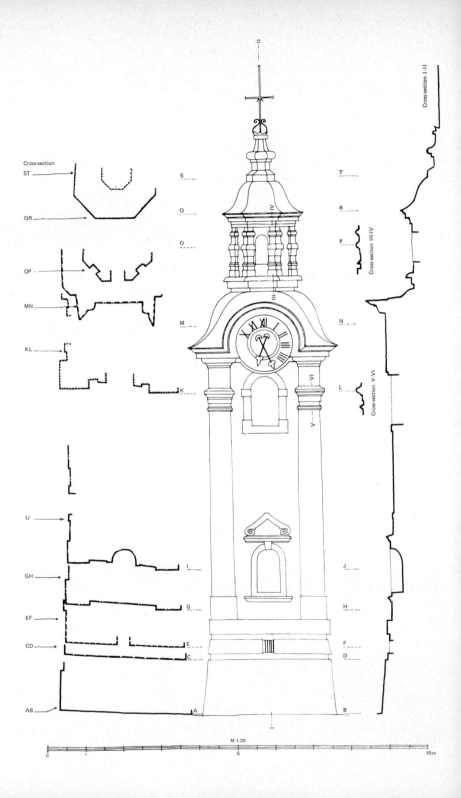

Cross-section
ST

QR

OP

MN

KL

IJ

GH

EF

CD

AB

S

Q

O

M

K

I

G

E

C

A

Cross-section J-II

T

R

P

N

L

J

H

F

D

B

Cross-section III-IV

Cross-section V-VI

M 1:20

0   5   10 m

◀ Fig. 29

Plotting of the belfry in Hohenhau, southern
Austria. The marked discrepancies between
the actual and the theoretical forms appear
very clearly in the cross-sections.

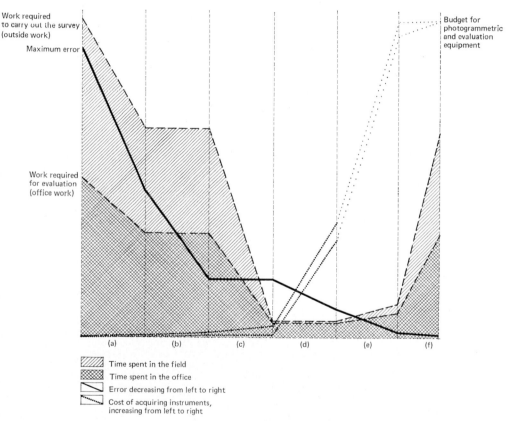

Work required
to carry out the survey
(outside work)

Maximum error

Work required
for evaluation
(office work)

Budget for
photogrammetric
and evaluation
equipment

(a)   (b)   (c)   (d)   (e)   (f)

⬚ Time spent in the field
⬚ Time spent in the office
⬚ Error decreasing from left to right
⬚ Cost of acquiring instruments,
   increasing from left to right

Fig. 30

Comparative costs of various methods used in
the surveying of old buildings: (a) classical
methods; (b) small instruments; (c) topographical instruments; (d) small photogrammetric instruments; (e) set of recommended
instruments; (f) large, high-precision instruments.

ECONOMIES

A graph, based on experience in Austria over the last few years, regarding the economies made possibly by using photogrammetry in conservation, is shown in Fig. 30.

Where classical methods allowed us to survey 3,000 square metres of façades a year, photogrammetry now permits 100,000 square metres which could be raised to 500,000 with the same equipment if the necessary additional staff are provided.

Photography increases accuracy tenfold and working speeds from 20 to 200 times as compared with traditional methods.

Stereophotogrammetric plotting is from 3 to 10 times faster than reproduction to scale, and from 30 to 100 times if working by rectification of the projected image.

Under favourable conditions an average of 3,000 square metres a day has been achieved—a whole year's work by classical methods. Recently, over 600 exposures have been brought back after a six-day expedition under difficult conditions.

Such a programme, and the advantage of being able to employ personnel without special qualifications, obviously entails capital outlay which, however, can be amortized within a short period of time. A judicious combination of classical methods with photogrammetry should be taken into account in training personnel. This will result in much more efficient and accurate records at a time when we are faced with new challenges due to the growth of population and changes in urban patterns of living.

Factors contributing to the deterioration of monuments

6

Surveys of an old structure reveal in considerable detail the changes which have taken place since it was built. Every building has its own life cycle and grows old with the ageing of its component materials. Its life cycle is affected by its location, and the purposes for which it has been used. The best means of preservation will not be through hasty *ad hoc* restoration but by continuous and careful maintenance, so that damaged and worn parts can be cared for before they become serious. Even with constant care, buildings, for a variety of reasons, inevitably deteriorate.

The next step in assessing the condition of a monument is to make a scientific study of historical and climatic factors which have affected the building, as a basis for deciding what type of restoration to carry out.

BAD REPAIRS AND FAULTY RESTORATION

Although conservation is the main purpose of restoration—this point cannot be sufficiently stressed—some of the worst architectural damage to buildings has been caused by faulty restoration. The administrators and technicians concerned are, in many cases, not qualified to assess architectural values and are guided by purely utilitarian principles, with the result that monuments of historical and artistic quality are often stupidly sacrificed because of unwarranted presumption and lack of skill. This may take many forms—the destruction of a whole series of mural paintings or carvings to the reconstruction of entire buildings in an archaic style, excavation without any precautions being taken to preserve finds, and so on.

However, the commonest case is that of operations undertaken for conservation purposes by incompetent or inexpert restorers. The damage caused varies in extent but could and should be avoided. Restoration is not something which can be done by any technician or lover of antiquity, but only by experienced and qualified experts. It demands supervision by the competent authorities and the work of skilled craftsmen (frequently using the techniques of a bygone age).

Valuable buildings can also be damaged by faulty consolidation of the structure or foundations. This may cause disintegration or instability or—even worse—make subsequent repairs impossible. The risk of inflicting such damage is at present greater than ever because of intensive building activities in many parts of the world, and especially in countries which have inherited large numbers of architectural and historical monuments from ancient civilizations.

Where consolidation is required on a scale that demands a preliminary investigation of the stability of the edifice concerned, technological considerations should not be allowed to overshadow the fact that the aim is to alter the nature and appearance as little as possible, and maintain the old structures if they are sufficiently sound. In principle a restored building should resemble the original as closely as possible in both structure and use. Even when it is obvious, in the light of our present-day knowledge of statics, that there are anomalies and defects, these should never be 'corrected' except where necessary to prevent irreparable damage, infiltration of water, and so on, for such 'anomalies' constitute an integral and 'documentary' part of the life of the edifice.

It is a very common mistake to consider that the main beauty and value of a building lies in its external and internal adornment, disregarding its inherent structural elements: there was the case of an ancient Arab-Byzantine cupola made of wood and lead that was 'restored' by being simply replaced in its entirety by a steel and aluminium structure, with no attempt made to conserve the original. If the principle of restoration (i.e. placing the accent on conservation) is accepted, the conditions under which rebuilding is justified should be considered very carefully. Erecting a new edifice is not restoration, even if it is copied from the original and stands on the same site. The new structure would, at best, be only a replica of the original.

NATURAL AND MAN-MADE DAMAGE

Preservation and protection methods must be adapted to the particular nature and cause of the damage.

The fact that restoration operations are undertaken at all implies that something is wrong. It may be as the condition of the ground beneath the foundations, the structure, or the building materials, or some single cause (e.g. subsidence of the foundations). Restoration methods cannot be classified in categories corresponding to the causes of the damage to be repaired, since a particular static defect may be due to a combination of causes. Determining the interdependence of the causes of defects is one of the main problems of diagnosis.

Since it is not possible to ascertain exactly beforehand how restoration should proceed,

it must always be closely supervised by an expert capable of taking decisions, so that changes can be made in the plans as the work progresses.

The preliminary thorough study of the monument should cover the nature of the materials used in the original building; the materials to be used for restoration work, whether permanent or temporary; the behaviour of these materials; methods of conserving them (this data will be useful also for other similar cases); the static condition of the structure, which may vary widely in different parts of the same edifice; the effects on the building of the local climate (different types of rainfall: warm and humid, warm and dry, moderate, wet, wet and cold; climate with marked diurnal differences); sun, seashore and other circumstances determining weather conditions which affect materials. Modern research methods make it possible to ascertain the reaction of building materials to physical, chemical, biochemical, biological, microbiological and botanical agents, and to calculate the resistance of different structures and materials to strains and stresses which are either inherent in each part of the edifice, or due to external factors of an exceptional character (*Plate 14*).

Damage can be divided into two main categories: damage due to intrinsic causes, connected closely with the original conception and nature of building, and extrinsic damage due to causes, deriving from the vicissitudes through which they have passed.

The *intrinsic causes* can be further subdivided into two main groups: those due to the location of the edifice—geo-topographical position and type of ground on which the foundations rest; and those, more numerous, due to the type of structure. The second group, generally speaking, relates to the type of building materials used (natural or artificial materials: stone and marble, wood, brick and terra-cotta, lime and binding materials); to faults in the design and construction of the edifice as a whole (e.g. wrong proportioning of the sections of the bearing structures), faults of execution (choice, use and working of materials, adoption of wrong construction methods, etc.), or technological faults, confined to the foundations, masonry proper, and to the roof. We shall later consider the main specific causes of damage which derive from these general causes, and determine the scale and the nature of their effects.

The *extrinsic causes* of damage to edifices fall into two categories: natural (long-term natural causes and occasional natural causes), and man-made causes.

The first of these categories (long-term natural causes) includes all the numerous physical, chemical, electrochemical, botanical, microbiological and other processes which slowly undermine the whole structure of a building, and may be summed up by the vague general term, 'ageing of the building'.

The second (occasional natural causes) includes exceptional natural phenomena, often very violent, which are virtually impossible either to foresee or to provide against earthquakes, bradyseism (slow upward or downward movement of the earth's crust), tsunamis (along coastal areas), volcanism, silting, etc.

The third category (man-made causes) includes damage done to buildings in time of war; and also, in particular, the changes made by man both to the original building and to the use made of it, as well as changes in the surroundings and in the condition of the subsoil. In this connexion, a distinction must be made between changes which relate to the nature of the building and fit into its general design, even though perhaps belonging to different periods; and changes which substantially alter the original conception and lead to damage classified as extrinsic.

The causes of deterioration of buildings may thus be divided into the main categories indicated below:

Intrinsic

Relating to the location of the edifice	Climate and geo-topographical location
Inherent in the structure	Ground on which foundations rest
	Constituent elements (materials)
	Building systems (design and execution)

Extrinsic

Due to natural agents	Long term
Caused by the action of man	Occasional

We shall now deal, one by one, with the seven main categories of damage listed above, giving indications for their identification and assessment.

INTRINSIC CAUSES OF DETERIORATION

CAUSES INHERENT IN THE POSITION OF THE EDIFICE

These include first and foremost the geo-topographical location and the nature of the ground on which the edifice stands.

The geo-topographical location

This governs the climatic conditions to which a building is subjected and against which it should be suitably protected; if it is not so protected, subsequent deterioration should be attributed to causes inherent in the building itself. The actual location of the building (in the vicinity of a stream, a reservoir, a precipice, etc.) may intensify the effects of the climate; so may its orientation in relation to the sun and the prevailing winds, which have a direct influence on its state of conservation. At the same time, a building's resistance to climatic conditions is not constant, but diminishes with age; hence it constitutes a feature in the life of the building and thus does not come under intrinsic causes of deterioration.

Plate 14

The church of San Michele in Pavia (Italy). An advanced case of weathering partially due to frost.

Plate 15

The monument of Borobudur was built during the Sailendra dynasty (eighth century) in central Java, upon a natural hill. The apex of the monument is off-centre and the difference is made up with fill. The fill gradually subsided and, as a result, the terraces are now badly tilted (Photo: *Unesco Courier*, June 1968.)

The nature of the ground

This and the formation of the soil on which the building stands are of primary importance, particularly as regards geo-hydrological features: the composition, lie and inclination of the rock strata, and the type of underground water table.

The building cannot be stable unless the unit load exerted by the foundations is commensurate with the nature and resistance of the ground. Other important factors are the apparent (or orographic) configuration of the land, determined by the slope, the nature of the surface, the natural run-off of surface water, and so on. All these factors affect not merely the durability and stability of the foundations, but in many cases the monument itself, and its general state of conservation *(Plate 15)*.

Preliminary investigation, using special methods, comprises the following checks and tests of the ground underlying the foundations.

Geological stratification check (in the case of alluvial land, the quality of the sub-soil down to a depth of 25–30 metres must be ascertained by taking core samples).

Load tests.

Consolidation tests (chemical, physical, mechanical).

Search for water springs, water-bearing strata, and possible planes of strata slip.

Identification and analysis of artificially laid soil, ancient or recent.

Such are the usual tests carried out in most cases; but they must naturally be supplemented by other specific investigations, including historical research, on the past and present use of the materials handled in any kind of restoration operation.

FAULTY MATERIALS

There may be defects in the materials of which a building is constructed; though not sufficiently serious to upset the static equilibrium completely, they constitute a threat to its stability, or at any rate to the state of conservation of individual parts of it.

These defects may, as seen above, be divided into two groups: defects in the actual materials and defects in the structure of the building.

Defects in the actual materials

This relates to the choice of the materials used for building: the size, shape, processing distribution and use of the pieces composing the bearing framework, including the binding materials and their ability to fulfil their static function, the most common weaknesses being insufficient resistance capacity, inability to stand the various stresses to which they are subjected, poor manufacture, poor binding materials, and so on.

In regard to materials, the following points must be checked.

Stone and marble: source of origin, quarrying methods (which may cause damage to the texture); methods used for transporting and processing. In addition, tests will have to be carried out in specialized laboratories on homogeneity, hardness, workability, resistance to frost action, conductivity, wear, compression, bending and shearing strengths. Stone which has already been used may have to be tested for impermeabilization and chemical hardening, and treated.

Bricks and terra-cotta elements: resistance tests as for stone, analysis of baking process and of the quality of the clay used, porosity, chemical inertia.

Mortar and binding materials in general: tests for hardening, shrinking, adhesiveness, compression strength and tensile strength, setting time.

Wood: tests for compression, bending and shearing strength, hardness, workability. In the case of wood, it is also important to know what insects they are liable to be attacked by (termites, various kinds of beetles, etc.).

Lime mortar may involve one of the causes

of the decay of materials which restorers tend to neglect. Obviously, the type of lime used varies widely from place to place as regards the proportion of water required, setting time, contraction, colour, proportion of aggregates required, and even methods of use in different seasons. All these points are of practical importance when, for instance, old lime plaster has to be repaired. Again, when we find old plaster which has lasted exceptionally long under ordinary conditions, it will be of interest to ascertain its composition and usage.

Lime mortars may show serious deterioration when subjected to heavy loads, particularly when used in large quantities. This may be due to poor quality, the use of unsuitable aggregates such as clayey or earthy sand, faulty proportions, presence of chalk in the paste, insufficient water, or excessively thick layers. Under these conditions, the lime, instead of being crystalline and at least as hard as brick, is powdery and does not adhere properly to the stones. It fills the gaps between the stones and is held in place by compression without contributing to the strength of the structure. It thus has no resistance to tensile stress and has a low coefficient of friction. This may lead to subsequent compression between the stone or bricks used in the structure, thus upsetting the load distribution, with consequent damage.

Again, the stone originally used for the building may be defective, although in theory stone blocks should emerge from the quarry in perfect condition: compact, unfissured, and neither violently battered in the hewing process nor exposed to fire. Moreover, stone should be cut into blocks which can be laid in a position corresponding to their original lie in the quarry.

Building defects

These derive, on the other hand, from the fact that the structures have insufficient resistance. This may be due to various causes: construction methods; errors in designing the different parts of the structure in respect of gravity and thrust, resistance and counterthrust, etc.

These two categories of defects, are frequently interrelated, for the equilibrium of the framework of an edifice may often be upset as a result of damage to their basic components and to a decrease in their resistance capacity and in the cohesion between the various parts. The equilibrium of a building depends on the observance of carefully defined and calculated requirements of form, dimension and position; once these requirements cease to be met, the building is in danger of decaying.

The commonest phenomena observed are of three kinds, depending on the nature the stresses to which the defective framework is subjected through the distribution of the loads:

Weakness or malformation of the foundations.

Excessive vertical stress in relation to the size of the supporting framework.

Non-vertical stresses or stresses not sufficiently counterbalanced by suitably resistant structures, i.e. defective framework.

At this point, some explanation of the nature of the different mechanical forces, and their relative strength, will be useful as a basis for identifying errors in the designing of buildings. The aim has been to present general principles applicable to a wide variety of monuments belonging to different types of architecture, methods of building and building materials, and specific examples have therefore been deliberately avoided.

Damage due to defective foundations. Since it was not until about two hundred years ago that a systematic method was worked out for calculating the foundations of buildings, defects in buildings prior to that time are due not to any lack of skill on the part of the architect but simply to the fact that the lack of scientific means of ascertaining the suitability of the various types of ground forced them to proceed by (often false) analogy (as likewise in deciding what types of building material should be used).

When, therefore, a building reveals damage which indicates that the foundations are at fault, steps must be taken to investigate the scope and methods of construction used. Usually it can be shown that (a) the foundations were inadequate from the start and have been reduced by wear causing parts of them to sag; (b) that the ground underlying the foundations has lost its original consistency through natural causes; or (c) that the foundations have become incapable of taking the extra load resulting from increasing the size of the building or from additions made to its height. The causes of damage to buildings are seldom evident at first glance, except in the event of explosion or earthquake; and a diagnosis of possible causes has to be made on the basis of the evidence available. As a rule, foundations are not visible and cannot be probed except by means of deep excavation. Where plans and a detailed survey of the edifice are available and the nature of the underlying ground is known, a check can be made on the basis of these documents; otherwise, the only indication of the cause of the damage is provided by the form it takes. Inadequate foundations may lead to damage in the rest of the building, but there are well-known exceptions, such as the Tower of Pisa, where the whole of the structure, together with the foundations, has tilted but the structure has remained intact.

Slight variations in the horizontal lie of the floors and the perpendicularity of the walls throughout a building are a fairly sure sign of subsidence of the foundations. An easy way of checking this is to place a glass full of water on the floor, and see whether it always spills over on the same side. In such cases it is not difficult to diagnose the state of the building; what is much more difficult is to diagnose the state of the ground underneath the foundations, and decide how to set about restoration *(Plate 15)*.

Generally speaking, any sagging or shifting of the foundations is reflected in the building in the kind of damage indicating the cause of the problem. The commonest defects are as follows: (a) separation of the elements due to poor construction; (b) sinking, due either to the original characteristics of the ground or to changes occurring after building had taken place *(Plate 16)*; (c) breakage due to additions to the building which have overloaded the foundation; (d) breakage due to disparities in the behaviour of the foundations (some parts better built than others), or else to faults in the underlying ground.

We do not intend to deal in detail with the consolidation of foundations, which is too costly to be undertaken except in the case of particularly valuable buildings and which, moreover, involves dismantling the actual building we are restoring. The great majority of such buildings are untransportable, though instances do exist where whole buildings can be moved without dismantling. This is, however, an extremely difficult and delicate operation.

Defects relating to vertical stresses. In buildings formed of structures placed horizontally one on top of the other, the load on each is composed of the weight of the superimposed structures plus the load resulting from any weights, objects, furnishings and so on pertaining to the use of the building. The total of such loads is exercised vertically and distributed, according to the architectural design, over the bearing sections of each structure. The static equilibrium of the whole is thus guaranteed by the unitary resistance offered by these sections to the load imposed on them, which is proportional to the total surface of their horizontal section.

When the weight exceeds limits imposed by the design, by the nature of the ground,

Plate 16

The megalithic temple of Hagar Qim, Malta.
The globigerina limestone has suffered from
windborne sea salts and rain.
(Photo: National Museum, Valetta.)

etc., structures are exposed to an excess load and undergo what is known as 'buckling', which results in various effects such as vertical clefts, bulging of the external surfaces, especially when covered with revetments; and, in the worst cases, detachment of the parts subjected to the heaviest load. Buckling occurs in vertical support structures, particularly where such structures are not homogeneous and their internal composition has deteriorated so that the weaker materials, under compression, become detached from the stronger ones. The latter have to bear the brunt of the excess weight and this increases the strain on their capacity to resist.

Excessive vertical load, which bears naturally on the lowermost part of a building, is common in buildings resting on piles which bear the greater part of the load, as for instance in the ground-floor colonnades of multi-storey buildings, or in any other buildings where the entire weight rests on a few relatively slender vertical supports.

One particular and important consequence of overload is the sagging of the foundations. This will be dealt with separately later.

Excess vertical load, when exercised not only on the vertical supports, but also on horizontal bearing parts with wide spans, may produce phenomena of a completely different kind. Bending and shearing stresses then develop, as so often happens with the beams of old wooden floors and the lintels of doors and windows. The effects produced will vary according to the material used: with wood, which is elastic, deformation due to load does not upset the static equilibrium unless it exceeds a certain limit and produces a progessssive rupture on the longitudinal fibres; stone lintels, on the other hand, being rigid, will break under the load, upsetting the static equilibrium immediately.

Defects relating to non-vertical stresses. Oblique stresses will occur in cases where, owing either to the particular structural conformation of the building or to special forms of incidental load, weights bear non-vertically on the structure.

Cases of this kind are rare, confined in fact almost exclusively to embankments, swimming pools, reservoirs, etc; in such cases there is oblique stress with a horizontal component, increasing towards the base, tending to impart to the structure a rotary movement towards the exterior. This may lead, on the outer surface, to horizontal shifting which may be general but is more frequently irregular, causing more or less horizontal gaps due to the slipping of the superimposed strata of the wall.

Much more frequent and more important are cases of oblique stresses due to poor design and reciprocal stresses set up in the various parts of the framework of a building.

Such stresses occur, above all, when loads or weights are transmitted to adjacent parts through non-horizontal contact surfaces: for instance, the voussoirs (or wedge-shaped elements) of arches or vaults and the trusses of a single-pitch roof in the absence of tie-beams or horizontal tie-bars.

In the case of arches or vaults, the cumulative loads transmitted by several voussoirs may produce, on the springing line (the line or plane at which the arch rests upon or springs from the column, wall, pier, etc.) a result which acts on the supports as an oblique force that can be divided into a vertical and horizontal component. The latter exerts on the pier or other support a force which tends to make it rotate towards the outside of the arch, thus causing static weakness.

The oblique action of the curved section of the arch is in fact the result of reciprocal pressure exerted between the numerous wedge-shaped elements and the horizontal component of the arch. It increases proportionately when the elements are far apart, as they are in arches composed of large squared blocks.

In the case of arches and vaults made of concrete compounded of small pieces of stone, or of tiles held together with some substance, the structure theoretically constitutes a kind of artificial monolith exerting an oblique force only. In view of the fact that its mass is in fact composed of a number of irregular elements, its general static behaviour depends not only on the effect of their reciprocal stresses, but also on the practical conditions of their equilibrium. Hence, to dismantle such structures into wedge-shaped elements, as is done for making a static analysis, is in fact merely taking an abstract hypothesis which is not applicable, except when dealing with the worst cases where the stability of the whole is affected.

Mention must be made, lastly, of oblique stresses of a simpler and more easily identifiable kind, most of them also less harmful due to the use of sloping roofs without the requisite horizontal tie-beams. This occurs mainly in the case of single-pitch roof beams which are simply supported at the ends, lacking tie-beams or cross struts—which is the usual design of half-truss roofs with vertical pressure.

The oblique stresses, in such cases, are concentrated on the main rafters which in turn impose on the supports beneath stresses which consist of a vertical and horizontal component, similar to those exercised by arches on their bases. Since they are not as heavy, however, the results of these stresses will be less than in the case of vaulted arches, but none the less considerable, especially as the thrusts are not counteracted by the weight of the walls above, and because the supports are thinner, as they are designed to support a smaller weight.

The subject of vertical and oblique stresses has deliberately been discussed in terms as general as possible, with a view to making the conclusions reached applicable to widely differing conditions. Hence, the present analysis should be valid for both of the two main categories of structural damage (defects of conformation and defects of construction) without any preliminary sub-division.

It is only by examining the building together with all data relevant to its construction that it can be ascertained whether defects derive from the original conception and design of the building or whether, on the other hand, they are due to the execution of the work, or to the use of faulty methods and materials.

After these general causes, we come next to specific causes relating to the main parts or the building: foundations, the above-ground section, and the roof.

It will be remembered, for example, that masonry foundations are very commonly subject to subsidence either at the time when they are built, or subsequently, as a result of the action of underground water or streams. With ancient pile foundations, there is also the danger of the wood rotting and ageing.

The best known and commonest causes of damage to the structure above the ground are due to excess loads, deterioration of binding materials and mortar, and the wearing out or decay of some of the materials used.

The main causes of damage to roofs are wear, breaking and slipping, and deterioration of the supporting framework. The old horizontal and terrace roofs used in arid or semi-arid climates suffer damage by not being properly watertight. Deterioration of roofs of all kinds contributes considerably to the decay of the monument as a whole.

EXTRINSIC CAUSES OF DETERIORATION

LONG-TERM NATURAL CAUSES

Every edifice standing on ground is surrounded by a particular micro-climate and is constantly influenced by a variety of interacting factors which may be classified as follows: (a) physical factors; (b) chemical and electrochemical factors; (c) botanical factors; (d) biological and microbiological factors.

Physical factors

Apart from the question of resistance to internal and external structural strains (which is part of the science of building), the main physical factor is the action of temperature, particularly very high levels due to fire, and to very low ones due to frost. The action of water likewise contributes to the physical deterioration of materials; as does also that of wind, wave motion, and bradyseism. In view of recent advances in methods of investigating the molecular composition of materials and electric and radio-active forces, it is to be hoped that new means will be devised for identifying other kinds of physical action exercised on the structures of buildings too. Most ordinary physical action, except that of fire, is slow, and difficult to reproduce under laboratory conditions. Hence the most practical means of proceeding is by repeated observations of the building itself.

Physical causes in general may be classified as temperature, water, wind and ground, all of them predominantly dynamic and leading to other, further effects.

Temperature. This action depends on the range and frequency of variations in temperature, the effects of which vary with the porosity and thermic conductivity of the materials. All damage due to frost action comes under this heading; as well as weakening and crumbling due to heat.

Water. Here action is of numerous kinds.

Apart from the action of rain-water and moist winds, masonry becomes humid as a result of percolation, absorption and condensation. The effects of capillary absorption, which is sometimes seasonal, may extend several metres above the level of damp soil, and may provoke chemical and static damage, soaking structures and so subjecting them to an overload.

In equatorial and tropical climates, the combined effects of temperature and humidity are very marked, facilitating chemical decay (most chemical reactions are based on the presence of humidity and favoured by a rise in temperature) and biological decay (favourable conditions for the development of moulds and the creation of favourable environments for certain insects, especially termites).

Various physical effects, such as currents and waves are also produced by rivers and seas.

The action of the wind blowing against or buffeting ancient buildings, and wind erosion, sometimes combined with sand storms, constitutes another cause of damage.

The last type of physical action is bradyseism, which occurs mainly in coastal areas, and is reflected in the slow rise and fall of the land.

Chemical and electrochemical factors

The effects of chemical agents on building materials can easily be ascertained by laboratory tests, which show the deterioration suffered by these materials and the ensuing radical change in their composition. Such tests, made on samples taken from various parts of the edifice, are part of the routine work of laboratories specializing in the analysis of natural stone and artificial building materials.

The main vehicles of chemical action are the atmosphere and water. One of the commonest atmospheric phenomena is oxidation, which does not damage buildings directly, but causes the iron and other metals subject to this phenomenon to corrode and swell, thus producing breaks and fissures in the stone in which they have been placed. Wood is also affected; it eventually loses strength, and pieces separate from one another.

Increasingly serious damage is caused by the combustion products of mineral oil and coal in the atmosphere; also, from time to time, by volcanic activity. The pollution of the atmosphere is due to the presence of gaseous and solid particles. As regards the most harmful are compounds of sulphur (sulphurous and sulphuric), which transform the carbonates in the building materials into sulphates, so causing an increase of volume which, in turn, leads to fissures and to the flaking off of pieces from the surface of the stone. Fog and mist affect buildings by depositing liquid particles of sodium chloride (such as are also transported by sea winds) *(Plate 16)*, together with solid particles (smog) which affect the form and colour of the external facings.

Water is an active vehicle of chemical reagents; even rain is chemically active since it contains carbon dioxide and various salts. Chemical compounds contained in solution or in suspension in water (produced by the disintegration of rocks, by industrial operations or by contact with sea-water) cause specific reactions which intensify the action of capillary humidity. Many monuments in semi-arid countries (e.g. Mohenjo-Daro in Pakistan) are affected by ground water heavily contaminated with various salts. This is a further example of deterioration due to combined physico-chemical action.

Chemical reactions are frequently caused or accompanied by electric currents in the sub-soil, which may change the composition of the foundation materials, weakening their specific resistance.

Botanical factors

These are easily identifiable as responsible for the damage caused by plants and parasitic vegetation. Plants growing in the immediate vicinity of an edifice may cause damage through roots which undermine the foundations and main walls. Again, seeds are liable to lodge in cracks in the walls, particularly where there are flat surfaces or ledges. The roots infiltrate and, as the plant grows, act as a wedge, pushing the masonry apart.

Parasitic plants either aggravate the effects of ordinary plants or adhere to the monument itself, and are particularly harmful because they affect the original facing and surface (e.g. ivy and other creepers), although a false romanticism has caused their insidious danger to be underestimated. Cryptogams also, small though they are, are likewise invariably dangerous (fungi, algae, mould and lichens).

Biological and microbiological activity

Biological and microbiological action which, like chemical action, transforms the composition of building materials, can be identified by specialized laboratory tests. Such tests show, for instance, that the ravages caused by the presence of micro-organisms (bacteria, etc.) and which, because often accompanied by chemical transformation, are termed biochemical, are due to the action of thiobacteria producing sulphuric acid.

Special mention should be made of xylophagous insects, which destroy structures and wooden ornamentation. Termites or 'white ants' are the greatest danger, because the harm they do is not visible externally and frequently not discovered until too late to be repaired *(Plate 17)*.[1]

Other types of damage include that caused by larger animals such as certain

1. See: Szent-Ivany, 'Insect Pests and Their Control', *The Conservation of Cultural Property*, Paris, Unesco, 1968 (Vol. XI in this series).

Plate 17

Mount Locust was built in the 1780s and is one of the oldest surviving buildings in the area. Additions were made to it in the 1820s and it was used as an inn on the post road between Nashville, Tennessee and Natchez, Mississippi, during the 1820s.

(a) The building before restoration. Deterioration mainly due to termites.
(b) Deteriorated sections removed.
(c) After restoration. The original structure and additions made to it in the 1820s was preserved and restored.

(Photos: United States National Park Service.)

17a

7b

7c

species of rats (and rodents of all kinds); and by bird droppings.

NATURAL CATASTROPHES

This category includes all natural events of a violent and unforeseen nature, occurring sometimes on a calamitous scale. It is not feasible to give an exhaustive list of these accidental factors, but the main ones are as follows: earthquakes; seismic sea waves (tsunamis); landslides, landslips and phenomena relating to land movements and disruption; volcanic eruptions and gaseous exhalations; cyclones, tornadoes, water spouts, typhoons; floods, overflowing and other phenomena caused by uncontrolled water flow; avalanches, snow-slips etc.; spontaneous combustion. Damage caused by frost is not included, since it is seasonal and so comes into the long-term action category. However, in places where frost occurs only at long intervals—once in several decades—it may assume an accidental character, all the more dangerous for being unforeseen.

THE ACTION OF MAN

This category includes, first and foremost, all the changes and transformations made over the centuries such as: enlarging and raising an original building, changing the original structures in varying degrees, and often upsetting the equilibrium of vaults and arches. When the resulting new loads are excessive, defects of various kinds appear and are easy to diagnose; some may be due also to poor repairs. Partial demolition, if unskilfully done, may likewise cause disturbance of the static equilibrium. Men may also, without realizing it, change the nature of the sub-soil by altering the water table through the use of wells and the construction of tunnels and underground passages, thus upsetting the foundations which perform the delicate task of bearing and distributing the heaviest unitary loads. Unlike that caused by nature, the damage

accidentally inflicted by man can or could be avoided. This includes, in particular, short-circuits and other harm caused by electrical installations, explosions of various kinds (including those due to inflammable gases for domestic use and deposits of inflammable materials); leakage due to neglect of roofs or water-distribution plant, water-filled radiators and water supply for industrial purposes; fires, whether deliberate or accidental.

We shall not deal here with war damage—due not only to projectiles of various types—the nature and scope of which, in view of the extraordinary advances in methods of destruction, is unfortunately impossible to foresee.[1] The points covered so far refer to direct damage, inflicted more or less knowingly; but indirectly, man's activities contribute in every way to increasing damage of all kinds, whether by the use of new kinds of lighting and decoration in the construction of new buildings or, at the other end of the scale, by wholesale transformation of the atmosphere, causing a violent change in the surrounding conditions of many, indeed almost all, ancient monuments.

The increasing volume of mechanical vibrations transmitted, during the past twenty or thirty years, through earth, air and water, the increase of road traffic and, even more serious, the installation of railways, underground railways and industrial plant all represent a dangerous threat to ancient buildings, sooner or later causing the appearance of signs of deterioration. The development of supersonic flight accompanied by the 'bang' or 'boom' has also proved hazardous. Modern civilization, if only indirectly, also undermines the solidity of monuments by polluting the atmosphere with industrial gases and fumes.

This makes it doubly necessary for modern man to do everything he can to repair the damage.

---

1. See: *The Protection of Cultural Property in the Event of Armed Conflict*, Paris, Unesco, 1958 (Vol. VIII in this series).

STRUCTURAL CLASSIFICATION

CAUSES OF DAMAGE CLASSIFIED BY TYPE OF STRUCTURE

Another way of analysing damage of the above-ground structure of edifices is by classification according to type of structure and type of building material. This gives the following groups, for examination one by one:

Structures of ashlar, various types of finishing: (a) large (with vaults [type I]; with frame [type II]); (b) small and medium sized (with vaults [type III]; with frame [type IV]).[1]

Mixed structures of wood and brick (type V); mixed structures of masonry and cast vaulting (type VI).

Structures of ordinary masonry consisting of rubble and lime (type VII).

Structures of cast elements of lime cement, *pozzuolana* and various inert substances (type VIII).

Structures of wood (type IX).

This classification cannot be applied with absolute rigidity, since no structure is completely homogeneous. The Egyptian or Peruvian pyramids are perhaps homogeneous, but even ziggurats are not, since they contain both unbaked and baked materials, sometimes also clay and stone. The monuments which we are concerned with restoring are all of mixed architectural type, and will therefore be classified according to their predominating features.

Mixed structures of stone and wood

In this category, we shall take first mixed structures of types V and VI and type VII (ordinary masonry) as being the commonest and most general.

In Europe and the Mediterranean basin, the mixed stone and wood category co-incide approximately with the great ecclesiastical buildings down to the Renaissance: churches, basilicas, mosques, monasteries; also schools and palaces. Houses and so on come under type VII (ordinary masonry), or wooden structures, type IX.

Type V (wood and stone) includes large edifices with vertical structures of hewn stone built with lime; and edifices with horizontal structures and wooden roofing. Such buildings seldom suffer damage from thrust, but are subject to damage due to defects in the foundations (already described), and disintegration of the walls (binding materials, limes and cements, of the stones or bricks, and ageing of the wood).

Deterioration of the stones may take various forms, according to type: soft stone, sandstone, tufa, badly baked or unbaked bricks. Gradual wear of the surface renders them unable to resist the load resting on them; and their increased porosity exposes them to the humidity of the atmosphere and of the soil which soaks in, producing secondary effects extremely damaging to surface ornaments and wood. This may cause different building elements to separate on account of their different capacities to resist. For example, the mortar disintegrates and eventually crumbles, and as a result pieces of masonry jut out from the building.

This shows that it is a mistake, in building, to use heterogeneous materials which behave in different ways; or in any case, that it is advisable to make sure that the same mateiral is used for the whole of each horizontal stratum (Byzantine masonry). Failure to observe this rule often leads to splits and fissures which result in damage, the gravity of which it is difficult to assess. Exposure to wind and weather for long periods, for thousands of years sometimes, inevitably affects the compactness of worked

---

1. For the sake of simplicity, structures made of tiles, considered as the most ancient type of artificial stone, can be assimilated, for all practical purposes, to stone structures types III and IV.

of sculptured surfaces. When the original stone used was unsuitable for its purpose, restorers have the further problem of conserving these surfaces as well as conserving the actual structures of the building. In this mixed type of structure, wood acts as a static binding agent, so that its resistance is interdependent with that of the stone.

The wood in such mixed structures (used for beams, attached lintels, wall decorations and wall facings) is subject to rot, especially in the joints between walls, and may cause collapse, this danger being aggravated by the fact that it is at the very points which are at once the most difficult to check and structurally the most vital, that the wall crumbles. Very damp wood is extremely vulnerable to attack by insect species known generically as woodworm, which accelerates its destruction and spreads to dry wood as well, and also to sound parts of the masonry. When this happens the wooden section of the structure gradually rots away until either the vertical stone structure or the wooden frame itself gives way, and part of the edifice, or the whole of it, collapses.

In cases of collapse of mixed wood and stone structures, the horizontal beams very frequently fall in because the ends notched into the walls have rotted away. Wood shrinks in both directions when not in contact with the air, particularly if not sufficiently seasoned originally; this makes it friable, less resistant and liable to break. According to the state of conservation of the different parts of the wooden framework of the roof (especially where, as in Gothic cathedrals, the large Renaissance roofs or the large Chinese pagodas, the bearing structures are of complex design, with long beams and a steep slope corresponding to the pitch of the roof), there may be oblique thrusts bearing on the vertical walls, either because the horizontal elements of the trusses are defective, or because they have sagged in the middle.

In these mixed structures, the points where disturbances of the static equilibrium are

most liable to occur (due primarily to decay of the materials). are first, the point of interaction between stone-bearing structures and wooden roofing and, second, all fulcrum points of the load-bearing framework. In this type of structure, consisting as a rule of vertical walls supporting wooden floors, faults in the dimensions of the load-bearing structures are rare, so that buckling seldom occurs; but walls may be forced out of plumb as a result of natural phenomena such as deterioration of the base of the wall, causing it to veer round on a horizontal axis. When this happens, the building will 'gape' *(Plate 18)*: vertical cracks appear, indicating that the walls are coming apart at the joints; and there is bulging due to disintegration of the lime or binding material. The wall then begins to lean, usually outwards, because of lack of support in a section of the base, dragging with it, eventually, those parts of the wall whose base is still firm. The way in which this phenomenon occurs will obviously vary according to the size of the wall and the processing of the building materials (see also *Plate 15*).

Structures of mixed masonry and vaulting

Structures composed of vertical walls or pillars topped by vaults behave in a different way. In view of all the possible combinations of wall types—with single-compound pillars, with monolithic or multi-block columns, with vaults of many kinds, from the single-barrel vault to complex ribbed double-capped domes, of brick or cast masonry or a mixture of the two, or having wooden structures of various shapes as in certain Byzantine cupolas and mediaeval or Renaissance vault structures—we ought, in theory, to draw up a list of categories more numerous, perhaps, than the types of building actually in existence; but shall confine ourselves to a few main types, to serve as a guide.

The first step is to make a distinction between continuous vaults on rectilinear supports and vaults on pillars bearing the balanced loads of entire systems of vaults (Roman baths, Lombard, Romanesque, Arabic and Gothic architecture, with cross vaults, barrel vaults, sail vaults, etc., with various types of finishing and thrust).

Cupola vaults, of all types of finishing and thrust, on walls with rings, either buttressed or unbuttressed (Roman, Persian, Byzantine, Arabic and Renaissance domes).

Vaults and domes overhanging or resting on walls with rings (pre-Hellenic, Roman domes).

Cast and monolithic vaults and domes (Roman domes and cross vaults) on walls with rings.

The conservation of the materials in the above structures has already been dealt with. The characteristic defects to which they are liable, because of either structural weaknesses or sagging, are related to the oblique thrusts transmitted by the vaults to their supports. In such structures, the sagging of the supports (foundations, walls, pillars) changes the thrust of the vaults, setting up new stresses and thrusts extraneous to the original system of balanced thrusts. This in turn leads to excess loads applied to the bearing structures, and to dynamic damage to the supported structures, which split, so upsetting the equilibrium of the entire system. This may occur over a long period, giving rise to slight but widespread deformations which can be diagnosed and remedied; or else the initial decay may spread at an increasing rate, accompanied by widespread damage that culminates in the complete collapse of the edifice.

There are very few buildings of this type anywhere which are undamaged, and a large number have collapsed altogether. The original flaws which lead to serious deterioration of such vaulted structures may derive from the sagging or compression of the foundations, or from defects in the masonry or structures; or may be due to natural causes (deterioration of materials, effects of thermic expansion or neglect in general) (Plate 19).

Generally speaking, large buildings are far more liable than small to damage through deterioration of materials, unsatisfactory solutions of the initial static problem, and neglect; whilst smaller buildings suffer mainly from carelessness, abandon and change of use. Indeed, excess thrusts and loads are found only where there are large roofs resting on tall supports.

One of the problems which the builders of ancient times were less successful in solving is that of combined bending and compressive stress; striking flaws resulted, unexplained because it was not understood that the crux of the problem lies in the ratio between the horizontal section and the height of the architectural member. An illustration of this, taken from antiquity, is the Sanctuary of Didyma in Anatolia, where the columns, which are more than 12 metres high, but bear no thrust, have survived; whereas the pillars of the new cathedral of Siena are already bending, so that the construction of the building has had to be interrupted. Historical records of the construction of the great vaulted buildings and their subsequent fate tell of the flaws that emerged and the accidents that occurred during building or during the dismantling of the scaffolding; and of defects which developed gradually until they reached a critical point (Plate 18).

One factor which must, in practice, be taken into account in restoration is the tensile resistance of well-set mortar, which is capable of counteracting the effects of thrust, especially in masonry composed of small regular quoins or, better still, of bricks or cast concrete. Though cast concrete is defined as 'monolithic', there exist within such monoliths, especially large ones, various internal tensions and shearing stresses which are held in equilibrium solely by the resistance of the casting. Thus the abnormal resistance of surviving structures of ancient edifices is to be attributed to the tensile strength of the mortar, and this should be taken into account in planning restoration.

Plate 18

The Roman theatre at Hieropolis. Note vertical cracks running through the vaults revealing stresses which have developed during the course of time.
(Photo: Sanpaolesi).

Plate 19

The theatre at Hieropolis.
(a) General view showing warping, lateral
    movements due to subsidence, etc.
(b) Detail of the arch.
(Photo: Sanpaolesi.)

19b

Structures of ordinary masonry

These are the most common, and differ from the preceding type mainly by their size (though large buildings also can be built in this way); also by the summary, careless way in which they are often built. As a result, they are more frequently subject to subsidence in the foundations, while the actual masonry will crack and fall apart. The solidity of such building relies more on the binding capacity of the lime as well as on the use of iron chains, wood and other means to reinforce the most vital parts.

In buildings of this type, stones are often used for door and window mouldings, string-courses and so on, which are roughly affixed to the masonry. The latter may contain pieces of all kinds of stone, broken bricks, bits of wood and so on, picked up from other demolished buildings and simply used again. While it is difficult to classify structures of this type, in view of the great variety of materials used, they must be mentioned, especially as they are very numerous—which means that the appearance of entire urban districts will be changed if they are neglected or abandoned.

Structures built of wood

This is the largest category so far mentioned. Building in wood is still common all over the world, and was even commoner in the past so that, despite all the destruction and changes which have taken place, wooden buildings still outnumber other. It has always been the main type of construction in Japan, China and Central Europe and, before the construction of buildings of reinforced concrete, was the only one capable of withstanding earthquakes.

Thus whole cities, such as Istanbul, were built of wood, with the result that they stood up to earthquakes but were, on the other hand, at the mercy of fire, which was even more disastrous. There are many types of wooden buildings (including the light Japanese type of squared, accurately dovetailed timbers and the similar but far heavier type found in the Alps and the Urals). The foundations are susceptible to damp, which causes damage that may lead to the buildings being abandoned or altered. In the humid tropics one of the main dangers comes from insects which attack the wood and cause it to disintegrate. Regular chemical treatment applied in areas where such insects are rife help to control the pests. Generally speaking, none the less, wooden buildings, though not as long-lived as stone ones, may survive in excellent condition for many years.

PHYSICAL FACTORS

NATURAL CAUSES OF DETERIORATION

Every building has its own micro-climate, which subjects it constantly to various chemical and mechanical influences. It was mentioned earlier that the physical environment may affect buildings through the nature of the ground, bradyseism, and so on. But apart from this, the atmosphere plays an important part in the conservation of the individual building materials exposed to it. There are, for instance, types of stone which are soft when quarried, but harden on contact with the atmosphere; and certain kinds of porous stone acquire a coating of microscopic vegetation which provides extremely effective protection against surface corrosion. However, the edifices with which we are concerned come into the category described in the foregoing section: bossages, columns, lintels, wall facings and floors of stone, marble and stuccoes; binding ma terials, plaster of various kinds including lime (plaster and *pozzuolana*), plaster of Paris, etc., combined with sand, wax, colours; structural elements and accessories such as flooring, fixtures, ceilings—wood of various types; accessory and structural elements—iron in the form of chains, locks, railings, chandeliers, wrought-iron fixtures, utensils; roof and wall coverings—bronze, lead and copper; glass is used for windows and for decorations such as mosaics, etc.

Building stone

The stones used for building may be of various types and origins, from the hardest granites and basalt to the softest tufa. Building technology has, from earliest times, overcome difficulties of quarrying, working and transporting stone. The commonest and most widely used stones all over the world are usually medium-hard to soft (lime and sandstone), which have the added advantage of existing in deposits in such size and thickness that they can be conveniently quarried in large blocks suitable for all kinds of building purposes. The large columns found in ancient buildings consist mostly of hard materials such as pink or white granite, marble of various types (including Greek and Carrara, and mixed types such as Peloponnesian and cipolin). Most sculptures are of white marble, porphyry, compact limestone or alabaster. The stones with which we are chiefly concerned are common limestone and sandstone. Four causes of damage to stone are given below.

Frost action. The main defect of these materials is their porosity, which makes them subject to damage from frost action.

Damage is lessened if there are no cracks in the stones through which humidity can penetrate, and if they have been worked so as to prevent the accumulation of small pockets of water. Common limestone is less subject to the penetration of humidity into the structure, and damage through frost action is less frequent. However, humidity penetrates to a depth of 2–3 centimetres in porous stones (such as sandstone), so that after the rain stops and the sun emerges the surface dries up, but the moisture remains within. If the temperature drops below 0° C ice crystals form between the surface and inner layers of the stone, usually resulting in damage. Some of the lime may also go into solution and, as the surface dries, the precipitates may cause disfiguring encrustations. On the other hand, atmospheric humidity promotes the growth of vegetation (mosses, lichens) which may help by retaining the humidity on the surface, thus serving both as a waterproofing agent and as an absorbent of excess humidity. However, this also increases the porosity of the surface and dissolves the connective tissue in sandstones, or in pure limestones such as marble. This leads to disintegration of the surface both in the case of sandstone, where the grains of silicon dioxide are freed and crumble away, and in the case of marble, when the calcite crystals become detached. This type of surface crumbling occurs in all porous stones. As for large-scale spalling and cracks, the causes are extremely varied and will be discussed later.

Thermic conductivity. Climatic conditions also affect stones because of their poor thermic conductivity. Take the case of a stone block which has been stabilized at a temperature externally and internally of 40° C. When placed in the summer sun, those parts actually exposed to its rays will gradually be heated to a temperature of 45–60° C, while the temperature inside the block remains stationary at 40° C. The difference of temperature will provoke sharp differences in expansion between the heated surface layer and the inner layer. This is a serious cause of damage, as stone is a very poor conductor of heat.

As happens in frost action, the expanded layer will tend to separate from the cooler layer. That the heat of the atmosphere produces marked effects is well known; but no detailed study has yet been made of the relation between cubic expansion and the extent of the tensions and reactions set up in stones.

Chemical action. A third cause of the surface disruption of stone is the chemical action of components added to the atmosphere by industrial fumes and domestic heating. The combustion products of coal and oil, the commonest fuels, add a constant stream of carbon dioxide and miscellaneous gases to the atmosphere, of which the most important include sulphuric and sulphurous sulphides and anhydrides.

Residues—particularly those of fuel oils—also contain unburnt substances which, being oily and adhesive, act as an excipient for anhydrides, sulphides, etc. Thus an increase in the amount of anhydrides will eventually intensify the scouring action of rain on limestones and atmospheric humidity, and the deposit of sulphuric residues will cause sulphatation of limestone and granite, though it has little effect on siliceous sandstone. Sulphatation produces what looks like the remains of a miniature volcanic explosion, with raised, chipped lips and a crater filled with dust and rubble. Marls and statuary marble are also affected by sulphatation, which inflicts fairly serious damage, ulcerating the stone so that it crumbles away at the slightest touch. Once started, it penetrates, and spreads over wide areas of surface. Like frost action, it is commonest on the outer surface, but may also occur inside at points where humidity condenses and atmospheric fumes penetrate.

In addition to sulphatation, which constitutes, for the moment, the most serious chemical danger, stone surfaces may also be attacked by nitrous and nitric anhydrides which have been pumped into the atmosphere. However, these anhydrides, being chemically less stable than sulphurous and sulphuric anhydrides, are more easily dispersed and neutralized and, moreover, do not affect so large an area. However, they may cause very serious damage, not so much to the actual structures of buildings as to their ornamentation, since they spoil the colours of wall paintings.

Winds. Winds are a fourth cause of damage to stone, often aggravating the effects of the other three. Prevailing winds, wet or dry, are one of the determinants of the microclimate surrounding a monument. Seasonal winds, and a seasonal climate, such as are found in temperate zones at all altitudes, in the monsoon regions, and in warm zones at high altitudes, are more harmful to buildings than the more uniform climate of cold regions. Serious damage is caused by sudden changes of the prevailing winds, bringing changes of climate in their wake. Take, for instance, the example of a house in a damp, warm climate, where the stones are soaked through: the sudden onset of a cold wind may produce more damage in a few hours by freezing the damp walls than normal wear and tear over a dozen years. Then again there are cases where, owing to a change of the wind patterns, the climate suddenly becomes extremely dry and the relative humidity drops from 80–90 to 28–30. When this happens, all the damp wood contained in buildings may split. All directors of galleries containing paintings executed on wooden panels are aware of the damage which changes of humidity may inflict on both wood panels and the frames of oil paintings. Apart from this, wind, when blowing at high speeds, may cause erosion because, as all rock-climbers are aware, it carries particles of solid matter. This, together with the effects of intense heat, is mainly responsible for the destruction of abandoned monuments in the hot, dry regions of Egypt, Mesopotamia, the American deserts, and so on.

Artificial materials

The effects of the atmosphere, combined with ground effects play a large part in the deterioration of baked clay materials which constitute one of the two main types of artificial stone (the other being concrete).

The damage they suffer varies according to hardness (depending on the type of clay used and the method of baking), even under identical climatic and siting conditions. For instance, some bricks in a wall may be almost entirely destroyed whilst others, apparently identical, are perfectly preserved; and again, some bricks, even though exposed to the humidity of the ground, may be in good condition whilst others, in a drier, better protected position, deteriorate.

The same applies to decorated terra-cotta elements, and to glazed tiles used for ornament and as a protective covering for roofs and cupolas; though in this case the double-baking of the glazed tiles and careful selection of the clay used usually make for high quality, and their thickness gives them better resistance to frost and chemical deterioration. On the other hand, in the case of paving tiles, *patera*, and exterior and flooring revetments, small non-glazed parts are always exposed to the effects of the atmosphere and deteriorate before the rest. The damage spreads, and sometimes leaves the glazed areas without support. This presents restorers with a difficult and very common problem—we have only to think for a moment of the majolica facings on floors, walls and roofs, of all the sculptures and pictures executed in glazed and unglazed terra-cotta, and of all the accessories and refinements of various kinds found in baroque or in Roman architecture.

Lime and other binding materials

By far the commonest binding material is lime-mortar, used in various mixtures and for a wide variety of purposes: for interior and exterior decoration, for binding bricks and stone together, and as the main substance in castings and concrete. Lime has to be processed according to the function it is to carry out, and small differences in the type of lime used and proportions of mixtures produces very different effects. The results depend also on seasonal and climatic conditions, both at the time of use and later, during the very slow setting process common to air-hardened lime. The behaviour of lime is also influenced by the inert substances with which it is mixed. The importance of its quality depends on the use to which it is put in a building. Combined with pigment for mural paintings; mixed with antimony oxide for graffiti or with a water soluble pigment for stucco and encaustic; or used for architectural moulding, it demands careful study as an object for restoration. The limes least subject to deterioration are those incorporated as binding materials in the actual texture of structures (bricks, stones, etc.), in which case they are liable to the same damage as the material—cracking and sagging. Once a structure has cracked, however, the limes contained in it are exposed, in the same way as stones or bricks, to the weathering effects of the atmosphere, and if they have not hardened sufficiently, the mortar may crumble more quickly than the rest of the structure, causing the whole to disintegrate.

Such cases are extremely frequent in ancient buildings; and in vaulted edifices which have been abandoned or neglected, it is the rapid disintegration of the limes or lime-based mixtures that is most often the cause of decay. If carelessly applied at the time of construction there will be undue shrinkage, causing flaws in the structure and eventually, when excess loads cause buckling, lead to water-infiltration and frost fissures. As a rule this is a slow process which, if diagnosed in time, can be halted fairly easily. Theoretically, good quality slaked lime (calcium hydroxide) is entirely transformed into calcium carbonate so that, mixed with good siliceous sand, it lasts practically for ever, becoming progressively harder through the absorption of carbon dioxide from the air.

This explains why the thick layers of mortar used by the Byzantine builders in many monuments from the third century to the thirteenth in vertical and vaulted struc-

133

tures are in excellent condition despite their poor location. The Byzantines used a mixture containing, in addition to sand, brick broken into small fragments about 1 centimetre in diameter, and powdered brick. This mortar was irregular in texture, and did not set fully; but the layers of bricks and stones are laid perfectly regularly, and absolutely horizontally. The mortar was applied with extreme accuracy, in layers 3–4 centimetres thick. The effects of shrinkage were foreseen and virtually eliminated by the use of stone broken up into many fairly large fragments (up to 3 centimetres in diameter). This layer of stones, bound together by mortar, protected the mortar against pressure from overlying layers but not against erosion by wind and rain. Hence vaulted edifices built with this type of mortar need to be carefully protected against humidity by roofs made of bent tiles fixed with pure lime mortar, or by roofs made of lead (or more rarely, copper).

In practice, however, if part of the lime does not contain sufficient water to set, or is mixed with clayey or rotting substances which prevent it from setting properly, instead of a compact mass of carbonate, a mixture of carbonate and powdery anhydrous lime results which contains harmful inert substances having no cohesive force. Badly made mortar deteriorates much more rapidly than good mortar does from exposure to air, and neglect.

Lime mortars, especially when they contain organic impurities, are an easy prey to many species of plants which differ from place to place and are too numerous to list here. They may, however, be divided into two main categories: climbing plants whose ramifying roots cling to the walls and draw nourishment from the lime to replace or supplement that obtained from the earth. This leads to the curious and common spectacle of plants—not merely herbaceous, but also arboreal—whose roots penetrate the layers of lime inside the masonry. Lime

mortar also provides a good hold for moss and fungi which in turn cause chemical deterioration or damage through infiltration but sometimes they may serve as a protective layer against further and more dangerous infiltration. The problem of plants growing in masonry has been mentioned in connexion with mortars because they are a common cause of damage to structures containing lime in considerable quantities. In addition, lime plaster is used as facing for masonry made of stone or baked brick or combinations of the two, in various forms, each of which needs to be considered separately. There is also ordinary plaster, on an average 2–3.5 centimetres thick, mixed with what is called hydrated lime (laid on in two stages, first a rough layer of hydraulic lime then a second, thinner layer of white, air-hardened lime). This method is used for many purposes; fashioning moulded cornices, distemper or fresco colour washing, and graffiti.

Alternatively, lime may be mixed with plaster of Paris (anhydrous calcium sulphate) to form smooth plaster for interiors; or with powdered crystalline marble instead of sand, to form stucco or artificial marble used for surface decorations such as panels, cornices, ornamental designs, and so on. There are also encaustic mural paintings dating from ancient times, which constitute one of the most interesting examples of successful experimentation.

Plaster revetments can be used to give the appearance of stone—as done to great effect in Palladian architecture—a method also very commonly practised throughout the ages, from pre-Hellenic times down to the present day. But in regard to the causes of damage which make the plaster fall off there is little to add to the observations already made about fresco and encaustic lime in general, and about special instances of restoration of the interior and exterior of edifices.

Stucco

Stucco is the term applied to mouldings made of special types of mortar as decoration for interiors and exteriors of buildings. It may provide the architectural and pictorial decoration of whole sections of edifice, and thus have great aesthetic importance. It may also be used to restore sculptures and replace the missing parts of a damaged capital, since it lends itself very well to making reproductions of carvings in stone or marble.

The mixtures employed for making stucco vary widely according to its use as an exterior coating of buildings, internal surfaces of walls, or for ornamental details. Slaked lime of varying quality is used in different combinations with sand, powdered marble, pozzuolana, gypsum (plaster of Paris), powdered brick, wax, oils and egg and size-based distemper. The usual method is to prepare the wall to be decorated with a rough preparatory layer (one part of slaked lime to two parts of coarse sand). The surface of this layer should be rough so that the next layer can be keyed in to adhere to it.

The second layer is made up of the appropriate mixture into a putty-like consistency, so that it can be modelled like sculpture (the pieces may also be manufactured in moulds beforehand) and applied—this is what is done in the case of the mixture made of pure chalk lime or mixtures of chalk lime with powdered marble and fine sand. Herein lies the weakness of this method. The main threat to stucco in the open is surface deterioration; on interior walls it is liable to suffer as the finer surface is detached from the first rough casting through humidity, subsidence of the walls, crumbling, or other causes. However, stucco can be extremely durable, as the paste can contain waterproof primings such as encaustic wax, oils, milk and egg-based distemper, etc.

Another cause of deterioration is rust which, in the long run, causes the nails and iron rods used for reinforcing protruding elements to expand and split the surrounding material. There are, nevertheless, surviving examples of extremely ancient stucco work, for instance the coloured moulding of Egyptian bas-reliefs in stone, the coloured facing of the Greek temples in Sicily (e.g. that at Selinunte), the interior of the underground basilica of Porta Maggiore in Rome, at Pompeii, on the inside and outside of many Roman buildings in Byzantine edifices such as St. Sophia at Constantinople, and in increasing numbers of more modern buildings.

Stucco affects the entire style of buildings and has therefore to be treated with particular care, even though it may be regarded as a modern technique. Hence its preservation is vital to the building to which it belongs ,and measures must be taken to protect it from the effects of the atmosphere, which damages it in the same way as stones: surface erosion obliterating outlines, frost action, deterioration through the infiltration of water, effects of fumes and gases, etc.

Stucco inside buildings may also be spoiled by constant condensation of humidity at the highest and coldest points: and, in particular, as a result of accidents, changes of taste, political events, earthquakes, and so on.

Mural paintings

There are various kinds of mural paintings. In Europe they may be divided into (a) fresco; (b) encaustic; and (c) tempera.

Frescoes. These are painted with colours dissolved in water on a dry wall freshly treated with a layer of lime plaster 10–12 centimetres thick, known as rough casting because the surface is left rough. This rough casting is composed of good quality lime and medium-grain sand (the lime must be slaked at least a month before, and the sand well washed and absolutely siliceous); the painting is then outlined on this surface, usually in red, though brown or yellow may be used. This outline traced with a fine brush, is called a sinopia as it is drawn in red; since it is dissolved in pure water, the colour fades when exposed to the air, and the dry casting to which it is applied does not fix it. When the whole of the composition has been drawn and the wall, if necessary, has been divided up into sections, a mixture is made of chalk-quality slaked lime in a liquid and fine sand. This mixture (lime putty) is smeared over that section of the painting which it is reckoned can be completed within a day, and smoothed over with a trowel.

Then the painting is begun, with pigments dissolved in pure water; if mistakes are made, they cannot simply be painted over: the plaster must be removed, and the new layer applied, before beginning that part of the painting again. The plaster will remain damp enough to work on all day, except in very hot climates, where it will have to be removed and renewed at intervals of three to four hours. The colour painted on wet plaster which has not yet begun to set soaks in to a depth of at most, half a millimetre and remains fixed; after carbonation the pigments (the most permanent mineral pigments are selected for the purpose—the Italians in the fourteenth century used at most seven or eight, including black and white) remain permanent, even when the surface is thoroughly washed with water. The original sketch in red remains beneath the layer of lime putty. Though hidden, it does not disappear—on the contrary, the damp layer smeared over it has to some extent the effect of fixing it in the rough casting, so that it can be recuperated later.

Fresco painting calls for skill and physical stamina as well as creative ability, engaging all the artist's faculties to an even greater extent than sculpture. The finished composition will consist of as many sections as days taken to paint it, distinguishable on close examination by the joins between the different applications of lime putty. Fresco paintings, whether exterior or interior, immediately acquire an appearance of great permanence, which was the reason why both Byzantine artists (in Roman churches) and Renaissance painters like Giorgione and Titian chose this method for the decoration of whole façades of buildings.

Unfortunately, plaster is perishable even when protected by the incorporation of colour and treated with special care; and the time comes when these precious paintings, forming an integral part of an architectural *ensemble*, begin to deteriorate. This is mainly due to exposure to the effects of water, frost and parasites, and to the changing fortunes of the building to which they belong. Apart from damage caused by fire, cracks or disintegration, the main causes of the deterioration of fresco paintings are surface erosion or the detachment of the plaster layer from the wall, when the painting begins to flake off, a process which, if not stopped in time, spreads to the entire painted surface.

Another danger to frescoes comes from changes in taste, which have caused many cycles of frescoes either to be whitewashed over, or else to be replaced by others of scant artistic value. Yet another danger comes from restorers repainting frescoes with unsuitable media (oils, casein lime) in order to brighten up the colours, or patch up parts which have flaked off (Leonardo's *Last Supper*). In any case, restoration depends chiefly on prompt diagnosis. A common cause of damage inside buildings is the condensation of humidity on cold walls (this also happens on the outside). Frescoes are also liable to be attacked by fungi which causes the compact surfaces to become porous and so prepare the way for further damage. When the plaster support crumbles and disintegrates, the thick surface layer containing the paint acts as protection for the layers beneath it, thus taking over the role originally played by the support.

A fresco technically well executed has a

rigid glassy surface. When this surface eventually succumbs to the effects of the disintegration of the underlying plaster layer, it breaks up into minute flakes which remain attached precariously to the grains of sand. They eventually fall singly or in groups, in the form of coloured powder, combining with dust, dead insects, cobwebs, and so on. It is at this stage that many inexperienced restorers decide that frescoes are beyond repair, and either abandon or demolish them. In fact rescue operations are possible and often produce miraculous results (see below).

Encaustic mural paintings. These differ from frescoes in their method of execution, but are liable to the same sort of damage. As to the technique used, recent research indicates that such paintings were done (as described by Pliny) with emulsified wax, or preferably, with wax rendered water-soluble by being treated with sodium and potassium carbonate (natron, which in Egypt is a natural product of the marshes in the valley of the Natron river). This treated wax, which Pliny calls 'punic wax' is soluble in water and can be applied with a brush either to cover large surfaces or to trace thin lines, in the same way as glue-based tempera. The encaustic paintings at Pompeii have fine even backgrounds of green, azure, red and yellow, decorated with black and white designs, and pictures executed with subtle shading and impasto effects.

The colour is first applied by the method used for water tempera, and then 'polished' by passing a hot iron slab over the entire painted surface. The heat releases the wax from its solvent and makes it insoluble in water again, as it was originally before mixing with natron; and the colours become deep, brilliant and transparent. This excellent technique makes the paintings themselves remarkably resistant, besides protecting the plaster against external damp.

All surviving ancient mural paintings (except the Etruscan) found in Egypt, Pompeii, Herculaneum, Rome, etc., including the funerary portraits found in the Fayum, were executed by this method. Many of them—such as those found in the House of Livia on the Palatine Hill and in the Domus Aurea—were buried for centuries under a layer of soaking wet soil without the colour being dimmed or the surface in the least eroded. On the other hand these paintings, once exposed to the air, deteriorate rapidly. This is mainly due to the disintegration of the plaster, which seems to begin as soon as the protective layer of earth has been removed. Accordingly—and this applies also to frescoes—excavations can be dangerous for, if precautions to conserve the paintings are not taken, they may lead (as at Pompeii) to the loss of invaluable evidence of the life of past civilizations.

Tempera. Mural paintings executed with tempera made from lime and various types of glue are the easiest to wash. This is a recent process, not employed for any major paintings, although it has been used, as being easier and cheaper, in certain edifices in Europe dating from the period between the sixteenth century and the present day. Here again, we need to know something about the damage liable to occur, so that measures may be taken to conserve these paintings.

Mural temperas are of various types, according to the binding material used: lime, starch, casein, dextrin, etc. The commonest is the white lime type. The pigment, combined with one of these substances, is applied to the dry wall, which is not very absorbent, so that the painting does not penetrate, but constitutes a layer superimposed on the surface which, with the passage of time, begins to flake away. In addition, the colours either fade or crumble because the pigments are not fixed and react to the chemical effects of the atmosphere. Needless to say, such paintings are further affected by the vicissitudes of the particular building to which they belong.

Unbaked, baked and semi-baked clays

Clay has been used in building from the very earliest times, especially for the floors of huts and for sealing wooden structures. The use of baked clay for making vessels to hold water and liquids was known during the Neolithic, and is much earlier than the invention of bricks—unbaked, semi-baked, baked or glazed—which play such an outstanding role in building. Glazing was commonly used by potters and it is assumed that the brickmakers took it over from them. The use of unbaked bricks continued for large buildings (ziggurats, Babylonia, many large pre-Colombian sites in the Americas) mainly for practical, but perhaps also for economic reasons, and still continues in many parts of the world.

Unbaked bricks may be of various types but the rule—as also for baked bricks—is that they must be small and light enough for one man to handle. Unbaked bricks may be fairly small but in the Americas (where they are frequently known as adobe) they may be 35–50 centimetres long. They are made, as a rule, of a mixture of adulterated clay and sometimes horse or cow manure, with straw or chaff added. Walls made of unbaked bricks were generally covered with a layer of plaster of one kind or another, on which paintings were sometimes executed, as in the case of the Etruscan tombs. In other cases, they were coated with plaster composed of pure earthen clay mixed with silica sand. Crude brick structures were used mainly to form compact, homogeneous walls, although the fact that the bricks were laid in horizontal layers prevented the existence of oblique slipping planes and also provided spaces for the insertion of wooden elements such as ceilings, lintels and so on. Hard woods such as oak and chestnut resist deterioration when thus used, but precautions need to be taken for soft woods such as fir and poplar. Unbaked brick is not suitable for facing (Plate 20).

All kinds of baked bricks, on the other hand, can be used for facing, including bricks baked twice (glazed) with various kinds of wood and other fuels, in a wide variety of furnaces designed to provide the minimum temperature required for transforming clay into terra cotta. The result of firing is that each brick remains separate, ceasing to coalesce with the adjacent ones. The change which results from firing forms the basis for one of the commonest and most effective manufacturing processes used in ancient times for a wide variety of purposes: vessels for containing and carrying liquids, cooking and table utensils, heating appliances, and, in architecture, roofs, floors, water-piping and, last but not least, works of art of great aesthetic value.

Bricks have been used in a variety of combinations—with mortar in modern times, with liquid clay and *pozzuolana* in antiquity, first in Mesopotamia and subsequently in the rest of the world. It is not necessary here to give a detailed description of the technology of baked clay bricks and of all the possible ways in which they can be used in architecture, in combination with crude earth, stone, marble and wood. Baked brick is an excellent building material in that, unlike stone, it is not as liable to damage from frost, blends very well with lime, lends itself to plastering, is chemically stable and adaptable to widely diverse physical and climatic conditions. The quality of the bricks will obviously depend both on the clay they are made of and on the baking process.

One of the most serious defects of bricks is under-baking: a well-baked brick should emit a ringing sound and vibrate when struck. A badly baked brick, when exposed to the sun, fails to meet requirements; it disintegrates, and when exposed to moisture, even to atmospheric humidity, it rapidly deteriorates beyond repair. Nevertheless, a wall where one or more bricks have disintegrated continues to resist unless one by one all the bricks give way.

The composition and thickness of brick

Plate 20

Part of the arabesque mouldings found on the walls of buildings in the Chimu (fourteenth century) city of Chan-Chan (Peru). The site covers approximately 18 square kilometres. The adobe structures have suffered considerable wear following their exposure, and in many cases such mouldings have disappeared completely.

structures may vary. With those of minimum thickness, the bricks, with the lime and cement, constitute the sole bearing elements, so that any anomalies derive from the structure and deterioration of single bricks. But for greater thicknesses—70–100 centimetres—rubble-filled structures are often used. These consist of two outer brick walls—which may either be completely detached or else joined by horizontal lime ribs—the space between them filled in with brick and stone fragments. Such walls are always a hidden threat to static equilibrium owing to their irregular formation, which leads to an uneven distribution of the stresses throughout the thickness, with consequent sagging and cleavage. The situation is frequently aggravated by the use of poor-quality mortar, by uneven shrinkage during setting of the different elements used in the wall, and by other attendant circumstances, such as imperfect perpendicularity, the insertion of high protruding elements the insertion of flues cutting vertically or obliquely through the load-bearing walls, and the rhythmic intercalation of rows of doors and windows one above the other, inadequately linked to each other and to the interior walls.

Apart from this, brick is often used for rustic structures to take bossages, decorations, supports for inlaid marble floors, mosaics, and so on, and its composition must then be such as to fit it for all these purposes. Otherwise, the revetments and masonry may often come apart, and pockets of moisture will form leading to deterioration of various kinds which are difficult to identify. Damage to vertical brick walls in the absence of obvious external causes such as earthquakes, explosions, or collapse of the foundations, invariably indicates disintegration and ensuing disequilibrium in the component parts—lime, individual bricks, etc. The disintegration of one brick quickly spreads, causing the appearance of visible cracks and so on, but these are the outward signs of damage, the causes of which lie elsewhere. Similarly, the rotation of a pillar or the bulging of a section of facing is merely the indication of collapse of the actual materials themselves, and never, save in the cases cited above, a sign of the collapse of the structure.

Bricks have been used also for the construction of vaults of varying thicknesses and shapes. Here bricks constitute an inert, resistant material, and they are used in combination with lime mortar, cement, *pozzuolana*, etc. All brick walls contain some form of binding material—lime, plaster, clay or bitumen as the case may be. Bricks can be laid in the most complicated and delicate designs in vaulted structures. Without the use of brick, the vast Roman, Byzantine and Renaissance domes could never have been built, for their standard conformation gives a regularity of static equilibrium which could never have been obtained with stone, however skilfully hewn and used. In these large buildings in particular, the conservation of the structures depends on the conservation of the materials themselves.

Assuming that there are no major errors in the construction and dimensions of the component structures, buildings fashioned from good materials will have a resistance in excess of the maximum theoretical figure. The distribution of the loads will differ from forecasts made on the basis of theoretical and experimental calculations (this is always true up to a point), and general stability will be guaranteed. If, on the other hand, part of the material is defective (fragile, frost-cracked, uneven), the stresses will increase constantly until they exceed the permissible limit, causing more and more damage which is often not apparent until it is too difficult and too costly to repair. If, for instance, the mortars used in a brick vault are ill-adapted to its particular shape, if the parts resting on the impost are exposed to attrition by rainwater which is not properly drained away, or if the lime mortar contains unsuitable inert substances where resistance to tensile strength as well as compressive stress is required, then deterioration will set in fairly soon. The root of the trouble must be identified and treated before undertaking further repairs.

Elements made of ceramic materials are widely used for a great variety of ornamental purposes. They may be modelled carefully before firing, modelled roughly before firing and finished off later, or more commonly, after being set in place. They may be made in various sizes and colours and arranged to form ornamental designs and patterns. Various kinds—stoneware, majolica, porcelain, painted terra cottas—of ceramic materials including glazed or unglazed vases have been used in architecture.

The different objects made by firing various combinations of clays, tempers, glazes, call for different conservation measures. Buildings and monuments in Mesopotamia, Etruscan temples, façades and courtyards of Lombard, Emilian, Sienese, Persian, Spanish, Arab and Chinese structures used materials made from baked clay. These decorative elements were invariably exposed to the effects of the atmosphere and suffered from frost, abrasion, mildew, and other weathering effects in the same way as ordinary bricks. On the other hand, the procedures followed for restoration, consolidation and conservation differ widely for each type. Specialized craftsmen are usually required, or may have to be trained for the purpose.

The ordinary baked clay used for decorative architectural features is less refined than that used by sculptors. The size, even when made by hand, is modelled on that of the brick; but terra cotta structures may be highly complex and be produced by what may be described as a system of prefabrication—as witness certain Italian Renaissance buildings where entablatures, string-courses and end blocks cast in the same mould are found in different buildings and even in different cities.

Majolicas are used in architecture in a large number of forms and for a wide variety of purposes. Vitrified surfaces found on terra cotta are used to introduce colours and may cover entire façades (the walls of Babylon), the scaled roofing of domes, individual ornamental objects such as paterae, entire floors and wall decorations, altar retables and fountains, and grave furnishings. Ceramic objects are virtually impervious to atmospheric effects, but the supports to which they are attached are usually more fragile, so that the greatest damage done to such objects is due to breakages occurring when their supports disintegrate.

Wood

Wood is used in combination with other materials for numerous structures (ceilings, roofs, facings, floors, staircases), besides which it forms virtually the only material used for the manufacture of fixtures such as doors and windows. The ageing of wood differs so widely according to species, climate and use as to make it impossible to define in detail.

The way in which wood used in building behaves, the times it lasts, and the restoration it requires depends on whether it is in the open or under cover, and whether its function is ornamental or static. Generally speaking, damp, especially where accentuated by heat, is very harmful, since the damp wood may be more easily attacked by parasites in the form of mould or insects which sap its strength. This is one of the most serious—and frequently insidious—causes of the deterioration of wood. Ceilings often collapse because the wood is eaten away by parasites which, in some cases, may have been living in the original tree and continue to multiply afterwards. The transport of timber from one part of the world to another facilitates the propagation of all kinds of parasites which, being unfamiliar, may be difficult to deal with promptly. The damage these insects can do is so serious that special governmental agencies have been set up to deal with them.

There are also other causes for the deterioration of wood. Wood used for trusses exposed to the air deteriorates as a result of variations of climate and of the stresses exercised by the structure. When wood is subjected mainly to bending stresses, the natural elasticity of the wood comes into play, relaxing the longitudinal fibres of stretched sections, and compressing the fibres of squashed ones. The effects are much more marked in the taut sections, where the fibres lengthen until splits appear and the natural clefts formed during seasoning are widened. If the wood is decorated, as often happens with ceilings, columns and bare roof beams, damage to the wood leads to damage to the decoration, which may be irreplaceable.

Such decoration may be treated like painted wooden panels because, though not executed with the same care, both the materials and the methods used are, technically speaking, the same. Wood is generally employed in combination with iron (nails, straps, brackets, bolts, etc.) to join the disparate structural elements together. The surface of the wood in contact with the iron—nails and bolts in particular—undergoes compression. This at the outset merely serves to hold the two materials together and protect them, but as time goes on and as the fibres contract either naturally or because of continuous stresses, the wood loosens its hold, allowing the damp of the atmosphere to penetrate and rust the surface of the iron. Rusted nails or bolts, for a time, hold better, but the moment comes when the amount of metal is so reduced that friction lessens and the nails work loose. The holes then have so much play that secondary shearing oblique stresses result which the wood is progressively less able to resist. The loosening of the structural elements and the resulting play between them may quickly become dangerous, especially where the wood is squared off

with fitted joints and where stresses are accompanied by vibrations produced, for example, by the wind. Other stresses such as the weight of a layer of snow may cause the roof to collapse or cause other damage calling for immediate measures. This natural process, combined with the effects of parasites, vibrations and rot may, without being noticed, cause extremely rapid deterioration, especially to large roofs, parts of which may be inaccessible.

Lastly, wood, being inflammable, is liable to serious fires, with damage both to works of art and the stone used. At one time or another most tile and wooden roofs or even the entire structure of ancient monuments have been destroyed by fires. In some cases prompt and skilful restoration can save what may seem to be hopelessly lost. It is a mistake to be swayed by first impressions, as is shown by the example of San Paolo fuori le Mure in Rome. The roof was burned and practically the whole of the left of the central aisle was destroyed by the collapse of several tottering columns. However, the remaining walls and columns and, most important of all, the mosaics which covered the whole of the immense walls and constituted one of the finest monuments of Christian art, remained intact. Nevertheless, the restorer discarded all that remained, and simply rebuilt the whole basilica in severe neo-classical style. Instead of attempting to save what was left after the fire, he merely added to the damage, his mistaken activity doing more harm than the fire.

Even extinguishing fires is a tricky process, for works of art can easily suffer damage in the process. The flames must of course be prevented from spreading, but the indiscriminate use of the hose to put out the last smouldering embers may ruin objects that had escaped harm.

Resinous species of wood are frequently used as piles in foundations, forming veritable underground forests supporting the edifice. This type of foundation is commonest where the soil is friable or where the surface of the ground is soft owing to water impregnation. In such cases, the method is to use tamping, a practice very common in the past.

It is very important to study the behaviour of wood that is driven into the ground, as it varies widely according to conditions. Experience shows that, as a rule, wood constantly exposed to humidity retains its resistance unchanged for centuries; but this is subject to certain reservations, and it is safer to assume that even when the stakes of pile foundations are, by and large, protected from contact with the air, some degree of rotting may occur, especially when the humidity of the sub-soil is subject to seasonal variations. It should be remembered that the condition of piles cannot be checked.

In places where the ground is damp, the water table is low and the nature of the soil such that the piles tend to work loose, and the foundations tend to lose their solidity. This may produce damage in the building similar to that deriving from other causes, so that careful diagnosis is necessary before a remedy can be prescribed.

Metals

Iron. Iron is one of the metals used in building. We take it first because it has, from ancient times, always been the most common. Down to the fall of the Roman Empire, the sole use made of iron in building (except in supports for stone modelling) was in the cramps holding blocks of stone together. In view of its oustanding resistance to tensile stress, however, it began to be used in building as a reinforcement for masonry which obviously had great tensile stresses to withstand. Iron chains (used first to reinforce damaged columns) soon came to be widely employed in building and, although subsequently discarded, this idea undoubtedly paved the way for later uses of iron in building. Needless to say, the chains running in the direction of the rise of an arch were designed mainly to indicate the line of the horizontal components of the thrust, so that the presence of such chains in an arched or vaulted building is of definite historical importance. Wholly metal structures did not make their appearance until the seventeenth century—the forged iron dome over the altar of Santo Spirito in Florence seems to have been the first of its kind.

One of the commonest purposes for which iron was used was for the manufacture of reinforcement rings and tie-rods (as were applied as an emergency measure on the dome of St. Peter's in Rome), and railings and balusters. However, examples of iron used in the form of bars let into structures are found from the fifteenth century onwards, e.g. the dome of Santa Maria del Fiore (1420–36); they were also used by Vassari to strengthen walls when building the Uffizi (1570). When in contact with lime, iron—even when wrought, and more or less rust resistant—becomes corroded, swells because of the formation of rust and, with the disappearance of the metal, loses its power to resist the stresses, the purpose for which it was intended. Metal chains used as tie-rods sunk into the masonry thus may, and often do, break off inside the wall. Even the connecting cramps of those parts which are embedded in stone, unless made of very good quality wrought iron, rusts, and the resultant expansion bursts the sockets holding the reinforced heads. Bronze cramps do not, of course, have this defect.

Another process connected with the use of iron is that of lead covering, i.e. pouring molten lead into the sockets of the iron clamps in the blocks to be joined so as to seal the head of the cramp in place. However, the electro-chemical interaction between the lead and iron in contact with one another—which is further accentuated by the presence of impurities such as sulphur or sulphates in the two metals—may lead to the formation of salts (carbonates, sulphates and sulphides) which will damage the iron and split the stone. Experiments using molten crystalline sulphur instead of lead have given fairly good results; but here it is recommended that bronze or stainless steel be used instead of iron cramps.

The discussion need not be continued further, since iron has rarely been used in restoration since the nineteenth century.

A few suspension bridges in forged steel have survived, but the majority have been replaced by others made of more suitable types of steel. However, steel merits consideration for the part it has played in the development of building, and should not be summarily discarded at the first indication of a decline of its functional qualities.

Bronze. Bronze as a building material was mentioned above in connexion with cramps. It is an alloy of copper and tin, mixed in varying proportions, to give different qualities, e.g. the bell-metal bronze used for statues and sculpture of all kinds. Depending on climatic conditions, bronze takes on a different patina and colour. Gilded bronze is protected by a layer of gold, applied either as very thin gold leaf which combines with with the bronze when heated (fire-gilding); or else by using mercury amalgam. This protective surface may survive very well (e.g. the statue of Marcus Aurelius on the Campidoglio in Rome, the four bronze horses on St. Mark's in Venice). Nevertheless, the bronze underneath may decompose because of the presence of impurities and, in time, powdered copper sulphide forms.

In building, bronze is used only for cramps, but bronze and copper were used before iron for working and quarrying stone, and the stereometry of ancient Egypt was based on these metals, which were also used for almost all utensils, as well as for decoration and roofing. Bronze decorations on marble were common in antiquity, but a more important use from remotest ages until today has been for the doors of temples and churches, especially in the Eastern Mediterranean, India, Italy and Germany. These bronze doors generally consist of two wings. Cast bronze panels may be fixed to solid wood and iron frames (outer doors of St. Sophia in Constantinople, those designed by Bonanno da Pisa at Pisa and Moreale, those of Barisano da Trani, and those at Hildesheim). Some were forged wholly of bronze, giving the impression of being cast in one piece, like those of the temple of Romulus in the Roman Forum, or those inside the Baptistry of St. John Lateran, or in the cathedral of Hildesheim; or else the parts are cast separately and then soldered on to a bronze frame, like the doors made by Andrea Pisano and Ghiberti for the Baptistry in Florence, those of the cathedral at Troia, and those of the Sacristy of the Duomo in Florence.

Because of their weight, these doors do not revolve on hinges attached to the door-post, but on a round-topped gudgeon resting on the threshold, with another gudgeon inserted in a hole in the lintel to retain them at the top. The lower gudgeon usually consists of an elongated forged steel spheroid, interposed between a fixed base consisting of a forged steel block hollowed out to take the lower half of the spheroid, and the base of the door frame, which is likewise hollowed out to take the upper half of the spheroid. The doors of the Baptistry in Florence and at Pisa Cathedral are hung in this manner and other examples probably exist.

The bronze carvings and decorations may be gilded as in Florence; coated with copper (St. Sophia); silver (doors of the cathedral at Troia, tomb of Bohémond at Canossa); or left unadorned (Pisa, Monreale, Trani, Hildesheim, Roman Forum, Rome). In all these cases, the bronze has acquired the characteristic green copper patina, of which careful account has to be taken before any restoration is undertaken.

Lead. Lead in the form of plating for covering roofs, cupola vaults and cornices, has frequently been used in architecture since earliest Roman times. The lead plates, which in modern times are hot-drawn to an even thickness of 2.5–4 millimetres were originally made by melting the lead in large receptacles and were then made into sheets, as evenly as possible, with a wooden mallet, giving thicknesses which might vary between 2 and 6 millimetres in the same plate. The plates were placed in position by ordinary large-headed nails driven into the masonry, or applied to a wooden frame (dome of St. Mark's in Venice). The plates, 50–70 centimetres wide, either overlapped a few centimetres, or were joined together with small bolts. The second method is fairly water-tight even for steeply sloping domes; the first is not. Soldering is impossible, for technical reasons, except in one direction and on condition that steps are taken, in the case of large roofs, to prevent deformation by thermic expansion.

Since contact between iron or copper nails and lead causes corrosion because of electrochemical reactions which decompose the lead and give rise to pulverization, use has been made of cadmium-plated iron nails which, having the same electric polarity as the lead, do not cause such reactions. Unless the lead plates are firmly fixed in place at the edges, they may easily be lifted by the wind, rolled up and eventually blown away. Lead is, nevertheless, an excellent roofing material because, upon exposure, a compact, whitish layer of lead carbonate forms which prevents further corrosion.

However, lead grows brittle with age, since the tiny crystals of which it is originally composed enlarge. The only satisfactory substitute is aluminium plating, anodized to give it a suitable colour and resistance. Lead in edges and shims provides the only means of adjusting the shafts of columns for absolute perpendicularity. In ancient times, lead was used on a vast scale to make pipes for drinking and washing water in towns, thermal establishments and so on, and is still used for such purposes to this day. This use of lead, however, rarely concerns restorers.

Copper. Copper, like lead, has long been used in architecture in the form of plating for roofs and as ornamentation; but despite the records (e.g. the Homeric Palace of Alcino, and the gilded copper and bronze roof of the Pantheon) no ancient examples have survived. In fairly recent times, copper, like lead, has come to be more widely used for roofing and for cornices. It takes on the green colour of copper carbonate, and is virtually indestructible. Yet restoration is seldom concerned with pure copper except in roofing, gutters, and the protective covering of wooden structures (in Gothic buildings in particular). The restoring of such fittings is perfectly straightforward: damaged plates can be repaired by cutting out the worn pieces and soldering on new pieces, using tin or, preferably, brass. Where possible, however, it is better not to replace the copper. As with bronze, a whole chemico-physical technology has been evolved for the regeneration of copper damaged by substances contained in the air and the ground and should be consulted for any information required on the subject.

ACCIDENTAL CAUSES

It is impossible, in the nature of things, either to give a systematic list of these causes, or to suggest remedies, save in the case of damage due to fire or war. It is difficult, likewise, to suggest measures for areas subject to earthquakes and floods, where steps obviously have to be taken for the protection of cities and homes as well as monuments. The example of Abu Simbel in Egypt cannot constitute a precedent; and remedies against the effects of cyclones have always to be improvised. As to damage by fire, the ordinary precautions taken are not sufficient in the case of buildings of artistic value, in view of the dangers to which their wooden elements are exposed as a result of electrical installations and heating systems, to say nothing of incendiary bombs in the event of war. A glance at the history of surviving monuments shows that the main cause of damage throughout the ages, has invariably been fire, whether at Chartres or Mainz, Ephesus or London, Peking or Istanbul.

It is naturally essential to take all possible precautions against the outbreak of fire, particularly in regard to electric and heating installations, which represent the greatest danger. Automatic alarm systems should be fitted at all crucial points, such as roofs, attics, workyards, and so on, to keep a check on electric plants. The importance of providing fireproof staircases to the most inaccessible parts of buildings cannot be overstressed. It is the job of guardians and keepers to study the premises and take all necessary precautions for the extinction of fires and removal of inflammable materials, and to make sure that long-handled grapples and picks are at hand with which to put out fires at the initial stages. All in all, such measures form part of the routine measures every country takes for the prevention of fires: it is a matter of selecting the best type of extinguisher, organizing their distribution and ensuring a satisfactory water supply. The importance of providing lightning conductors for tall buildings is worth mention in this connexion.

During the Second World War the damage inflicted by military activities and riots sometimes assumed catastrophic proportions, partly because of the scale of operations and still more, because of indifference.[1] If military men were better informed they might show more consideration for the preservation of local monuments, at least so far as they do not compromise their own safety. Many fragile objects (sculpture, stained-glass windows and majolica objects) were removed to safety, and steps were taken to protect at least some of the monuments which could not be transported, with the result that the damage inflicted was less serious than in wars prior to the First World War. During the Second World War, experiments in the belligerent countries included the construction of reinforcing walls and roofs, and the protection of monuments with reinforced-concrete shelters or heaps of sand-bags filled with a mixture of earth and sand (though siliceous sand had the disadvantage of damaging monuments in the event of fire). They had some good results, saving, for example, invaluable treasures like Leonardo da Vinci's *Last Supper* in Milan. It is best to use a metal rather than a wooden frame to support sand-bags, and to build a brick or stone wall round the outside; though complicated, this is worth doing. It has also been suggested that measures be taken to increase the mobility of certain categories of art-works—frescoes for instance—so that they may be similarly protected. There can, of course, be no absolute guarantees, especially if atomic weapons are used—although even then it might be possible to save art treasures by concentrating them in a few, clearly marked places. Technical progress has made it perfectly feasible to remove frescoes from their supports and protect them at much less expense *in situ*.[2]

Other accidental causes of damage to buildings in ancient cities are changes in the underlying ground and general surroundings as a result of modifications in the underground water régime caused, for instance, by major drainage schemes, the extraction of gas from the sub-soil, the diversion of fumes, the construction of artificial underground reservoirs for electric power plants, aqueducts, water-distribution systems, and so on. Such operations may produce general effects difficult either to identify or to prescribe remedies for, so that no restoration should be undertaken until a thorough study has been made of these effects and their variations. During this preliminary period, emergency measures only should be

1. See: *Sites and Monuments: Problems of Today*, Paris, Unesco, 1953 (Vol. I in this series).
2. See: *Protection of Cultural Property in the Event of Armed Conflict*, op. cit.

taken, to ensure that no further damage ensues.

A point to be noted is that even small construction works in the vicinity of ancient buildings (such as the building of underground railways or drains, the repair of other nearby buildings, the construction of water wells) may have harmful effects on ancient monuments. Then again, pollution of the ground by the infiltration of chemical substances, or the constant running off of drainage water may damage the foundations of valuable buildings, so affecting the buildings themselves. Thus some accidental causes of damage operate slowly and gradually, others are sudden and demand urgent remedies. Even when it is not possible to make a precise diagnosis, any data obtained furnishes a basis for deciding what remedies to apply: if, for instance, the ground under foundations has weakened, tests have to be made to ascertain the degree of danger, and the foundations then rebuilt accordingly; but it may be years before the causes can be properly ascertained. In such instances it is best to extend the foundations beyond the minimal safety limit so as to stabilize the situation for some time to come.

Conservation and restoration: operational techniques

7

Conservation refers to the systematic measures taken to keep monuments in good condition—including measures needed for the care of particular parts, such as roofs, fixtures, and so on. Restoration means restoring the structure to its normal static and functional condition in order to re-equip it to fulfil its original function or to fit it for a new purpose.

This distinction does not imply that conservation is more important than restoration or *vice versa*. Indeed, conservation often depends on careful everyday use; efficient maintenance, with due attention to heating, lighting, water distribution, refuse disposal, ventilation, glass installation, varnishing, and so on; and replacements necessary to keep pace with technological advance. Restoration architects should be consulted when new fixtures are installed, for the technical specialists may be unaware of problems involved when changes are made to old buildings. Central heating has, for example, frequently caused extensive damage due to the changes in the microclimates of old buildings which had, over the course of years, achieved a stable relationship with cold or damp.

Can an ancient building, taken over for practical use, be conserved in its original form? Any building so used which has survived must have been the object of certain conservation operations, and many parts of it will already have been replaced. This applies even to the large religious edifices built of stone, wood and masonry. In any masonry building over 200 years old, the floors, if of ordinary material, will most certainly have been replaced; whereas floors of exceptional value—made of precious marble, mosaics or decorated terra-cotta tiling—will have been the object of special care. It is easy to pick out parts of a building which have been repaired—exterior walls covered with plaster, decorated or plain; parts of the stonework damaged by frost, heat or wind; roof timber, flooring, fixtures and facings, and so on. In short, practically no surviving buildings in practical use are literally intact, with a few rare exceptions such as the council chamber of the Biblioteca Laurenziana in Florence, which still has its floors, ceilings, walls and fittings; the Raphael Rooms in the Vatican; part of the Escurial outside Madrid; and a large part of the royal palaces at Versailles and Caserta.

CONSERVATION

An important monument which has survived so far must be preserved intact at any cost. Routine maintenance should affect structure and appearance as little as possible.

Even small repairs should be executed by specialists who are fully conversant with the monument.

Large public buildings and religious

edifices (including monasteries) may have their own conservation specialists who can supervise repairs to masonry and stonework, but such operations tend to be expensive in view of the special precautions and the expertise required. However, it is a mistake to skimp on everyday upkeep repairs. Minor routine repairs are not emergency measures, and should be carried out with as much care as restoration proper.

Major maintenance, involving larger budget requirements, is necessary for those parts of a structure which need periodical renewal or which are particularly liable to damage due to wear and tear. These include work on: (a) foundations; (b) façades (internal); (c) roofs; (d) floors and interior fixtures (doors, revetments, fire-places, staircases, toilet fixtures, plumbing, lighting, etc.).

Let us now take these items one by one.

FOUNDATIONS

The main forms of damage to foundations were discussed in Chapter 6. Repairs may have to cope with (a) the disintegration of foundations through faulty construction or (b) collapse due to the weight of later additions made to the building. If the strata upon which the building was erected are level and firm the disintegration of the foundations may not imperil the building; if the strata are irregular, serious damage may follow, because of tilting and the loss of equilibrium.

Foundations may be neither deep nor extensive enough. Remedial measures depend on the nature of the ground and the type and size of the building, and may involve exploratory boring to investigate the sub-soil to define the cause of the damage to the building; after which the damage can then be repaired section by section. Excavations can be made along the walls over long stretches provided they do not go deep. If the walls go down 3–4.5 metres, the stretches must not extend 3–3.5 metres, and the walls of the excavation must be shored

up. The old foundations will then be demolished across their whole thickness (half the thickness when excavating on both sides), in 70–80 centimetre sections. Each time, the new section of foundation must be rebuilt immediately.

The new foundations may be in brick or reinforced concrete. Various patent systems utilize iron units combined with piles which can be placed in position rapidly and embedded in cast concrete. For speedy construction, the casts in high-resistance concrete can be made after the metal frames and the stays (trimmed to measure) have already been laid in place; but the surest method is to lay bare as small a section as possible at a time, and replace the foundations bit by bit. If necessary, the wall above can be shored up with metal, wood or masonry supports. These will always be necessary if parts of the wall overhang. No settling of the ground must be allowed to occur at the moment when the load of the building begins to bear on the new layer, as otherwise further damage may result, particularly if the ground beneath the foundations is not homogeneous or if the rebuilding is done too hastily.

Such operations must be carried out under expert supervision. Short sections may be cemented with the help of pressure pumps and injection borers. If the ground contains abundant water, the excavations will need a coffer from which the water can be pumped. The casts should be made with quicksetting, high resistance cement. Provided the ground is sufficiently firm, it may be possible to build on to existing foundations laterally by securing the new cast concrete to the old sections by steel cables and plates. One of the commonest methods of consolidating ground is by building a coffer-dam about the foundations—a very ancient practice perfected through experience. Though used mainly for consolidating the bottom layer of the original foundations, it can also serve to consolidate the ground around the existing foundations in preparation for sub-foundations. Coffers (made of resinous wood stakes, stakes embedded in concrete, and various types of bored or cast stakes) usually give good results even in ground which has a high water table; they may be sunk to a depth dozens of metres below the actual foundations. However, routine maintenance is usually on a small scale, and does not necessitate shoring up the walls.

The next step, after replacing damaged parts of the foundations, is to repair damage to the building proper. Where the collapse of the foundations is caused by overload resulting from additions to the original building, the situation can be remedied by demolishing the whole or part of the additional sections. If the foundations can be extended, the added parts of the building can be kept, provided that the original building can bear the overload and distribute it satisfactorily over the new foundations. With continuous foundations, breaks will be indicated by the appearance of visible cracks in the walls above, which may subsequently spread further. Breaks in foundations destroy their continuity. The cracks can usually be cemented over after the foundations have been repaired by one of the methods described above or by others suggested by local practice. It may be preferable not to do this if the foundations have been satisfactorily consolidated, so as to leave a certain amount of play between the sections formed on either side of the split.

For larger-scale operations, full investigations, tests and experiments will be necessary.

FAÇADES

Façades may be subdivided into external façades which include all of the faces of a building exposed to the elements, outer surfaces of a building, the walls facing inner courtyards or gardens, etc. Inner façades include those which are sheltered from the elements by being completely roofed over. In turn they may be subdivided according to the materials used.

Ashlar (or dressed or carved stone) façades

The most commonly found are built of limestone and sandstone. Marble, granite, rocks of volcanic origin, etc., are also used. All stones may be damaged by frost, heat, wind, atmospheric pollution, bird droppings, etc. Settling of the foundations and other stresses may cause splits or fractures.

When single parts of the facing disintegrate, restoration simply means replacing the damaged bossages. But this, in the long run, may alter the whole original façade, its specific colour, style of workmanship and patina. Every effort must be made to preserve the original material. The widespread practice of restoring a building by making a copy of it, even when the new materials used are similar to the old, is to be condemned. New parts incorporated in an old building are always disagreeably evident, however much care is taken; differences of detail, which the ordinary observer may not detect will subtly change the whole general appearance and character, eliminating something that can never be restored. The façade furnishes the key to the whole colour and form of a building, and must therefore not be altered.

One problem in restoration is whether to try to imitate lost original parts and so deceive the eye of the observer; whether to go to the other extreme and actually emphasize the replacements, which then upset the architectural harmony of the whole; or whether to compromise with the so-called neutral colours and neutral forms that are still used in restoring paintings *(Plate 21)*. The only reasonable way is by grading restoration according to the state of preservation of each particular part. Take for example the case of a façade where the artistic value of sculpted mouldings and cornices is not less than that of the building as a whole. Even if the façade mouldings and cornices are all of the same quality, colour and material and all are equally damaged, they cannot all be treated in the same way. The original mouldings cannot be exactly reproduced, and so must be left as they are or, at the very most, treated in some way to halt the disintegration of the surface. The main blocks, unless so deteriorated as to be unable to fulfil their structural purpose, should likewise be left untouched, except for repairing an occasional block by cutting away the damaged part and replacing it by small cubes, made of similar material, inserted in boxes into the original block and fixed in place by common Monaco or Meyer putty or some other new type of resin or silicone-based putty. This kind of selective restoration will give good results provided that no attempt is made to reproduce the missing parts, or conceal the repairs; and that the new pieces used do not mar the harmony of the whole *(Plate 21)*.

Such work must obviously be supervised by a skilled architect who is qualified to decide how far individual parts and the monument as a whole can and should be restored, without falling into the error of polishing up and renewing objects whose beauty has been enhanced by age—material changes can have ethical and spiritual repercussions.

The worse the damage to the decorative elements, the more important it is to limit operations to consolidating what remains, for while a chipped cornice can be patched up, a missing capital cannot always be replaced by a copy; and mouldings, carvings and paintings are an integral part of the façades of many buildings—the great Gothic cathedrals, Greek and Hellenistic temples, Mayan and other pre-Columbian pyramid or temple structures, Byzantine and Romanesque buildings, Moslem mosques, and so on. In many cases mosaics survive, but only very small parts of exposed paintings, whereas carvings may last for thousands of years. Even these, however, when incorporated into buildings of hewn stone may deteriorate, especially if not encased in the actual building but executed on slabs or panels affixed to the walls in the most usual way

with claws, lime and scarfs. The Indian cave temples form a special case: the sculptures are cut into the natural rock, which itself has deteriorated. Generally speaking, none the less, the most serious damage is to facings consisting of sculpted panels.

When the damage is due to flaws in the underlying structures, every effort must be made to avoid dismantling the decorations. Crumbling vertical walls, as already said, can be consolidated by injecting cement of various types and compositions (grouting) at high or low pressures with drilling machines. Such operations demand expert supervision.

Pressure applied to badly crumbling walls should not exceed two atmospheres, so as to avoid setting up dangerous internal stresses and strains, and to ensure that the bulk of the mixture remains inside the masonry. This is important both for economic and for aesthetic reasons. Cement may sometimes be injected also into arching or vaulting masonry, but it will be preferable, as a rule, to have skilled workmen rebuild, little by little, with special materials. In dealing with walls built of brick, tufa or small stone blocks, special attention must be paid to the consistency, quantity and uniformity of the mortar. It may be necessary to demolish small sections of vaulting (40–50 centimetres wide, up to a maximum of 1 metre) and to shore up small parts of shaky wall with wooden splints cut on the spot, and then rebuild the demolished section immediately. Such patching may give excellent results in inside walls, but is generally to be avoided in visible sections of masonry (we shall discuss later when, and within what limits, this method can be used for façades, either stone or brick).

Once the bearing structure has been consolidated by one of the methods described above, the carved sections of the facing can be put back in place, after repairing any damage they may have suffered through disintegration of the supporting wall. It is essential to use the same method as the

Plate 21

The theatre of Marcello, Rome. The restored
areas follow the original design without
attempting to duplicate the aged original. The
contrast is therefore striking.

original builders, either fixing the panels with cramps, or attaching them, superimposed one over the other, to the underlying wall. The cramps must be made of non-rusting metal (bronze, copper or stainless steel) and fixed with putty, cement, melted lead or sulphur. In the visible parts of the structure, the first consideration, when replacing sections of masonry, is to avoid altering the appearance of the building in any respect—the colour and tone scheme of the facing command respect as an irreplaceable example of a certain artistic technique. Scrupulous care must be taken in the selection of materials (origin, colour, working), and the use of any new binding materials is absolutely excluded.

Particularly to be avoided is the very common but deplorable practice of using ordinary Portland cement instead of lime plaster when repairing facings. The dark-grey colour of such cement clashes disagreeably, for most lime plaster, whether old or new, is either white or creamy yellow. The facing cannot remain homogeneous if cement is injected into one section of the underlying structure; this, if done at all, must be done to the whole of a particular element—a pillar or lintel, for instance, and never to one part only; if one doorpost needs consolidating, the other must be treated as well. Apart from serving for cast structures, which is its main purpose (for which it may be used in restoration as well), cement may be unsatisfactory because the sections do not adhere properly. Samples should first be taken and subjected to laboratory test. The use of cement for repairing worn stucco on facings is to be avoided at all costs. Walls may be consolidated by cement on the inside, but on the outside, nothing but the original building materials should ever be used.

The types of ashlar facings are too many to describe in detail. Badly damaged parts of squared block facings can be replaced by identical new ones, but no attempt can be made to refurbish the whole surface to look like new. However, ashlar facings (especially sandstone, marble and limestone) may be treated by hardening with substances in liquid form that are readily available on the market, and usually have a base of fluo-silicate acid salts, with various additional substances. This treatment should only be undertaken if it is sure that the substance will penetrate the stone either after immersion or continuous application over several weeks.[1] The substance must never be applied with a spray or a brush, as it then forms an impermeable surface film which subsequently falls away, taking part of the surface layer with it, or at the very least part of the surface patina.

Ashlar facings consisting of slabs used as revetments on masonry composed either of concrete castings of brick, or else of ordinary lime and stone masonry, behave differently. Expansion rates, adherence, and so on are different. Pockets of humidity form, cramps break, slabs crack and detach themselves from the wall and the revetment. The question of repairing walls was dealt with above. As regards slab revetments (which may also, in a more general way, include floors constructed of split stone, 'lithostrotons', mosaic or inlaid marble floors, marquetry or flagstone), restoration may range from the consolidation of small blocks and the replacement of the odd cramp here and there, to the dismantling of whole sections of the walls. The criteria to be followed here are the same as for facings in ordinary ashlar; but it must be remembered, in addition, that many such slabs are engraved with insets of semi-precious stones in artistic designs and colours in which jasper, chalcedony and other coloured stones are used and carefully selected by the artist for grades in shading. The original material, therefore, must never be replaced, even though it may be broken into fragments,

1. See: P. Sanpaolesi, *Le Pietre dell' Architettura*, Firenze, Vallechi, 1965.

but simply be joined together again with some kind of putty (Meyer or silicone) on a slab, and fitted back into place. In this sense, the term 'slab' may also be applied to mosaics made of tesserae, though the restoration of such mosaics calls for special methods (described separately below). They have this in common with slabs proper—that the constituent parts must be preserved in their original position.

To take a practical example: repairing a broken pavement involves not only restoring the original shapes, colours and materials (slabs, fillets, combinations, tesserae, etc.), but also reconstituting the irregularities of the original surface. Hence such surfaces, and in particular, pavements, should never be mechanically planed or polished, save by methods similar to those employed in ancient times.

The only way to preserve the irregularities of surface and design is to remove and to treat the pieces in need of repair. This procedure is described below in the section on frescoes and mosaics.

Façades of ordinary plaster, or plaster decorated with frescoes, stucco or scratch work

Plasters play a very important part in architecture, and their restoration may present difficult problems. Plaster has been used for interiors since remote times; and, more recently, for exteriors. In the latter case the methods of using are very diverse. Lime plasters are of four main types; common plaster, plaster which is frescoed or otherwise painted; plaster decorated with stucco or mouldings of various kinds; and scratch-work plaster with engraved patterns. Before lime became the main constituent of plaster, *pozzuolana* and chalk were used. The paintings on most Etruscan tombs, for example, are executed on backgrounds containing mainly chalk; Hellenic and pre-Hellenic paintings are done on plaster composed of chalk with a negligible quantity of lime. Lime began to be commonly used in masonry first in Hellenic buildings and then in Roman. From then onwards, all buildings, large and small, have used plaster for protecting and decorating interiors and exteriors alike.

Plaster on the outside of buildings has a limited life time in ideal conditions, even in sheltered places, it does not last more than 150 or at most 200 years. Hence the problem of totally replacing old plaster arises. This may prove disastrous unless the same materials and methods are used. The walls of buildings in good repair and in use cannot simply be left as they are if the surface plaster falls off without serious aesthetic detriment to the building—unless of course they are to be classed as ruins. But the replastering must be done as unobtrusively as possible. Fortunately, on outside walls in any case, the fresh appearance of the new plaster will soon wear off. The work should be done by skilled, conscientious workmen with the same tools and techniques as were originally used.

There are three types of wall paintings: frescoes, distemper and encaustic. Technically and aesthetically the restoration of painted plaster presents greater difficulties because the plaster itself deteriorates and the painting may be damaged when the plaster comes loose from the supporting structure.

The pigments used in frescoes are highly stable chemically and are practically always mineral paints (hence known in Italian as 'earth' colours), dissolved in pure water and applied to the final layer of plaster while it is still damp (a day or at most two, depending on the season). The colour takes part in the chemical transformation of the lime contained in the plaster, in the course of which it hardens and changes from calcium hydroxide into calcium carbonate. Thus, frescoes too, once they have set, become insoluble in water, the pigments being imprisoned in the body of the plaster when it is transformed into a carbonate. This chemical action occurs mainly in the first few

155

days while the plaster is drying, but it continues over a fairly long period. On the surface of the plaster, a layer never more than half a millimetre thick is thus formed, and impregnated with colour; it is compact and crystalline, and provides excellent protection for the rest of the plaster. This explains why we find ancient plasters of this kind which have survived for over 1,000 years. On the other hand, when the fresco disintegrates and begins to flake off, it is because the underlying plaster is crumbling; and no means has yet been found of consolidating the plaster support without spoiling the painting on it. The only remedy is to remove the painting to another support, rendering it mobile instead of fixed. This method can likewise be used for saving paintings in buildings about to be demolished, or removing them temporarily from structures in need of repair or consolidation.[1]

Mural paintings executed in oils or various types of tempera can also be removed. Their pigments may be soluble in water (hot or cold) and have to be rendered insoluble by treatment with some substance such as shellac, or synthetic resin (vynilic or acrylic) before being removed, as with frescoes, by means of canvas glued to the surface. Another, far older, method is to remove the painting together with the whole thickness of the wall on which it is painted; but this can only be done when the building itself, as well as the fresco and the plaster, are in good repair. Cutting away the wall (stacco a massello)[1] is a major operation requiring special techniques.

The method for encaustic painting was described above. The rest of the wall and underlying layers are treated as just described, but the only way of restoring an encaustic painting in situ is by the same encaustic method: using pigments dissolved in punic wax and applying heat to the finished surface to seal it off.

Walls may be covered with plaster or stucco—either painted or simply moulded.

Damage to stucco and relief mouldings must be repaired by the methods recommended above for smooth plasters. For figured stuccoes, special precautions are necessary; the main ingredient in interior stuccoes is chalk; external examples are usually made of lime mixed with powdered marble (statuary or some other type) rather than with sand. A framework of iron wiring or hard wood is sometimes used. It is difficult to recommend any standard method save for flat stuccoes which can be detached. The only general recommendation is that, when stuccoes are badly damaged and in danger of being lost altogether, they should be removed to safety and the wall behind them repaired.

Generally speaking, the rules are the same as for the restoration of sculpture: stuccoes should be consolidated rather than replaced in toto. Chalk is an excellent binding material for joining together detached pieces, but the correct first step must always be to determine the composition of the stucco.

Monochrome scratch-work decorations appear mainly in Tuscany, and are not very common. They represent a special form of double plaster: an underlayer applied with a paste containing powdered antimony oxide. making it dark brown, practically black; and a thin overlayer of almost pure lime. While the overlayer is still soft, the design is executed by means of a pointed iron rod, scraping off the lime so that the dark underlayer shows through. This type of plaster is extremely hard. Some examples still survive after being exposed to the air for 500–600 years. To restore such designs, the same methods and materials as for the original can be used without any risk of the new parts clashing with the old, since the new scratch work will take on the same colour as the old as soon as it dries.

One final observation must, however, be

---

1. See: 'The Conservation of Wall Paintings', *The Conservation of Cultural Property*, Paris, Unesco, 1968 (Vol. XI in this series).

made on the subject of common plasters, some of which are smooth surfaced but the majority of which, particularly on the outside of buildings, are irregular both as to application and as to the composition of the paste, and moreover, often contain one or more colours. For uniform colours, the sole possibility is to use one of the many existing types of tempera (lime, glue, casein, and so on). The colours have to be mixed into the final layer of plaster—only a small quantity is needed and it must be a mineral pigment. Alternatively, the fresh plaster may be given a very diluted wash of pigment to produce a pale, transparent colour, preferably using one of the seven or eight colours listed by Cennini.

Façades of brickwork or of baked materials

Bricks are one of the commonest building materials. As the types of brick façades are too many to be described in detail, very general rules are given here, applicable to all climates and types of bricks.

Baked bricks were made when the necessary raw materials—clay, wood and straw—existed; those used in restoration should be made of the same materials as the originals so that, despite the differences in baking methods, they will have the same colour and texture. However, bricks acquire a distinctive patina, and the general colour of a brick facing will depend to a great extent on the processing, the quantity of lime, the colour, thickness, compactness, and so on, of the bricks used. In patching small areas, therefore, the aim should be to match the new pieces with the old, imitating the original workmanship; but when there is a large surface to restore, no attempt should be made to copy the original. Such attempts in the past have been failures. The only reasonable course is to differentiate clearly between the old and the new, taking care, however, that the latter do not clash. This applies both to smooth façades and to those consisting of baked, moulded material,

mixed stone and brick or bricks of various shapes and sizes.

Bricks may be worked before baking, with moulds; or after baking, in much the same way as stone, with chisels, rasps, etc. The first step, in each instance, will be to investigate the techniques used in the originals, and proceed accordingly. It should be noted that the flat bricks used in ancient building are very different from modern bricks, which are usually perforated and not suitable for use face outward. Thus in most cases bricks of the requisite colour and shape, modelled on the old ones, will have to be specially baked and the workmen will have to be shown how to lay them.

Façades of mixed masonry and timbers

The last type of façade, very common all over Europe, is made of brick or plaster, enclosed in a framework of timber visible on the outside; such façades form a large category that has many variations. The main problem is not in restoring the timber (which, technically, is simple) but the brick and plaster surfaces and, generally speaking, the plugging material used between the timbers. The material used should be the same as in the original building—brick or plaster. If brick rubble was used, mixed with insulating material (fragments of wood, oakum, hemp, etc.), it should be used again, in view of the importance of the part it has played in the history of building.

ROOFS

Roofs are normally considered to have two component parts: the supporting frame and the covering.

The supporting frame is, in some cases, visible from the inside of the building, of which it then forms an integral part. The materials and structures should be conserved, provided they are sound and do not constitute a fire hazard. As it may often prove difficult to obtain wood of the same kind and dimensions for buildings which have been seriously damaged—as many were in the Second World War—other materials, such as reinforced concrete or iron may, in the last resort, be used to replace the roof timbers. In such cases, wooden casings of the same dimensions as the old framework can be used to cover the new material or else the old timber can simply be replaced by the new material, with no attempt to conceal the change.

There are, on the other hand, many instances where the framework is concealed, in which case it is preferable, in the interests of both safety and maintenance, simply to replace it by a frame made of reinforced or pre-stressed concrete or of steel. This is frequently advisable when the roof has no specific value in itself, but serves only as a protection, and there can be no objection to taking measures designed to prevent fire and deterioration. It obviously does not apply to the large wooden roof frames of Gothic cathedrals and mosques which, though not visible, constitute an integral part of the actual roofs, and must therefore be protected by all possible modern means against fire and accidents. We have already dealt with the subject of painted and carved decorations, which should be treated not as secondary accessory elements, but as an inherent part of the whole.

Roof coverings may be of various materials: brick and metal (lead, copper, zinc and, more recently, aluminium); slabs of various kinds of stone; pozzuolanic plaster; or cementite (when the coverings of vaulted structures are not surmounted by a roof, but form a roof themselves). All roof coverings are adapted to the framework supporting them; so that any wooden roof can easily be adjusted to take either a heavy brick covering or a much lighter lead or copper one. It may not be adapted to bear a very heavy stone slab roofing (for which a vaulted structure is best suited). Such roofs do however exist, as do also flat roofs which consist of wooden frames covered over with protective layers of earth and straw; span roofs consisting of thick layers of straw or cane; roofs made of the bark of trees; and other types, which vary from region to region and use various local materials and techniques. It is important to prevent these particular local techniques from dying out. It is not possible to make any general recommendations, except as regards materials which are used in virtually the same way in various places, such as baked clays, which are extremely common, in various forms, all over Europe and Asia, America and Africa.

Baked clay has great aesthetic and practical possibilities, suits a wide variety of landscapes, plain and mountain requirements, and climates hot and cold. Its characteristic red colouring is universally valued. Where its use is traditional it is the favourite roofing material, especially as a baked tile roof gives excellent protection in all climates. Tiles that simply overlap and are held in place by their own weight are bound to harbour all kinds of plants and insects; but most large and inaccessible roofs, such as that of the dome of Santa Maria del Fiore in Florence, are brick tiles.

When roofs are covered with small lead or copper plates, the joins must be absolutely waterproof. This is the reason for the ribbing which is characteristic of such roofs, whether sloping or dome-shaped, and which constitutes an extremely important feature of the design. It is essential to retain this feature when restoring old lead roofs, although it may now be technically possible, with modern modern materials such as aluminium, to dispense with these joins. The ancient wooden Dome of the Rock in Jerusalem which, after being completely destroyed, was replaced by another dome with a metal frame and aluminium covering, looking like an astronomical observatory. In contrast, we have the example of the leaden domes of St. Mark's in Venice, where the restorers first reinforced and consolidated the old wooden framework, then covered it over with a new sheeting of lead to make it watertight, and finally put back the old lead sheeting so as to retain the design of the old roof with the patina it had acquired through centuries of weathering.

FLOORS AND INTERIOR FIXTURES

Floors and pavements can and do play an important part in determining the character, not only of the interiors, but of entire architectural ensembles such as squares, gardens, terraces, and so on. They can be of a great variety of types: simple mud floors, patterned floors in two-coloured tiles such as those in the Bibliotheca Laurenziana in Florence (an example of refined sobriety), richly patterned mosaic floors—similar in type to the mosaics found on walls and domes—adorning Roman palaces, churches and sanctuaries. One general recommendation can be made: avoid changing either the materials or the style.

A word should be said here about the widespread practice of using polishing machines for finishing off floors, and for dressing and polishing marble and bricks. This artificial smoothing process has the effect of opening up the joins between bricks and so spoiling the design and general appearance; it serves no purpose, either practical or aesthetic, in restoration work, and should be avoided.

The polishing, inside buildings, of floors made of stone or marble slabs is likewise undesirable.

Another point restorers should note is the importance of the colour of floors, whether plain or patterned. The pattern of some floors, simple though it be, may echo the whole structural design (as in Brunelle-

schian architecture, or Arab buildings); to alter it is to destroy something of the building itself, for the interplay of coloured sections and stone fillets is of unique significance. In the case of such famous examples as St. Mark's in Venice, which is extremely variegated, and Saint Sophia in Constantinople, noted for the stark simplicity of its all-white slabs of Proconnesso marble, the floors fit into the general scheme of the building and, moreover, have unique historical significance. They must be conserved as they are. In the case of Saint Sophia, a broken slab of marble could be replaced or mended; but in St. Mark's, not even the tiniest of the tesserae forming the mosaic floor can be changed, but only fixed more firmly in place.

However, the commonest method of restoring floors is to replace them. This is usually done with materials similar to the originals in design, shape and colour. Cement mortar turns dark and should not be used. Lime mortar remains white, and gives a better general appearance to the floor. Old floors should not be wholly replaced except where completely worn out, or destroyed by accident, and even so, only if they are not unique of their kind. Floors of outstanding artistic value should, wherever possible, be protected by planking, resilient mats, or by carpets. In extreme cases, floors may be dismantled and pieced together again in a safe place. This is what is generally done with majolica pavements worked with a unique design when they begin to lose their glazed surface and cannot be repaired. There are thus only two ways of protecting priceless floors against wear: covering them over, or removing them to safety.

RESTORATION

Restoration operations do not allow any rigid classification into categories: each case must be considered on its merits. It is impossible to decide beforehand, on a purely theoretical basis, what form restoration is to take: consolidation, isolation, completion, etc. The first step after deciding that restoration is necessary is to carry out a detailed investigation of the condition of the monument. Only when this has been done can the plans for restoration be decided.

Simply freeing a monument from surrounding later additions, in order to expose the original portions, will seldom provide an adequate solution. For instance what is to be done about façades that were previously hidden? Have the buildings it is proposed to demolish a supporting or containing function? Take the very simple and common case of an edifice standing on ground that needs consolidation. It will often be wrong to stabilize the foundations only (which can sometimes be done without touching the monument), since some restoration of the monument may often be necessary. The planning and budgeting should not be so rigid that the architect is unable to adapt his plans when it is often the monument, during the course of the work undertaken, which imposes its needs on the work to be carried out.

ANASTYLOSIS (RECONSTRUCTION BY REASSEMBLING)

Anastylosis is the term applied to the process of reconstructing an edifice which has been demolished as a result of accidental causes or has collapsed through neglect and abandon.

The etymology of the word is simple (from the Greek $\alpha\nu\alpha$ = up, upwards, and $\sigma\tau\nu\lambda o\varsigma$ = column): to reconstruct from (fallen) parts.

The background circumstances vary widely. If the monument has simply collapsed through neglect, parts of it get scattered and gradually deteriorate; reconstruction is impossible unless their original form can be ascertained. If destruction is accidental or violent (earthquake, fire, bombardment), most of the component elements may, nevertheless, survive virtually intact, and the positions they occupied will probably be known.

Reconstruction demands a detailed study of any data on the monument recorded prior to its destruction (either by accidental causes or by deliberate demolition with a view to reconstruction); or else the methodical analysis and experimental assembling of surviving elements—a proceeding of questionable validity unless based on sufficiently precise data.

Vast reconstruction projects have, nevertheless, been carried out, often on the basis of archaeological excavations and finds. The Roman forum is a well-known example. Drawing on his own knowledge, skill and taste the restorer takes the individual elements excavated and attempts to reconstruct missing structures (shafts, columns, capitals, and so on) in such a way as to form sound units (with simple masses) or individual details (mouldings of sculptures) that convey a true idea of the original.

Generally speaking, of course, this is easier in the case of stone edifices; they undergo less damage, and their original positions and functions can be determined with greater certainty.

Reconstruction—which cannot be regarded as restoration in a broad sense—is most commonly undertaken in the case of edifices built of clearly identifiable materials, such as dressed or carved stone or a wooden building whose major structural elements are still in place. When the structure consists of highly perishable materials (e.g. thatch, mud, rubble, etc.) which retain neither their solidity nor shape, they may be replaced by new buildings of the same or similar materials. However, this would constitute a more or less accurate copy of the original and in this sense would not be authentic. A new edifice or structural element has been built on the model of the model of the original, incorporating such of the original parts as may, in the most favourable conditions, be fit for use again.

Rebuilding a more or less faithful copy

cannot be considered as reconstruction when virtually nothing of the original has remained intact. This is what happened, for instance, in the case of the excavations undertaken after the discovery of the famous 'Qumran scrolls' in Jordan. The foundation walls of a very rudimentary building, constructed of extremely poor material, were revealed and identified as a monastery belonging to the Essenes. The plan of the building and the fragments of the rooms discovered provided valuable historical information on the life of the community; it would therefore have been enough, without attempting a vast and unrewarding task of reconstruction, to ensure the safety of the excavated masonry instead of undertaking the reassembling of doubtful elements. The whole modern trend is against such attempts which can only be justified, for practical or sentimental considerations, when valid fragments of the original monument have survived.

The reconstruction of cities has been discussed often and at length, but no general agreement has ever been reached, each country drawing its own conclusions, and adopting its own methods. Since individual buildings form an integral part of the town as a whole, the same criteria must be applied to buildings and towns alike, and the same restoration methods followed, i.e. conservation, partial demolition, transformation for other uses. The restoration of a city may be simply the sum of the restoration of its individual buildings, except that the whole must always be positive, constituting an improvement and not a worsening of its appearance. Unfortunately, there are more ways than one of interpreting this injunction, and though people very often declare that it is incumbent on us to save what we have inherited from the past, to enhance the value of outstanding treasures, it often happens, when it comes to agreeing about the means of doing so, that what some regard as enhancement, others regard as destruction.

There is no general solution to this problem, which is the key to restoration work, having a bearing on both principles and methods. The solution adopted in each will depend on the views held and the resources available (including financial)—though funds should be forthcoming if it is the government which is interested in the project.

Let us take the case of Warsaw, one of the cities most severely damaged in the Second World War. Warsaw dates back largely to the eighteenth century. Most of the centre, the Old Town, was completely destroyed. About 1790, Bernado Belloto (Canaletto the Younger) painted twenty large detailed views of Warsaw, including the Market Square, first laid down in the thirteenth century. The accuracy of details is probably due to his use of camera obscura, a technique highly developed by his uncle, Canaletto, under whom he had worked. Systematic surveys had also been made as a practice over the years by students and professors of the school of architecture, so that plans of practically all of the old buildings existed.

The decision was taken to rebuild the Old Town and reproduce the façades of the buildings lining the Market Square and of other important monuments in accordance with Belloto's paintings. Similar decisions were also taken in respect of Gdansk, Wrocław and other badly damaged towns, regarded as unique symbols of the cultural and historical heritage of the Polish people; while the restoration of Warsaw, the ancient heart of Poland, was a proclamation of faith. The whole of the Old Town has now been completely rebuilt, down to the smallest detail, even to street lamps which obstruct modern traffic. The work was undertaken by the government so that it was in the interest of private individuals to recover as much as possible from the ruins of their former houses in order to help in restoring the original appearance of the old buildings; and it was they who were mainly responsible for assembling the scattered materials subsequently used anew for the reconstruction.

A question springs immediately to mind: what were the architects' criteria in reconstruction interiors? Were they modernized? In very many cases, the interiors were planned in accordance with the requirements and tastes of the future tenants, who could make any changes they wished provided there were no major alterations to parts scheduled for conservation.

The next question is whether the Warsaw of today is the same as the old Warsaw, or is it merely a copy? This is a very difficult question. We must consider what a townscape in fact is. What does it mean to us, and to what extent does it depend on the nature and treatment of the materials of which the buildings are made? A copy is a reminder; and since the imprint of the creator borne by the original work of art gives it its unique quality, and if the original has been totally destroyed, the copy must inevitably possess different values from its predecessor.

Let us now consider another case, that of Rotterdam, which until the Second World War, was a city similar in appearance to Warsaw, though far older—this mercantile city dates back to the sixteenth and seventeenth centuries. The main difference was that it had canals running down the centre of many of the streets which, lined with houses and warehouses, with no pavements, resembled the quays of a port. Rotterdam was destroyed in the war, just as Warsaw was, but the Dutch decided on a completely different policy; they simply cleared away all that remained of the old city and built an entirely new one in its place instead of building a replica of the old.

In general the reconstruction of buildings should be largely confined to cases of outstanding importance, such as the Parthenon. Although it had been used successively as an orthodox church and a mosque, the Parthenon had undergone no major alterations: the naos, the colonnade and the roof had survived. It was substantially intact in 1667 when the Venetians were besieging Athens and the Turks had retreated to the Acropolis and were using the Parthenon as a powder magazine. A Venetian shell fired at short range by the troops bombarding the Acropolis hit the magazine and blew up the Parthenon, demolishing the bulk of the walls of the naos and both sides of the central colonnade. Except for the pieces salvaged by Lord Elgin, the debris remained, and was still there some forty years later, when it was decided to piece together the broken parts of the Parthenon.

This operation, a typical example of anastylosis, concentrated on the lateral colonnades, and was carried out successfully. The difficulties were considerable, since every column of the Parthenon is composed of eleven pieces; there were also the capital and the frieze, the cornice, the entablature and the interior frieze (known as the Panathenaic Frieze, sculpted by Phidias). The piecing together of the friezes (if all the pieces had been recovered which was, alas, far from being the case) would have been very simple.

The anastylosis of the columns, however, presented a far more difficult operation: the columns were elaborately worked, and highly complicated devices were used by the ancient builders to correct the apparent irregularities of the diameter. The eleven pieces of each column had all to be fitted exactly in place, and a part belonging to one column could not be used in the neighbouring column, however similar. Incorporating the damaged pieces presented a further problem. It was decided not to make any attempt at copying, but rather to leave the traces of the damage suffered by the Parthenon which now forms part of its history. The restorers adopted the sound practice of replacing the core of the column by material designed to guarantee its solidity, and facing it, on the outside, with plaster containing powder of the same Pentelic marble as that originally used, to match the colour as closely as possible. No attempt was made to reproduce the design. The exterior of the monument, after the repairs to the great breach, was completely restored *(Plate 22)*. The anastylosis of the Parthenon may be said to be wholly successful, allowing a general view of the monument as a whole and an uninterrupted view of the outer colonnade.

A similar problem was presented by one of the temples at Selinus (Sicily), older even than the Parthenon, which was probably destroyed by an earthquake. The whole of the lateral colonnade lay in pieces on the ground, but as they consisted of large blocks of local travertine, it was possible to piece them accurately together again after an interval of over 1,000 years. This is one of the most astounding examples of anastylosis ever recorded—the colonnade was re-erected completely despite the 90-degree rotation caused by the earthquake. At the same time, unique and most interesting evidence of seismic destruction of a monument was discovered during the course of the operation. Nevertheless, in this case, anastylosis also destroyed all evidence of its past history and raises doubts about the necessity for the reconstruction of the monument, which had been partially undertaken in the belief that it would be an easy one—which, in fact, it proved not to be.

An example, similar to that of Selinus in that the monument had been destroyed by an earthquake, is provided by the oval-shaped forum of Jerash in Jordan. The columns were shattered, but remained in the same place when the city was destroyed. Restoration was justified, reconstituting as it did the majestic architectural proportions and volumes of the original forum.

Another interesting example of reconstruction—this time of a building still serving its original purpose—is that of the theatre at Sabratha (Libya), a former Punic and Roman sea-port. This large, two-tiered Roman theatre, with a fixed stage in tiers and decorations of rare beauty and refine-

ment, is without doubt one of the finest surviving examples of this type of architecture. Until a few years ago, the stage was in ruins, with only a few surviving traces at ground level. It was found possible to reconstruct the stage and the tiers of steps; the original parts were reassembled and new portions added where necessary.

The magnificent structure of the altar to Zeus crowning the Acropolis at Pergamum, near Izmir (Turkey) was found in a fairly good state of conservation when the ruins of this city were excavated about 1865. A part of the altar and surviving reliefs were taken to Berlin and pieced together with some difficulty as it was partially disfigured. It is now installed in a large hall of the Pergamon Museum in Berlin. However, when we recall its original position on a ledge at the top of the mountain of Pergamum—surrounded by the ruins of the theatre, the Temple of Apollo and, lower down, by the royal palaces—it is hardly possible to maintain that as a work of art it can be as fully appreciated in Berlin as it would be there.

As the above examples show, views vary between two extremes: total reconstruction, or conserving the monuments as they are found. Many take the view that conservation is the more scientific and should be the general rule. But the situation is complicated by the fact that an architectural monument is not only a work of art to be enjoyed, but also may have utilitarian functions. There are exceptional cases when it is absolutely necessary to demolish monuments and then reconstruct them, but in principle this should be done only as a last resort when the pieces can be put back in place with absolute accuracy. The reconstruction of the theatre at Sabratha did not wholly meet this condition, but it was carried out so that it could meet its original purpose. On the other hand the reconstruction of the temple at Selinus reveals a spurious sensibility often found in conjunction with a coldly pseudo-scientific attitude which is incompatible to an approach in which a monument is a work of art and has a historical role as well.

TRANSFERS

The transfer of monuments or parts of them was once very unusual and was generally done, if at all, for town-planning purposes. An early example was the transfer of a frescoed vault by the architect Paoletti at the end of the nineteenth century from the Medici villa at Poggio Imperiale outside Florence using a temporary frame and strong, complicated scaffolding. The removal of monuments to new foundations nearby or to another site is possible only if they are of exceptional importance.

The best procedure is straightforward removal of the entire structure. The first stage is to consolidate the structure for protection during the transfer. The new foundations are prepared, the building is fitted with a supporting frame or cradle, complete with special trolleys or chassis. If it is small, it might be fitted on to rubber-tyred trailers and towed. A large building would have the ground between the old and the new site levelled, tracks laid, and the cradle and its contents moved using, as a rule, hydraulic jacks joined in circuit with one or more pumps. At times such an operation would last for months as the unit is slowly moved over the countryside. All the elements of an old building can thus be preserved.

Alternatively, the architectural units of a building can be dismantled and reassembled on the site selected. Unless the building is entirely made of well-worked materials in good preservation, however, traces of the move will always remain on the reassembled building. One of the earliest known transfers of this type was that of the Holy Steps (Scala Sancta) reconstructed in the Sancta Sanctorum outside the basilica of St. John Lateran in Rome. Another, rare for its time, was that of the Romanesque door of Santa

Maria Soprarno in Florence which, when the church of San Jacopo degli Scopeti outside the town was deliberately demolished before the siege of Florence in 1527, was dismantled and rebuilt within the city. This, though, was a case of dismantling and reassembling rather than a transfer in bulk.

Generally speaking, the first procedure is preferable. If the edifice is very large, or consists mainly of ordinary masonry or painted decorations and stucco, successful reconstruction is almost impossible.

Size is a limiting factor in both procedures. The second is recommended only if the edifice can be dismantled without such damage to individual parts as to necessitate their replacement. An edifice built entirely of wood can be taken to pieces fairly easily, whereas one built of stone and plaster necessarily loses the plaster during the dismantling, and has to be replastered after reconstruction. The combination of old and new materials is generally to be avoided, as the two can seldom be combined to give the same effect as the original. This applies likewise, as we shall see, to partial repairs and repainting.

A case worth mentioning is the eighteenth-century façade of the theatre at Amiens, one of the few buildings in the old part of the town to survive the Second World War. The theatre formed the only obstacle to a scheme to widen a street by 6 metres, and it was decided to move it. A casing was constructed of reinforced concrete (which proved more economical than using a pre-stressed structure), to act as a prop for the front of the façade. Props were also erected on the other side (the interior of the theatre was completely destroyed), so that the façade was entirely encased on both sides. The next step was to build permanent sub-foundations between the old and the new structures, with breast walls built at the required intervals apart, each fitted with a track to take a series of wheels which had already been placed in position when constructing the foundations

Plate 22

The Parthenon, an early and one of the most
successful examples of restoration by anastylosis
(Photo: Sanpaolesi).

under the façade. The entire façade was then slowly and with extreme care pushed back 6 metres, with the help of hydraulic jacks. The operation took two days, the façade being moved about 8 centimetres an hour. It was moved into place and sunk into reinforced-concrete foundations; after which the props used to brace it were removed.

Such operations obviously demand the greatest care. The façade at Amiens was not very high—14 metres only; the props were separate, and could not be less than 5.5 metres wide at the base, so that the ratio between the height and the base was sufficient, in the event of the façade tilting out of the vertical, to offset any excess load that might be caused by the movement.

The façade was built of soft Marne stone. Particular care had to be taken, while the props were being removed with the help of pneumatic hammers, to avoid damage to the reinforced concrete base of the prop. Buffers made of light material (thin wooden cases filled with compressed glass wool) were used, resting against the façade, and so arranged that the filling dropped away automatically if necessary, so that the pressure of all the props could be kept constant.

Even now, however, removal operations like this are very rare, because the expense is justified only in the case of artistic monuments of outstanding value.

When the Fonta Gaia in Siena, designed by Jacopo della Quercia, was moved from the centre of the square to the loggia of the town hall, it was decided to dismantle it and piece it together again on the new site. An operation like this involves minute organization and painstaking execution. Each stone and carved element is marked and identified so that it can be replaced in exactly the same relative position it occupied before being dismantled.

THE MONUMENT AND ITS SETTING

A monument, whatever its artistic or historic value, seldom exists in isolation. The problem of freeing monuments or groups of the miscellaneous buildings (usually houses) that gradually come to surround them has been tackled in various ways.

The Arch of Augustus, for example, is an outstanding architectural monument that at one time formed part of the walls enclosing the city of Rimini. These walls were, in part, late Roman. The triumphal arch must have originally stood alone, and was perhaps erected outside the earlier city. It had been used for so long as a city gate that the main arch was eventually partially walled up and a smaller gate, with two wings, was built inside it. After the destruction of some of the surrounding buildings during the Second World War it was decided to isolate the arch. This might have been reasonable had it not been for the fact that certain buildings in the background do not harmonize, and the disappearance of its surroundings has left the arch without any relation at all to its present setting. The retention of selected buildings would have provided a better background combination of space, volume and colours, and recalled historic associations.

Sometimes internal parts of a monument are removed in order to adapt it for a different purpose. The cathedral in Lerida (Spain), which is part Romanesque and part Gothic, was incorporated into the nearby castle, and transformed, during the eighteenth century, into a barracks by building intermediate floors in the vast space of the nave. The whole building was seriously damaged during the Napoleonic wars and, later, during the Civil War.

A decision was since taken to remove all of the added structures and restore the cathedral to its original state. The effectiveness of the operations carried out can be judged by the sheer beauty of the architecture, unmarred by any inside structures or fixtures. It is to be hoped that, irrespective of the use to which this magnificent edifice will be put, such additions as may have to be made will be kept to the strict minimum.

In the case of Lerida, measures had to be taken immediately. Diocletian's Palace in Split is quite another matter. Here the problem is complicated by the large number of houses built inside the Palace—many of which date back to the Middle Ages—which now form an integral part of the monument. Certain extraneous portions have been removed, and the Porta Aurea and Porta Argentea sections have been partly cleared; but traces were left as evidence of its historic development, and the temptation to reconstruct the original façade was avoided.

The theatre of Bosra in Syria (one of the cities of the Decapolis) was a somewhat similar case. An Arab village of clay huts was built on top of the tiers of the theatre and fortified with towers. Under a recent project all the Arab additions were removed, bringing to light one of the best extant examples of an ancient theatre.

Operations of the type described above are justified only when a monument has to be freed of later, temporary structures which were added to it for some other purpose (as at Lerida). In other cases, where the monument is in an excellent state of conservation, it may not be necessary simply to sweep away age-old buildings (even of secondary importance) in order to expose the whole monument to view.

What general criterion then, can be laid down for clearing operations? How far can restoration give satisfactory results, more or less independently of individual taste and the dictates of necessity? One rather special example can be cited to show how overconcentration on historical or documentary considerations may lead to the forfeiting of the artistic value and architectural beauty of a monument. The Strahov monastery in Prague was founded in the twelfth century. Adaptations and additions, mostly seventeenth and eighteenth century, had so altered its appearance that no traces of the original building seemed to have survived. It was then decided to adapt the monastery in order to house the Museum of Literature of the Czechoslovak Socialist Republic. It was found that much of the building still consisted of twelfth-century Romanesque walls. Without any attempt to preserve the general effect made by the juxtaposition of the various elements, everything else was removed, leaving only the remains of the Romanesque buildings, isolated like a laboratory specimen. Scientifically speaking, this was perfectly correct, but this type of restoration, interesting though it is in theory, is not feasible save in very rare cases. In any event, the original structure would have to be very valuable indeed to justify sacrificing the general architectural ensemble in order to satisfy the purists.

PROVISIONAL OPERATIONS AND PRECAUTIONARY MEASURES

SUPPORTS

Temporary supports or props are frequently required urgently. A building in danger of collapsing, an unsound façade, a corner about to rotate which would undermine the whole structure, a sagging floor, and so on, require props to prevent collapse and buy the time required to plan and carry out the necessary restoration.

Propping has to be adapted to the particular situation. An arch that is not sufficiently solid can be supported by inserting a temporary frame under the intrados, the frame in turn being propped up by stays made of various materials (iron, wood, masonry). There are other ways: the arch can be filled up with a brick wall if the weight it bears is heavy. A small wooden or iron truss surmounted by a sheath of wood (3–5 centimetres thick, maximum 10 centimetres wide) can be wedged firmly in position, and supported by two or more vertical stanchions. Single props seldom suffice; as indicated, temporary frames are built to extend over the whole inner surface (*Plate 23*).

Usually the most difficult part of this operation is to arrange the supports on the ground in such a way that they can be removed when restoration is complete, but meanwhile rest firmly on the ground and do not obstruct work on the building. When working on the arches of a portico one of whose pillars shows signs of damage, the props must be placed under the two arches on either side of the damaged pillar, and not in a line with the pillar itself, since the ground beneath it would probably give way under the load. A fairly large platform can be erected; alternatively the points of support can be displaced by means of structural steel girders which rest on new foundations some distance away, so that room enough is allowed for the excavations needed in rebuilding the pillar.

In such cases, the foundations are usually laid bare, or demolished and rebuilt later, so as to provide enough space in which to work. The props must be arranged accordingly. Each case has to be dealt with separately, and no general estimates of costs can be given.

When the props need not be left in place for long, wooden ones can be used. Otherwise they must be stronger. Metal may warp and may be suitable for fairly small loads only. Something more solid, such as reinforced concrete, may be needed.

Reinforced-concrete props were used in the Arena at Verona, one of the most interesting post-war restoration projects in Italy.

Jacks are needed to shift the load on to the props and remove them afterwards. They should be connected in groups controlled by a single pump, so that the props can be removed uniformly without upsetting the static equilibrium. For simpler operations, the load can be transferred to the props by means of ordinary wooden or iron keys driven underneath the prop base-plates. If metal scaffolding is used, dismantling must always be done by first relieving the tension of the props and easing them slightly away from the wall so that, if necessary, they can be quickly dropped back in place in case of sagging.

Other precautions are also necessary when replacing an edifice on its permanent foundations after temporary removal. At all critical points (such as the joins between new and old structures, metal or reinforced-concrete trusses supporting damaged elements, etc.) sighting stakes, tensimeters and deflectometers must be used to determine the behaviour of the new parts inserted into the old and to make sure that the various elements are solidly joined together.

DRAINAGE

Drainage may take various forms, such as permanent measures to drain ground water away from a building when crypts or basements are subject to permanent or periodical flooding; or temporary measures to drain water out of excavations made for the laying of foundations.

In the first of these cases, flooding is due either to the sinking of the ground beneath buildings by natural compression, or to bradyseism. An example of this is Venice which, it is reckoned, is sinking at the rate of approximately 20 centimetres every 100 years. The only way of dealing with this phenomenon would seem to be to lower the water by means of dikes, locks, and so on; but the measures taken in every case depend on local conditions and the available resources.

Far commoner is the case of buildings sinking while the ground around them rises. There are various ways of dealing with this. A small structure, for instance, a crypt or an underground passage of

Plate 23
Temporary scaffolding used as a support in
the Chapel of Rucellai in Florence
(Photo: Sanpaolesi.)

particular importance, can be surrounded by a 'floating' concrete tank protecting it from the rise and fall of the water table. Some of the other measures used for this purpose, such as pumping, are positively harmful, and the effects of a pump are only temporary and intermittent. In many cases, the water level may be lowered by installing drains.

The commonest case is when small areas have to be drained for purposes of laying foundations or investigating the sub-soil; this is done by simply pumping out the water accumulating in the excavations, or by isolating the area with plastic sheets to reduce the infiltration of water.

It is important to remember that draining ground under a building alters the load-bearing characteristics of the soil, and allowances must be made for this.

PERMANENT MEASURES (CONSOLIDATION OR REPLACEMENT OF INDIVIDUAL STRUCTURES AND ELEMENTS)

Preliminary measures include the operations described above, such as propping, preparing scaffolding and obtaining the necessary tools (jacks, winches, dismantling devices), drainage of water, etc. We shall now deal with permanent measures, such as the consolidation of damaged parts and the materials and methods used for the purpose: cement, concrete, iron, and chemical substances for hardening crumbling stone or destroying animal or vegetable parasites.

CEMENTATION

In the case of buildings standing on ground whose solidity is impaired by the infiltration of water, the ordinary procedure has invariably been to drain off the water. This, however, does not always prove satisfactory, since it may lead simply to changing the conditions of the soil rather than consolidating it. There is also the danger that some earth will be carried away together with the water, no matter what means of pumping are used. In view of this, a new system, initiated in the course of the nineteenth century, has gradually spread: that of consolidating the ground by cementation. This is done by boring down to the required depth, blocking off the area to be consolidated, and injecting under regular pressure a liquid, slow setting, Portland cement mix-

ture. This method too is unfortunately risky and must be applied with the greatest care. There is always the danger the cement will fail to set because it contains too much or too little water and, unfortunately, it is often impossible to check this during operations. This method is suitable for very sandy soil. But even in places where it can be used, it may increase volume as the mass into which it is injected is already compact and subjected to the load of the building standing on it. The cement should therefore always be injected with the minimum of pressure; if it has to be injected deeply and over a wide area, more and deeper borings should be made so as to avoid having to increase the pressure.

In other types of ground, where siliceous sand does not constitute the predominating element, this method is not advisable because clay, which is almost always present, does not lend itself to cementation. A different method is therefore used: the clays are subjected to treatment which decomposes them and transforms them chemically from colloids into hydrates, thus causing pulverization, or disgregation of the clays. The appearance and composition of clay molecules depend on their percentage water content.

When the water is drained out of clayey soil, its volume will obviously be reduced, so that the strata are compressed. Certain clay strata, however, such as those formed of compact blue clays, are excellent as foundations, and should not be treated in this way. This treatment should be applied, in particular, to surface clays, which swell very rapidly when wet, and shrink again directly they dry up, producing fluctuations of volume and resistance which may provoke such dangerous phenomena as displacement, landslips or rupturing.

For these surface clays, the usual method is treatment with chemical (usually acid) substances or electrical agents to transform them into sterilized, compressed and compact ground, reduced in volume—this last is important since a drawback of this type of clay is that it is easily washed away by water, so that cavities are formed.

Another recent method now being perfected is that based on electro-osmosis: treatment of clay by a low-voltage, high-frequency electric current provoking electrical compression of the molecules, which then lose their molecular water. This is done by setting up a negative and a positive pole between two points in the ground. The results depend upon the nature of the ground itself.

Soil which has been consolidated, either by cementation or by electro-osmosis, may form a compact mass (distinct from the surrounding ground remaining in its natural state) and forming, as it were, one piece with the building above it. The result may be—though this should obviously be avoided if possible—that this monolithic structure is too heavy to be borne by the unmodified ground surrounding it or, in other words, that the problem of the stress between the foundations and the ground is merely transformed into one of the stresses between the treated ground and the natural ground. Hence cementation and electro-osmosis are successful only on condition that the bearing capacity of the natural soil surrounding the processed area is not exceeded.

Since every type of ground behaves differently, any such operation must, in each case, be preceded by tests and controls to ascertain the nature and reactions of the ground underneath a building's foundations.

GROUTING

Portland cement can also be used for many other purposes in reconstruction. It has a large content of anhydrous calcium silicate which, with other constitutents, reacts chemically with water, hardens and strengthens. Many variations exist, and care must be taken to specify types which are chemically neutral and will not provoke damage. Cement has been employed as grout—a liquid mixture which can be pumped through pipes—to meet particularly difficult problems of repairing walls and damaged and disfigured structures in general. The utmost care must be taken not to alter the external surfaces and to adapt operations to the general scheme of restoration. An example of this is the work recently done of the basilica of St. Mark's, Venice, where the bearing structures, which were in danger of collapsing, were renovated *in toto* without touching the precious mosaics adorning the façades.

The interior of St. Mark's is faced entirely with marble slabs, cornices and, in particular, mosaics, which for a long time concealed the real nature of the inside walls. In the past, the outside of the church had been repaired and all the facings, to a depth of about 50 centimetres had been replaced; but nothing had been done to consolidate the great pillars supporting the large domes. It was discovered in the course of these operations that, as a result of past subsidence of the church, affecting different parts of the building in different degrees, the material forming the core of these pillars was splitting. It was no longer resistant, and was on the verge of collapse. This situation was rendered doubly dangerous by the fact that it was concealed by the precious marble and mosaic facings. A previous attempt had been made to repair this damage, and patch up the walls under the mosaics. However it was difficult to put the mosaics back afterwards. While small mosaics are easily dealt with, large ones have to be removed in sections of, at the most, 1 square metre, and in replacing them, the greatest care has to be taken to ensure that they are properly matched so as not to break up the design. Even so, traces of the joins where mosaics had been replaced in this way were still visible, and this made us hesitate about making another attempt.

It was decided to leave the mosaics untouched and inject grout into the masonry from behind, using fairly strong pressure. The work on one of the large pillars supporting the dome was completed in a year. Work began at the base, moving up in horizontal layers. A fixed pump was used, and the pipes through which the cement was pumped were progressively lengthened in order to reach the top. All of the parts faced with mosaics were left virtually untouched, but the marble facings, being large and easy to fit back exactly in place, were removed.

A different method was employed for the consolidation of the vaults, which were made of brick. They were not only disintegrating and had large cracks, but were completely deformed by the shifting of the pillars. Instead of the old system of removing the mosaics, mending the underlying wall, and then replacing them, the procedure adopted was as follows. A solid frame was set against the outer surface of the intrados, with a system of props, thus immobilizing the whole of the vault to be replaced. The inner structure of the vault was then demolished from behind, brick by brick. This exposed the back of the mosaics without their being moved out of place or rearranged; care was taken to leave the back rough, to ensure that the new mortar would adhere properly. The vault was then rebuilt, ring by ring, using the same materials as before

(bricks and mortar), fitting on the intrados in exactly the same pattern as the original. The same deformations were followed precisely, taking due account of the condition of the mosaics. The frame propped up the vault and ensured its absolute rigidity during these operations. After the vault had been rebuilt, tests were made to make sure that the mosaics were securely fixed to the new masonry. The scaffolding together with the protective covering between it and the mosaics was then removed. There is now not the slightest trace to indicate that the whole of the wall behind the mosaics has been rebuilt and the original surface is preserved, unaltered.

This operation owes its success partly to the use of the new method of grouting for strengthening the pillars, and partly to the lessons learned from past attempts to restore the mosaics, the traces of which are still clearly visible. It shows that restoration must very often be based on a compromise: in this particular case, a new structure was erected beneath the old skin as it were, the greatest care being taken to avoid the loss of the original elements except where absolutely necessary.

Grouting can also be used to restore crumbling stone masonry. Such masonry frequently consists of two walls (an outer and an inner), originally filled in with cast lime and rubble. The disintegration is frequently due to the poor quality of the lime, which in time becomes a sort of loam. When holes are bored in such walls, to take samples of the interior, it is sometimes found that even the 'loam' has leaked out, so that the obvious way of consolidating the wall, while leaving both the inner and the outer surface intact, is by grouting at low pressure to fill up the space. This would appear to be an ideal method as there is no need to touch the surfaces of the wall, and the grout, on setting, will both consolidate the structure and seal up cracks between any sections of the facing which may have become detached.

However, it requires the greatest care. Complete success still cannot be guaranteed, although considerable progress has been made, and the defects resulting when too high a pressure is used have been eliminated. The first step is to pump in sufficient water to wash out all the fine dust (which would otherwise prevent the cement from setting) between the two wall faces, and to dampen all surfaces of the stone or rubble and the inner faces of the walls thoroughly so as to ensure that the grout will penetrate completely, adhere, and set quickly and firmly. Tests are necessary to ascertain whether the inside of the wall will take the grout, and to decide what cement mixture to use.

In hot weather, care must be taken to keep the cement and the area to be repaired damp as otherwise it may not set properly. The pressure used in injecting the grout should be very low (not over one and a half atmospheres) so that it is pumped in slowly and fills all interstices without seeping through the joins or exerting outward thrusts which will damage the surfaces of the walls.

Grouting, then, is one of the most effective methods of consolidation, but requires careful execution. It is important to wash out the inside of the structure beforehand and, since the cement must be kept damp until it sets, it is best to do the work in wet weather. The grout should be injected at low pressure in successive layers from the bottom upward, but without making too sharp a break between the layers. This will prevent future shifts, without eliminating those which have occurred in the past, and have therefore, so to speak, entered into the history of the edifice.

REINFORCED CONCRETE

In recent years, increasing use has been made of reinforced concrete for consolidating edifices by total replacement of their bearing structures. Its capacity to assume any shape required makes reinforced concrete ideal for the total replacement of foundations (bed-plates, piles cast on the spot or prefabricated, inverted beams, foundation plinths, and so on); and for the consolidation of vertical bearing structures: (a) by the insertion, into the masonry (ordinary type of wall) out of sight, of a frame consisting of pillars topped by girders capable of taking the whole of the load which bore on the weakened original structure; (b) by the erection of a permanent system of external props and stays (rams, struts, etc., to offset dangerous thrusts); (c) by the total or partial replacement of horizontal-bearing elements such as floors and roofs (especially large wooden truss roofs which are so deteriorated as to be no longer serviceable). Reinforced concrete can be used for repairing roofs without changing either their appearance or the materials—the inside of the original beams, which are often painted and carved, is hollowed out and replaced by a reinforced-concrete core.

In a more general way, an attempt should always be made to re-employ original materials so as to preserve the external appearance of the edifice unchanged. Fragments of parts damaged by accident or natural causes and which can no longer serve as bearing elements may often provide a basis for reconstituting the original design of an individual part of a building (e.g. a capital which appears at first sight to be damaged beyond repair). It is, in fact, extremely difficult to make an exact reconstruction of an ancient capital (e.g. a Romanesque or fifteenth-century capital, or an Indian capital with lotus flowers). If it has to be removed, as often happens, it may be possible to replace the inner core (which constitutes the local bearing element) by reinforced concrete or metal, and then use remnants of the original material simply as a façade or protection.

BEARING ELEMENTS OF METAL (PINS, CHAINS, TIE RODS, RIVETS)

The portico of San Lorenzo in Milan was badly damaged during the Second World War. It was further weakened by vibrations set up by heavy traffic. It has been bound several times, but the equilibrium of the whole entablature was extremely unstable. Little information was available regarding the foundations under the columns, the load distribution as between one column and the next, and the degree of lateral equilibrium of the portico as a whole, since the surmounting entablature had come apart.

It was even suggested that the whole church be dismantled and transferred elsewhere, away from the traffic. As an alternative, drastic steps had to be taken. On closer examination, the columns proved to be thoroughly unsound: the marble was splitting along its natural lines of fracture, and the joins between the blocks had worked loose. The insides of the columns were removed and replaced by a core of reinforced concrete, cast to measure, to act as the bearing structure.

Steel is commonly used instead of concrete for this purpose, with equal success. The procedure is as follows. The outside of the part to be hollowed out is enclosed in a rigid casing (usually made of thick plaster) applied on top of a layer of aluminium foil which protects the surface of the original from damage when the casing is removed. Wax was formerly sprayed on as a means of protection, but it penetrated the surface and proved difficult to remove. The casing, enclosing the entire column, is secured with a sufficient number of wooden staves to keep the shaft immobile while the core is being removed by a drill that can cut into the marble.

The most interesting example of this type of operation was that carried out on the Arch of Constantine in Rome, which is composed of a core of large masonry blocks to which are affixed, on either side, four large columns surmounted by an entablature and resting on a tall stylobate. The components differ widely in origin, date, processing and degree of deterioration. The core consists of rough masonry. The outside is faced with marble slabs (Carrara, Peloponnesian). In view of the large cracks that had appeared, it was decided to hollow out the entire length of the local bearing elements (from the cornice, capital, column and base to the plinth).

A tubular-steel column was fitted into the hollow cylinder thus made, cemented in position, and fitted with a wide cap which was bolted to the lower surface of the entablature. All this was done *in situ*, as it was impossible to dismantle the columns and remove them for processing as at San Lorenzo in Milan, where the damage was equally serious.

When the operation was completed, and the steel core had taken over the bearing function of the columns, the old hoops originally used were put back again, and the surmounting entablature replaced, on top of a reinforced-concrete head designed to hold the columns firmly together.

The hoops which often encircle old pillars and columns date back in most cases to the period of construction. Strictly speaking, they should not be removed even when the columns are consolidated by other means, as they testify to the history of the monument. In point of fact, monolithic and well-designed columns are perfectly capable of bearing extremely heavy loads and the hoops were used only because the builders of the day had no means of making even an approximate estimate of the bearing capacity of their materials. The method of making the hoops was quite different from that now used; either they were put on hot and left to cool so that, in contracting, they tightened; or else they were put on cold, and the ends were then made red hot and beaten together so that, on cooling, the hoop was drawn tight.

Large pieces of cornice on the Arch of Constantine were on the verge of falling. It was at first thought that they would either be removed, leaving obvious traces, or replaced by new pieces that would be secured by brackets. However, although some of the pieces weighed several hundredweight, it was found possible to consolidate by piercing them with long pins and securing them to the solid, underlying parts of the monument. The first step was to bore holes 15 millimetres in diameter at suitable points and insert into each a pin composed of an outer steel tube containing a steel core longer than the tube, which was topped by a leaden knob. The tube itself is split lengthwise into three sections. When the pin has been inserted into the hole in the marble to the required depth, the leaden knob is screwed round, so as to press against the inside edge of the end of the steel tube; this causes the tube to expand and grip the surface of the hole cut in the marble. The knob is turned further until it flattens out laterally, gripping the sides of the hole in the marble; after which the head of the pin is fixed to the crumbling part of the marble by means of a nut. The whole patch is then covered over, for greater security, with a layer of liquid cement, and the top of the hole is filled in with a small, round piece of marble identical with the marble originally used, so that no traces of the metal pin remain. By inserting three or four such pins, it is possible to consolidate even large elements and so avoid having to replace them.

A striking example of restoration effected by means of metal structures (in this case, temporary metal tie-bars) instead of the traditional disfiguring props is offered by the Trecento Palace at Treviso, which was seriously damaged by bombing during the Second World War. The top of the front wall, which had been damaged at the base, twisted outwards, making the wall obviously unstable. Steps were immediately taken—even before the war was over—to prevent further damage (there was an overhang of at least 65 centimetres), and

three large raking shores of masonry were erected. When the time came for proper restoration, it was decided not to demolish the walls since the Palace was built of small pieces of stone and bricks which would have been difficult to piece together again. In fact, the wall was structurally, virtually undamaged. It had merely rotated. It was decided to try straightening it with metal cables. The entire wall was encased in a solid frame that rested on the existing shorings, and it was pulled round into position again following the natural horizontal axis. The working load required to pull the wall back into plumb (which was a minimum percentage (5 per cent) of its total weight, owing to the fact that its angle of rotation, and thus its horizontal component, was very small) was not excessive—iron stretchers with a left-handed thread sufficed; but the operation was difficult because of the need to flatten down and smooth out the base upon which the wall had rested before rotating. This involved careful removal of all the broken fragments which, as a result of the violent displacement of the wall, had become embedded in the edges on both sides of the break. After the upper part of the wall had been pulled back into position, the join had to be firmly mortared over. This delicate operation was successfully carried out by placing, along the axis of rotation, a number of jacks which 'let go' one by one as the wall slowly returned to its original position.

Another significant example of new techniques now available to restorers was employed in the Arena at Verona, where pre-stressed metal elements were used for consolidating a crumbling section of wall. The foundations were wholly unaffected; the problem was an outward displacement of the centre of gravity of the peripheral structure, with consequent compression of the mortar.

The Arena at Verona is built of local white and red limestone, which is very hard but has one drawback. As its surface

175

is liable to pulverization, corners and joints get worn away, the bearing surfaces become uneven, and the structures give the appearance of being made of cobblestones without a natural bed. Plants lodge in the cracks, and erosion gradually spreads to the inside of the structure.

In this way, a piece of wall 16 metres high and 80 centimetres thick, though itself in a state of perfect conservation, began to rotate outwards and was in danger of collapsing. This had been prevented by bracing, an operation facilitated by the curve of the structure as a whole, using courses of blocks of local travertine, which is not liable to frost action and is very durable. To straighten up the wing which had an outward inclination of 30 centimetres, it was originally proposed to demolish and rebuild it, or else to try supporting it with tie-rods. Meanwhile, light reinforced-concrete trussed struts were placed in position to prevent further damage. Subsequently, pre-compressed metal came into more general use for purposes of consolidation, and it was decided to use this method here. The base of the threatened wing was cut open and a thick reinforced-concrete girder was inserted in it, with a corresponding girder in the upper part of the wall (crown). Thereupon, a series of holes was bored throughout the entire height of the wall, twisted steel cables were inserted, and attached to two pre-cast beads, one at the bottom and one at the top of the wall. These cables were then drawn taut by means of jacks, and cemented in position. When the jacks were removed, the tension of the steel cables came into play, automatically, exerting such pressure on the wall as to pull it back to the vertical.

The effects of this operation (a kind of test case) could be seen by the naked eye thanks to the props previously placed in position. The Verona example would tend to discourage permanent measures unless adequate technical means are available; it is far better to take temporary steps to halt the damage and wait until a really effective solution is available.

But even the Verona example cannot be regarded as definitive—first because of the inevitable slackening of the tension of the cables (the well-known flaw whereby tension eventually diminishes by as much as 15–20 per cent); and second, because the constituent materials of the monument will inevitably continue to deteriorate, causing further erosion which will eventually make the present measures ineffective.

HUMIDITY CONTROL

Let us now consider the effects of water on the exposure of historical structures, and the ways of eliminating them.

The effects of prolonged contact with soil soaked with water (either salt of fresh) on the classical types of masonry are considerable, though varied. Masonry composed of limestone and good lime, for instance, may actually be hardened by contact with water; whereas brick masonry, on long exposure to water, shows widespread corrosion, both on and beneath the surface, with the formation of saline crystals, formed either from salts contained in the water itself, or by salts released from the materials by humidity. The most dangerous of these deposits are those of sodium or potassium, whose effects are particularly evident where there are stucco or fresco decorations, or marble designs.

Humidity usually spreads along the surface layers of plaster, spoiling the surface and causing patches of damage, though the wall itself may be in good condition. In order to save the frescoed or decorated part of walls when it is not possible simply to detach and remove them to safety, various other procedures have been suggested: drying the walls; cutting them at the base and inserting a layer of some isolating material to prevent capillary action; lowering the water table. Since a wall which had once been soaked through will obviously be more vulnerable to damp in future because it becomes porous, investigations have concentrated on methods of cutting into the wall at the base and insulating it from the foundations.

One method tried was to insert a layer of lead, but this was based on the assumption that lead is damp-proof, whereas it frequently yields hygroscopic salts which retain humidity, so that the corrosion penetrates below the surface. For the construction of roofing on wooden frames, on the other hand, lead is suitable because the rain causes the formation of a protective whitish-coloured layer of lead carbonate which hardens in combination with the carbon dioxide contained in the atmosphere; whereas the humidity which attacks a layer of lead inserted in the base of a wall, due to the capillary action of water rising from the foundations, ends by eating through the lead and penetrating the wall above.

In view of this, glass sheeting was used instead of lead for insulating the base of walls; this is absolutely damp-proof, but the disadvantage is that there have to be joins between the sheets, through which moisture moves easily. The water also runs along the lower surface of the glass and emerges on the upper surface, so circumventing this obstacle.

The Knopen method of drying out walls, based on the use of slow natural drainage, has been used with success in such large buildings as the Palace of Versailles. A series of small pipes of porous clay are let into the wall to a depth of about 30 centimetres, at intervals of about 1 metre (at Versailles, very porous pipes approximately 3 centimetres in diameter were used). These pipes, which lie at an angle, are closed, on the surface, by small perforated grids. This method relies on the formation, inside the pipes, of a draught which keeps them absolutely dry; and as they are made of porous material, they can absorb and remove moisture from the surrounding wall. Unfortunately, the effects cannot be checked; more-

over, frescoed walls cannot be bored to take the pipes—though they might possibly be used at the back of a wall.

There is one outstanding example of the consequences of misinterpreting the effects of humidity on walls. In the convent adjoining the church of Santa Maria delle Grazie in Milan, Leonardo da Vinci's *Last Supper* was protected against bombing by a casing built round the refectory, but left for a long time exposed to the effects of damp. It was decided to heat the adjacent room in the hope that this would dry the wall on which the fresco was painted—with the result that moisture condensed on the frescoed surface, increasing the risk of damage.

Various methods can and have been used to eliminate moisture in walls. The best is to set up, inside the masonry, dry draughts which operate continuously and remove the humidity.

CONSOLIDATION OF FROST DAMAGE

Stone (e.g. sandstone and tufa, not such types as Istrian stone, travertine, or porous stones with cavities) which has been damaged by long exposure to damp and temperature offers other problems. When water within such stone freezes, the resultant expansion causes the surface to crack and separate from the rest. Marble and sandstone suffer particularly from frost.

In order to avoid having to remove and replace an entire façade (a questionable proceeding, in any case, and tantamount merely to making a copy of the original), attempts have recently been made to harden the constituent materials *in situ* and render them proof against further damage.

The first step is to try waterproofing the surface by, for example, silicone treatment to protect against humidity and consolidate damaged material. Solutions of silicone dissolved in water are, at first, fairly effective but as silicones are colloidal and subject to natural shrinkage, cracks subsequently appear in the surface of the silicone film, allowing moisture to penetrate and the damage to continue. No substance free from the disadvantages of silicones and capable of giving permanent results has yet been discovered.

Another method is to treat stone and other natural materials with chemical substances similar to those of which they are composed so as to replace the natural binding matter (which, in the case of marble, is weak and fragile) by another. Marble, for instance, is composed of calcite crystals bound together by a cement of anhydrous calcium carbonate which readily deteriorates; if so treated that all the cavities in the crystalline mass are filled and the crystals are bound together into a single block, the stone will be consolidated and proofed against further deterioration.

Chemicals are injected in the form of a solution (usually aqueous) together with substances designed to cause its precipitation so that, after entering the stone in liquid state, it is deposited and consolidated.

The same is done for sandstone, argillaceous varieties of which are composed of a mass of siliceous crystals held together by a connective tissue of clay softer than the mass of the stone (which consists of a deposit of crystals of silicon dioxide or sand). As a result of atmospheric humidity and frost, this clay, contained as binding material in sandstone, increases in volume and causes disaggregation of the stone. If it can be replaced by a silicate, the condition should of course improve.

Here again, we are still at the experimental stage, and care should be taken to ensure that any measures taken will not cause other damage.[1]

Incidentally, we do not know at present what steps will be necessary when the iron frame of a reinforced-concrete structure exposed to the air becomes exposed as a result of rusting following the infiltration of water. The increase in volume of iron when transformed from a metal into an oxide is such as to split the structure (even concrete).

Experiments on stone may reveal suitable methods for consolidating reinforced concrete.

Parasites

Another danger to building materials (described elsewhere in connexion with wood) is systematic destruction by insects. The most dangerous are termites (white ants) against which early and vigorous measures must be taken, for with their voracious appetites they quickly reduce timber to a thin shell riddled with tunnels. Several commercial means of treatment exist, varying from the injection, under pressure, of insecticides to dismantling affected wood and immersing it in solutions which will kill the insects and destroy eggs and larvae. Subsequently, affected parts may be soaked in wax to fill up all cavities made by the insects and prevent further eggs being deposited in the holes left open after treatment. Various types of varnishes which seal holes in the wood and make it impervious to further attack also exist.[2]

PATINA

One of the first noticeable things about a town, particularly if it is old, is its general tone and predominating colour. We talk of the colour of Rome, of Venice, of Kyoto, and so on. In each case this results from a subtle combination of many factors: local climatic conditions (including the kinds and degree of atmospheric pollution); the original materials used in construction; the original shades of the colours of exposed materials; the types of paints used, and so on. Oxidation, the action of humidity, the formation of salts from metals, changes in the

---

1. See: 'The Conservation of Stone', *The Conservation of Cultural Property*, op. cit.
2. See 'Identification and Control of Insect Pests', *The Conservation of Cultural Property*, op. cit.

mineral composition of stone, the weathering of wood, growth of organisms from bacteria through lichens, moulds, mosses and the leafy plants all help to change colours. All this produces the characteristic patina of ancient buildings. Laboratory analyses may trace the original material used in construction, the source of a marble, for example; the kiln and the clays used in certain kinds of brick; the type of wood used in construction, and so on. But the individual contribution of the various factors involved in changing the appearance of materials from their original state not easily defined, or reproduced either in the laboratory or on buildings.

The first problem to be tackled is technological: rediscovering the techniques which produce specific effects. Until this has been done no progress can be made. Ruskin's poetic and aesthetic writings on Venice covered every aspect of its colour—except the technological. But restoration architects need to know the exact techniques for reproducing the original colours and to be acquainted with the properties of the materials involved. It should not be assumed that colour does not play an important part in restoration. On the contrary, the colour of an architectural *ensemble* must always be considered carefully. The use of colour is, in fact, one of the subjects with which many contemporary architects are least conversant, though it is an inherent factor not merely of the architectural, but also of the natural setting. Colours can cause a group of houses to blend with or, if unskilfully used, to clash with its setting. Generally speaking, it is the initial planning that is the most difficult, for the final result is the outcome of careful research into contrasts, the effects of walls against a background of verdure, the relative merits of different materials, and so on, albeit the solution suggested by the particular surroundings may sometimes prove the most successful. Colour must be used consciously as it plays a vital role in restoration—even in roofs.

They should not attempt to introduce modern roof covering but use the materials and styles of the original builders. The flat or domed roofs, untiled but coated with waterproof plaster, that are common in Egypt and Asia Minor, for instance, suit local conditions and should obviously be copied; the introduction of metallic or synthetic materials would greatly modify the harmony of the whole.

The patina acquired by the individual parts of a building differs according to the component material, and will be affected by rain or atmospheric humidity. Fungi and micro-organisms lodge in cavities in stone and cause seasonal changes of colour. Stone and bricks simply become dirty from dirt of the atmosphere, part of which may be periodically removed, but a certain amount always remains.

To remove fungi and micro-organisms, chemical weed-killers are sprayed, so as to penetrate and kill the roots. There are various possible ways of cleaning façades. The patina should be left, since its removal—if too radical—may spoil both stone and appearance. The current method of dealing with the effects of dust and smoke is to spray the surface with powerful jets of water, but this should in fact be avoided because it may also detach particles of stone and harm the surface and is entirely out of the question for carved façades—it might be compared to the former method of cleaning paintings with a soda solution or alcohol.

Generally speaking, patina should be preserved in the same way as damaged parts and decorations of a building in which the stone has deteriorated.

However, there are cases where it becomes essential to substitute new material in places where the old is beyond salvaging or where an ugly doorway, for instance, cut into a building at some later stage, has to be filled in, and the traces of this operation should be concealed.

The patina acquired by an edifice over the ages has a value of its own, and constitutes an essential element of its history. It must not be destroyed save for very good reasons—any more than the wrinkles of old age can, with impunity, be masked by make-up.

INTRODUCING NEW ELEMENTS

Materials must be selected for the restoration of any artistically important monument: stone to patch up facing, wood to repair a beam, bricks for parts built in brick.

The choice is between the original and modern materials. Take, for example, the case of a mullioned window with an over-layer of masonry, where the capital of the centre column is missing, and there is nothing to indicate the design of the original. There are three possibilities: (a) to use a rough equivalent of the original, made of the same material, to replace the lost capital; (b) to use a rough equivalent made of a different material; and (c) to use a bearing element made of any material, even metal (iron, bronze), so introducing a frankly modern element (as has been done in numerous restoration operations). This last method should be employed with circumspection since there is no such thing as a 'neutral' shape, and any 'shape' used is necessarily affected by the new material; its sole merit is that it makes no attempt at copying and there can be no doubt about its origins. Or take the example of glass windows where either the original glass or the gratings have completely vanished. Some form of glass must obviously be used, but which? Small panes with lead inter-ribs; single panes, with or without frames? As in the case of other modern materials (such as reinforced concrete) should the new material be left visible or encased in material similar to the original? In each case the architect must decide: the only valid general rule is that no parts must be replaced unless they are beyond restoring.

If new material has to be used, it must be remembered that it imparts to the monument the imprint of a certain phase in its existence; it is important that future generations will retrospectively approve of its use, and be able to distinguish between the original elements and those which have been added. This is not to say that new materials should not be employed for restoring and reinforcing lost or damaged parts; but only that all such additions should be at once clearly evident and made with the greatest discretion, taking full advantage of the wide range of colours and materials that are now available, and skilfully disposing volumes and surfaces. There are now many different ways of processing brick, stone and wood for use in restoration and reconstruction, and of building new edifices on traditional lines to fit in with a given town or landscape.

The architect-restorer must decide whether his work blends in with existing buildings; whether the relations between parts of a building and between buildings themselves can legitimately be altered; and whether or not structural modifications are justified.

ORNAMENTATION

The term 'ornamentation' can be used to describe everything which is applied to a building at the last stage and is visible on the surface. Individually, decorations may have no artistic value. They may be liable to damage because of humidity, poor quality, neglect, hooliganism and so on. Their restoration requires expert and perhaps artistic skill. It may need supervision and co-ordination by an architect-restorer if it involves the work of various specialists (stucco, gilding, marble, picture restoring, and so on).

For instance: a craftsman engaged to restore the gilding on the structures (facings, railings and gratings) of a baroque building must be able to select the right type of plaster and the right tint for the mordant (white, red, ivory yellow) to match the gold, yellow, green or red foil (which are shades of gold-leaf, not 'colours' of gold if the results are to be satisfactory, especially when the old gilding has retained some of its colour). Similarly, decorators and even whitewashers must match their colours, so as not to jar with the existing ones, and make sure that the concentration, transparency, and so on, are the same.

MURAL DECORATIONS

Important murals are considered in another volume in this series[1] in connexion with fresco and encaustic paintings. Mural paintings of minor importance are very common and should, by and large, receive the same treatment. However, they may not always justify the cost of extensive restoration. If so, provisional measures may be adopted: inserting small broad-headed nails to prevent the plaster from dropping off, stretching nylon thread or gauze over the surface, or spraying it with a fixative such as Paraloid or Rhoplex in a 1–5% solution with toluene (an acrylic emulsion which has given good results).[1] Similar measures can be used if the plaster is in good condition but the painting is flaking off, but only with substances which can subsequently be dissolved and removed. Damaged murals and sometimes very valuable paintings are usually found on walls which have absorbed damp that deteriorates the lime beyond repair, taking the painting with it.

Most frescoes are painted on plastered walls fined off with well-cast lime slaked at least two months before, using the ordinary fresco or encaustic technique. This latter process (used at Pompeii) has given rise to a great deal of discussion. The binding medium contains wax, rendered soluble by one of the materials which in Egypt, where this technique originated, is known as natron (a natural substance that is really a solution of sodium carbonate or potassium carbonate), which has the property of making wax soluble in water. Wax thus treated can be mixed with pigment to form a solution similar to water or egg distemper, and can be applied to walls; a hot slab is then applied to the surface to restore the plasticity, resistance and insolubility of the wax.

To conserve the surface layer, the same method has been tried as for encaustic painting, applying a wax varnish to the surface. This is a very old practice, but is not wholly satisfactory, as the addition of even a very thin film of new wax may revive the effects of the original wax and so destroy the porosity which is essential to allow the moisture to come to the surface and evaporate, and so keep the painting dry.

One of the commonest methods of safeguarding mural paintings nowadays is to remove them from their supports. Means have been devised for doing this without the slightest risk, so that a fresco can be removed from the wall and put back on a new support, rendering it mobile.[2]

Paint applied to fresh plaster undergoes a chemical change, in the course of which calcium hydroxide (slaked lime) is transformed into calcium carbonate (plaster) through contact with the carbon dioxide contained in the air, and thus becomes insoluble. This explains why frescoes, once the wall on which they are painted has dried, are insoluble in water.

The method of removing a fresco (*strappo* method) is as follows. A very thin piece of canvas is spread over the surface of the fresco, fixed in place with ordinary carpenter's glue, and left to dry; subsequently further layers of thick canvas are glued on to reinforce it, and handles are sometimes attached to large frescoes, to assist manipulation. When the glue, which must be laid on very hot, is thoroughly dry, the canvas is eased off the surface of the wall with the help of a long blade. As the painted surface is by then fixed more firmly to the canvas glued to it than to the plaster forming the

---

1. cf. 'The Conservation of Wall Paintings', *The Conservation of Cultural Property*, op. cit.
2. ibid.

original support, the fresco comes away with the canvas, and it can be rolled up like an ordinary easel painting except that it has the remains of the plaster adhering to the back of it. After the back has been thoroughly cleaned, the traditional method was to transfer it to heavy canvas. It was glued to it by means of an insoluble adhesive. This last point is important because the canvas attached to the surface of the fresco with carpenter's glue is subsequently removed with hot water.

The operation thus consists of two glueing operations, the first designed to remove the fresco from the wall, the second to attach it to a new support made to last as long as the painting itself. Until a few years ago the second operation, obviously of vital importance, was executed with casein glue obtained by mixing casein with lime (in ancient times it was called 'cheese glue' and was obtained by mixing cheese with quicklime). Since casein is insoluble, the canvas glued on to the surface of the fresco could subsequently be removed with hot water. By this means the whole of the thin top stratum of the plaster on which the fresco is painted is again fixed and consolidated by the putty. Provided it is carried out correctly, this method is always successful; canvases which have been carefully glued on to the surface of a fresco can subsequently be removed with the simplest of appliances.

New synthetic adhesives[1] are now on the market which possess the same properties as casein glue, without the disadvantage of its tendency (unless very carefully prepared) to putrefy and crumble. Similarly, the use of thick canvas to provide a permanent new support for the fresco (as distinct from the thin canvas used for transferring the fresco to the new support) has now been discarded almost completely in favour of slabs made of Eternit (asbestos insulation board) or Masonite (board made of compressed wood fibres) which, provided they are rot-proof, give better results. If Eternit is used, it is important to make sure that the cement in the mixture contains neither chlorine salts nor sulphides. The transfer of the fresco to a frame containing a slab of Eternit, Masonite or other similar material is effected in the ordinary way, and retains the original shape better than when canvas is used for the new support. For large frescoes, which have to be divided up into sections, it is easier to fit the pieces together again and conceal the edges when a rigid support is used. Recently, successful experiments have been made with rigid supports of glass fibre and polyvinyl esters, which constitute a light and rot-proof frame easily adjustable to fit the shape of a fresco painted, for example, on the underside of an apse or a vault.

MOSAICS

Mosaics, like frescoes, can be removed for transfer, but their special feature is that they are composed of large numbers of stone or glass tesserae which the mosaicist pieced together on fresh mortar, deliberately leaving irregular lines or surfaces for chromatic effect. It is essential that this irregularity should be preserved when transferring the mosaic to a new support; apart from which, the position of every single tesserae in relation to the adjacent ones (and these tesserae may vary in size from 3 to 4 millimetres to as much as 1.5 centimetres each way) must remain unchanged. In view of their considerable weight, mosaics (whether on walls, ceilings or floors) need a bed of lime putty 2–3 centimetres thick, topped by a rendering of lime plaster or *pozzuolana*. Unlike fresco painting, which requires a thin layer of plaster applied the same day, the bed for a mosaic is prepared the day before, so as to harden slightly before the tesserae are placed in position. Each piece is pressed down slightly, to squeeze out the water between one piece and the next.

---

1. See the Appendix to *The Conservation of Cultural Property,* op. cit.

In order to remove a mosaic for transfer, a canvas, consisting of numerous thin layers, is glued to the surface. In the past, sheets of thick paper were used, wetted to take the shape of the surface, smoothed out and then covered over with a piece of coarse hemp. The mosaic then adhered firmly to the paper. The disadvantage of this method was that, when putting the whole back into place (mosaics are hardly ever removed and set in frames, but practically always put back in place) by pressing it gently into the damp coat of prepared plaster, the surface tended to level out, losing the characteristic irregularities of the original.

Instead of using paper only, it is possible, to apply one sheet of paper, and back it with several layers of coarse canvas to form a rigid structure, so that the surface retains its irregularities when the mosaic is put back in place. When the lime has set, and the mosaic is firmly in place in its new bed of plaster, both paper and canvas are removed, as usual, with hot water. What makes this operation particularly difficult is that mosaics have to be removed bit by bit, in sections of at most 1 square metre (and even this represents a heavy weight); so that supports have to be provided in order that they can be lowered without breakage and without chipping the edges. Where a mosaic covering an entire vault has to be removed and then replaced without the joints between sections showing, the greatest care must be taken to ensure that the sections are pieced together again with absolute accuracy at the edges, so as not to break the continuity of the design. This is done by making reference marks on the back of the mosaics.

Another problem which arises is due to the contour of the vault or wall from which the mosaic is removed. A layer of plaster of as much as 10 centimetres thick may be removed together with the mosaic, and this must be accurately replaced afterwards, to produce precisely the same contour as before. A further difficulty is that the original mosaic levelled out all the nooks and crannies in the wall, acquiring in the process a certain irregularity of form which cannot easily be reproduced by the new, rigid support to which it is transferred.

SCULPTURED ELEMENTS

Many buildings are decorated by carvings incorporated in the architecture—Gothic cathedrals are a striking example. The edifices themselves belong to the general category of works of art which can be neither added to, or even worse, replaced, but must be left as they are, regardless of their state of preservation. But since sculptures of value must be handed down to posterity, the question arises whether to leave them where they stand after consolidation, or transfer them elsewhere.

Each case must be considered on its merits. When the point is decided, it will be clear whether the carvings need restoration; if so, the method selected must alter both the carving itself and the building as a whole as little as possible.

Sculpture is both a decorative element and has intrinsic artistic value. When it is possible simply to consolidate, the work can be done by the methods ordinarily used for marble (reconstitution of damaged parts, repair of parts already restored previously, chemical treatment for hardening, reinforcement with cramps, protection on the spot, and so on), the aim being to leave the general appearance of the edifice unchanged. If climatic conditions render such measures ineffective, it is preferable to remove the sculpture to another site in the vicinity, where it can be protected whilst still being easily accessible to the public. For groups which need to be displayed as nearly as possible in their original setting—archaeological finds, for instance—a special museum may be provided. When this is not possible, pieces of sculpture may simply be transferred to a more suitable place in the same building (palace, church)—an inner room, porch, or loggia where they can be protected from further damage.

There remains the problem of what to do with the niche or lunette from which the sculpture has been removed. Sometimes it may simply be left empty. In other cases (e.g. Gothic cathedrals, where the sculptural decorations constitute an inherent part of the building), replicas can be made to take the place of the original which has been removed.

The removal method will depend on the nature of the particular piece. Free-standing sculptures which are simply placed in niches or fixed in position by cramps or bolts can easily be removed, precautions being taken to ensure that they suffer no damage in the process. Sculptures incorporated into the masonry, on the other hand (such as, to cite an extreme but very improbable case, the Royal Portal at Chartres) would necessitate a series of operations on the structure of the edifice in order to isolate, remove and replace the carved blocks. This would amount to reconstitution on a different site rather than eliminating the causes of damage.

Copies to replace originals should as a rule be made of the same material; but most sculptures thus designated for removal have their surfaces damaged by centuries of exposure and a faithful replica cannot be made so that the only solution is to make a cast, reproducing the sculpture, not in its original state, but with the traces time has left on it.

The first stage is to take a cast of the carving with plaster of Paris; this is then reinforced by inserting a metal frame and filled. The surface of the mould is treated to prevent the casting material from adhering to it. The cast is made of a paste of highly resistant white cement, mixed with a specific quantity of a fine powder of the same stone as that used for the original so as to give it the same colour. To obtain good results, the casting should be done in successive layers of not more than 2 centimetres thick, and certainly never more than 6–7 centimetres in all. In these conditions,

the cement will set perfectly, and no cracks will subsequently appear. As the cast will be hollow, it will weigh infinitely less than the original. Special attention must be paid to the setting, compactness and laying on of the successive layers. This process ensures durability and colour. Casts made of epoxy resin reinforced by fibre-glass, suitably mixed with powdered stone, also give excellent results.

STAINED GLASS

Stained-glass windows are frequently found in buildings in Europe and the Mediterranean region. Usually a steel frame, sometimes a very large one, is fixed in the masonry, panes of coloured glass, usually 2–3 millimetres thick, are enclosed by single- or double-grooved lead ribbing, and attached to the main steel frame by steel rods fastened to the lead ribbing with copper wires which are soldered to the lead wound around the rod and twisted tight. The lead ribbing may disintegrate, or the frame itself may become detached for various reasons (faulty construction, exposure to wind, variations of temperature, fire, wilful acts of destruction, damage by falling stones or lumps of brick, breakage of panes of glass, disintegration of the lead due to age).

Small repairs to the lead ribbing or the devices for fixing the frame to the masonry can be done on the spot; but when large pieces of lead have to be repaired, or panes of glass, it will usually be wise to remove the window and then piece it together again with new leading, clean and straighten it out, and put it back in place. Great care must be taken not to break the panes, in view of the difficulty of manufacturing new glass of precisely the same colour and transparency as the old. The work must be done by highly skilled specialists with long experience. Damaged windows are, as a rule, taken to pieces entirely. To replace broken or missing panes, glaziers try to produce glass of the same colour and intensity as the old, but this is not easy. A piece of plain glass in a stained glass window makes a patch of light which ruins the effect of the whole.

After a window is repaired, a second window, of plain glass (preferably tempered) is often fitted in, on the outside, to afford protection, with a space between the two to allow airing and cleaning.

In another type of window very common in Turkish and Arab mosques, the panes are fitted into a frame made of cast plaster. Restoration involves making a cast of the decorations on the plaster frame—a delicate operation, since the decorations are an integral part of the architectural design, and may be the product of skills now vanished.

TEMPORARY SHELTER

There have been numerous cases of archaeological finds being lost by exposure to wind and weather; and it is absolutely essential that as much valuable material as possible, including such objects as painted walls, should either be removed to safety or, if left on the site, at any rate protected by a temporary shelter. This was done in the case of the House of the Mysteries at Pompeii, the mosaic pavement of the Imperial Palace in Constantinople, and numerous Egyptian mural paintings. Nevertheless, finds are ruined and lost all over the world because of exposure to sun, wind and rain, and the depredations of unscrupulous souvenir hunters. They must be protected, whenever possible, by shelters. Mosaics on walls or pavements should be kept under light conditions that correspond, as far as can be judged, to those of their original setting, since any change in the direction or intensity of the source of light may affect their appearance.

It is no simple matter to provide shelter for large-scale excavations. When the objects are of exceptional value, it may be necessary to reconstruct the whole of the original edifice—indeed, this is the ideal way of proceeding for all major excavations, as it will then no longer be necessary to uncover roofs, demolish walls and remove carvings unprotected from rain and sun. But this is not always possible and prefabricated units or wood, corrugated iron or plastic and fibre-glass shelters can be used to enclose the site while restoration is in progress.

Piero Gazzola

The restoration of bridges of artistic and historic interest[1]

8

Bridges are inseparable from the development of civilization but, more than most forms of monuments, they are subject to the violence of natural and human agents. Their resistance is constantly being tested by the innumerable shocks they must bear and the action of the water courses they cross, from the slow dissolving power of water itself and the constant friction of its movement to the assault of materials borne by currents which at times serve as veritable battering rams.

Economic, social and military factors also operate. The more useful a bridge is, the more it is exposed to damage and change. Vehicles—from clumsy ox-drawn wagons with steel-bound wheels to the heavy lorry cause stress by weight and vibration. Essential in time of war as in peace, vital and sensitive points in road systems, they are usually the first targets in any attempt to paralyse or destroy a country's military or economic strength.

Utilitarian features have to be taken into account when a bridge is to be rebuilt: its usefulness; present load-bearing needs; anticipated growth in traffic. If it is historically or artistically important other criteria must also be considered, including its previous role and history. Reconstruction must respect the past, and any new elements introduced must be carefully integrated if all that the old bridge represents is to be preserved for posterity. But before this elementary principle of respect and of humility gained widespread acceptance among restorers, many monuments were subjected to deplorable attempts especially during the nineteenth century, and many historically important bridges were mutilated. Even during the twentieth century, many such bridges have either been badly restored or else simply condemned out of hand and replaced by modern ones.

The Porto Capuccina bridge at Ascoli Piceno was the most important historic bridge restored in Italy before the Second World War. Such restorations occurred only sporadically before 1945; after that date formidable problems had to be faced. In many countries, bridges headed the list of the monuments which were destroyed. In Italy, the bridges scheduled as historic monuments which survived were the exceptions —apart from those of Venice which had no strategic value, and those of Rome which were spared to a certain extent as it was declared an open city—all others were designated victims for which there was no escape.

This brief summary deals only with the most spectacular restorations.

1. Based on a paper presented at the International Congress for Architects and Technicians of Historic Monuments, Paris, 6–11 May 1960.

COVERED BRIDGE OVER THE TICINO AT PAVIA

Background

The bridge was designed by Giovanni da Ferrara and Jacopo da Gozzo (who were probably the architects of the bridge of Castelvecchio at Verona). The work began in 1352; in 1353 the first five arches were raised, and the bridge was completed under Galeazzo II. The debris of an ancient Roman bridge were used in the construction (the main walls being of brick with stone profiles); it comprised seven arches of varying size, the third and fourth starting from the left being semi-circular, the others more flattened. It was 206.28 metres long and 7.10 metres wide, and rested on six piers, the first of which, starting from the right bank, was entirely sunk into the ground while the others faced their prow-like shapes into the current. The most original feature was the gable roof, supported throughout its length by small granite pillars *(Plate 24(a))*.

In September 1944, the bridge was hit by bombs. The first arch starting from the right bank, as well as all the roofing, collapsed and the remaining arches were badly damaged, especially the second one on the right, which eventually gave way in August 1947 *(Plate 24(b))*.

Proposed reconstruction

At the end of the war historians, restoration specialists and hydraulic engineers discussed the restoration. On purely technical grounds, and with no regard for the historical and artistic aspects, the hydraulic engineers proposed demolition, and reconstruction elsewhere. They pointed out that the arches were lower than originally because of the raising of the river bed in preceding centuries and, under flood conditions, would not be high enough to channel the enormous mass of water that would then spill over the banks and flood the nearby village, as had already happened in 1868. They stated that restoration would be extremely costly; that difficulty of access, the narrowness of the thoroughfare and the low roof would make the bridge unfit to take heavy lorries; that, if the decision was to make a complete reconstruction, it should not reproduce the old form but be totally different in character so as not to create a false monument.

After once again pressing for a complete restoration, the historians and specialists, supported by the Trusteeship Office, answered the points raised. The high-water dangers could be countered by opening the arches then buried in the earth and by providing a diversion canal (a project had already been studied by the specialists); a new bridge would cost much more than the restoration of the old one; heavy lorry traffic could be diverted nearby, to the new bridge of the Impero.

Solution adopted

The engineers' suggestions prevailed. In 1951, the old bridge was completely dismantled, and a new one was put up slightly downstream. But it lacks the authenticity of a modern design. It might be called a parody of a reproduction, generally resembling the old bridge, but differing from it intolerably in details.

It is located some 30 metres downstream, perpendicular to the river, whereas the location of the old bridge was slightly oblique.

The bridge's historical and practical role in the life of the town was neglected. At one side, the Corso dei Partigiani had to be turned north by creating a long, narrow and absolutely disproportionate square along the river; the other end no longer meets the Via dei Mille; a second square allows traffic to reach this street by taking two turns—a most unfortunate consequence—that distorts the flow of traffic, which was once well planned. The flow is further complicated by the useless hiatus created by each of the new squares.

Pavia thus got a new covered bridge: the useful length and width were increased, the number and span of the arches changed, the parapet balconies made symmetrical, the piers made regular, the little chapel altered, the two portals redone in an entirely different manner. The reinforced-concrete arches have been covered with stone paving and small granite pillars—completely different in their proportions from the originals—have been used to support the roof. The new bridge is not the original which had been restored, nor an exact copy, nor is it in contemporary design ... it represents an anachronistic attempt at 'improving' the original design with fatal results *(Plate 24(c))*.

ROMAN BRIDGE OF PORTA CAPUCCINA AT ASCOLI PICENO

Background

This bridge crosses the Tronto at the beginning of the large bend north-east of the town. It was built in a narrow part of the valley where the banks are abrupt and tend to narrow together.

It is 62 metres long and 6.50 metres wide and rises 25 metres above the water. It has a single semi-circular vault and is faced with locally quarried travertine blocks.

The powerful structure of the bridge and the discovery during the restoration of the Roman pavement confirm its probable importance as a terminal point of the part of the Via Salaria linking Ascoli to Fermo.

Preliminary surveys

In 1930, repairs to the foundations of the abutments were first undertaken, but it was not until 1938 that it proved possible, after careful surveys, to complete the consolidation of the bridge.

A frame supported by the projections of the foundations was made in semi-reinforced concrete in 1930. Its regular watertight covering contrasted well with the masonry, and it allowed operations to remove anything that was foreign or inert in the internal structure of the bridge without risk to its static equilibrium.

Dismantling of the two sides to maintain a balanced weight at the bridge extremities and centre revealed a Roman pavement some 80 centimetres below the level of the roadway; it was removed and numbered block by block. Several other discoveries were also made.

1. Traces of a pavement of fired briquettes in *point de Hongrie* placed above the Roman pavement on a bed of sand; this has been conscientiously preserved.
2. Examination of the irregular travertine blocks, which were of quite different proportions from those of the other surfaces, suggested that the outside surface of the left upstream abutment must have been entirely rebuilt throughout its length and up to a height of 3 metres starting from the impost of the arch. Inside, at thicknesses of between 50 centimetres and 2 metres, good masonry was exposed, made of stones and *pozzuolana* roughly joined by an ordinary quicklime mortar.
3. Various left-overs of iron and fired clay materials.

Discoveries affecting statics

1. There was a total absence of mortar between the hewn blocks of the arch and the outer surfacing, except for the wall of the left abutment upstream (see above).
2. Deterioration and fractures from crushing in many travertine blocks in the arch.
3. Perfect regularity of the arch downstream; upstream, it had been subjected to a slight straightening movement. The portion most damaged was the outer surface.
4. Corresponding to the irregularity just mentioned was a deep, irregular and continuous longitudinal crack, causing distinct separation between the upstream

189

Plate 24

The covered bridge at Pavia (Italy).
(a) Appearance before the Second World War.
(b) War damage.
(c) The new bridge, resembling the old, but
    differing from it in many details.

c

and downstream portions of the right semi-arch.

5. The surfaces of adjusted hewn blocks in good condition were well preserved.

6. Complete fragmentation of the mortar in the masonry filling between the layers of strongly sloping tuff nearly 3 metres below the level of the impost.

These data suggested that the bridge's solidity was compromised by the disintegration or absence of mortar, and by pressure from the heterogeneous filling material.

In view of the discovery of the Roman pavement, it was decided to superimpose a new traffic level over the old and adopt a system of demarcation which would clearly differentiate the modern and old portions.

Consolidation and reconstruction: stages

1. Preparation of provisional reinforcements, and construction of a foot-bridge for pedestrians.

2. Preparatory consolidation: injections of grout or liquid cement under pressure between the hewn blocks of the arch and the outer surface, and where necessary in the reinforced arch.

3. Consolidation of the abutments up to the level of the impost. It was necessary to remove all the fill, pressure wash the resultant space, angle the support on the tuff, and fill in with concrete, to provide solid support for the successive consolidation operations and eliminate the pressure on the external structures. Highly resistant grout was injected in the travertine joints of the outside portion.

4. Consolidation of the arch of the bridge and the walls of the parapet up to the kerb of the Roman pavement. Two supporting arches in brick were also constructed, with an opening of 6 metres for the left abutment and 5 metres for the right.

5. Recomposition of the Roman pavement, which had to be made accessible to specialists and to the public. The road level

had been raised 1 metre, so that the pavement could not be seen easily. The problem was solved by the use of two internal arches and, for access, two rooms (one on the ground floor, the other below ground) of a neighbouring house immediately upstream from the left abutment. From there, an ingenious system of small galleries at different levels led the visitor to the Roman pavement and to the ancient and modern structures inside the bridge.

6. New bridge superstructure, composed of a scaffolding in reinforced concrete supported by brick pilasters. The raising of the road level facilitated both the link up with the access road and the draining of surface water, which had previously poured into the bridge in great quantities, whose level had been lower than that of the adjacent roads.

Finally, the public and vehicles of all categories could again use the bridge without any risk to its static equilibrium; and the old Roman structures were made visible and accessible.

THE BRIDGE OF BASSANO

Background

The first more or less reliable documents go back to the thirteenth century. They record that it was made of wood, and consequently subject to wearing by the current and by floods. In seven centuries, the waters of the Brenta destroyed it many times. It was also ravaged by fires, but always rebuilt. Palladio designed the latest version in 1570, following Roman techniques, after reading Vitruvius' treatise on the bridges over the Rhine. The bridge is built of wood and comprises five spans, each 13 metres long, which are supported on vertical piles bound together in the form of trapezoids, and so set that the current flows along their parallel sides. It is covered by a roof supported on wooden posts throughout its length.

Its useful width was 7.70 metres (total width 8.30 metres); length 65 metres; height between the roadway and the surface of the water: 9.50 metres.

Reconstruction

The bridge resembles that of Lucerne and certain covered wooden bridges in Alpine towns in southern Austria. It was destroyed on 29 April 1945. Photographs, models and documents were used to reconstitute it exactly as had been designed by Palladio. The reconstructed bridge was inaugurated on 3 October 1948 *(Plate 25)*.

ROMAN BRIDGE OF VAISON-LA-ROMAINE

Background

This restoration set and followed exemplary standards.

The bridge was built in large blocks of local limestone; it consists of a single arch 17 metres long. Its height, from the level of the impost to the pavement is 10 metres, and its total width is 9.50 metres. In 1944, explosives intended to blow up the bridge succeeded only in shattering a number of blocks near the keystone of the arch. After summary consolidation, restoration proper began in 1954.

The explosion damage did not particularly threaten the bridge's stability. The technique used by the Romans facilitated reconstruction. Vaults of square blocks are supported by juxtaposed arches; it was fairly easy to replace any shattered blocks or those affected by splits and cracks.

Apart from the blocks forming the key of the vault, its upper part was formed of five practically independent arches. The arches at the extremities were intact. The central arch was in a serious state, and the intermediate arches considerably damaged. Seventeen blocks, each 1 cubic metre in size, needed changing.

Reconstruction

Sudden floods made it impossible to rest the scaffolding on the bed of the Ouvèze, the river the bridge crosses, or on the bases of the abutments; but by traversing the modern parapets it was possible to construct a suspended scaffolding, supported by the extrados of the arches which were intact. A platform was then suspended from chains, under the vault.

When the bridge was freed from later superstructures it could be seen that the extrados of the blocks of the vault had directly served for some time as a carriageable road; the blocks had been worn down by the continuous passage of wheels which had left deep, rail-like grooves in the stone. All the blocks were joined together by cramps that were still quite effective, despite their age and the then condition of the bridge.

A restoration that respects history has another highly important advantage: with the help of modern technology, which is indispensable to complete success, it can provide details of ancient techniques that hitherto had been known only approximately, and so improves our understanding of past civilizations. The pattern of vanished civilizations is slowly reconstituted, and we obtain details that later repairs and additions have modified or even disfigured.

BRIDGE OF CASTELVECCHIO AT VERONA

Background

This bridge was begun in 1354 and completed in 1356, on the site of a demolished Roman bridge; traces of the latter have been found, confirming the information contained in documents. The plan of the bridge is attributed to Giovanni da Ferrara and Jacopo da Gozzo (presumed designers also of the covered bridge of Pavia).

The Adige describes a large bend, 120 metres across, as it enters the city. Here the

Plate 25

The wooden bridge at Bassano del Grappa,
designed after Roman bridges built over the
Rhine.
(a) The bridge during the Second World War.
(b) After reconstruction.

bridge is located. Because of its gradient the
river does not leave deposits, nor does the
current flow strongly enough to erode its
channel. The present level may therefore be
considered as approximately the same as it
was six centuries ago.

Except for the edges of the arches and the
bases of the piers, which are made of limestone from Sant Ambrogio, the three-arch
bridge is of brick. The two cutwater piers
are respectively 12.3 and 6.3 metres wide
and 19.4 and 17.3 metres long. The total
length of the bridge is 119.9 metres; the
width of the roadway varies from 6 to
6.5 metres. The slightly convex arches face
upstream.

The bridge was part of the system of fortifications of Castelvecchio built by Can-
grande to protect against internal enemies
and ensure a possibility of retreat towards
the friendly North, i.e. towards the Empire.

The bridge survived almost intact to our
times. Under the Austrian occupation, a
substantial restoration was ordered by Francis I of Austria as the bridge was 'threatened
by corrosion'. The underpinning of the
large pier was strengthened on the castle
side; the large ornamental facing stones of
the pier itself, which had been loosened by
the current, were put back into place; the
dismantled superstructures were repaired;
and the battlements were patiently reconstructed (though hardly in conformity with
present restoration principles) and changed
back to their original form.

The retreating German army mined and
blew up the bridge on 24 April 1945 *(Plate
26(a))*.

The bridge formed part of a whole of
which only the castle, and the abutments
and piers of the bridge remained. The arches
and battlements above them had been destroyed, but the battlements were not authentic (nineteenth-century restoration, see
above). The bridge was a small but significant part of the whole panorama, so much
so that its absence would compromise the
general architectural harmony.

Reconstruction

It was accordingly decided, after thorough
reflection, to undertake a complete reconstruction. Most of the Sant Ambrogio limestone blocks, the arches and piers, and a
portion of the bricks, were recovered from
the bed of the Adige. From the models made
before the destruction and detailed photographic documentation, the bridge was reconstructed as it had originally been, each
stone which had been saved being replaced
in its former position.

Before the work began, it was noted during a check that, in the lower reaches of the
piers, formed of large blocks of Verona
stone, the only foundation was a base composed of superimposed layers of solid red
bricks of normal size, joined by a simple
mortar of white quicklime used hot. In the
case of the small pier, the base was 60 centimetres thick and rested on a layer of conglomerate 80 centimetres thick which in

turn lay on a thick bed of natural gravel. In the large pier, on the west side, erosion by the current had removed the whole layer of conglomerate and seriously loosened the blocks whose base was at water-level. In places, the current had even created alarming breaches which had formerly been filled with natural rock.

The small pier was surrounded by new underpinning which, at a depth of 3.3 metres below the former foundation level, was inserted horizontally 1.3 metres under the old base of fired bricks so as to form a buffer for approximately 60 centimetres around it. The whole stone wall was reconstructed and cemented, and the circle about the foundation was completed. The cavity was deepened in order to have a more solid subjacent position strengthening the supporting surface. In this way the unitary stress did not exceed 5 kilograms per square metre in the foundations.

The same method was used in the large pier. One of the layers of big blocks forming the base at water-level is in Sant Ambrogio stone. These blocks probably date from the Roman construction and their workmanship recalls those of the Porta Borsari. The stones of the foundation and of the lower edges of the arch were identified scientifically for colour, type and treatment, so that the best replacements could be chosen from various quarries (some quarries that had long been abandoned were even reopened to obtain the same type of stone). In addition to the bricks recovered, others were obtained from sites in the province, and elsewhere where mediaeval buildings were being demolished; when necessary, new bricks were ordered from local brickworks, the fineness of texture and colour being carefully specified.

Ancient building techniques were followed. The idea of inserting a reinforced-concrete framework in the bridge was rejected. The original was followed, even as regards the structure—so, incidentally, avoiding the damage which would no doubt have developed from the difference in the coefficients of thermic and elastic expansion as between reinforced concrete and the stone and brick facing.

The work began on 2 March 1950. The two small arches were first reconstructed, then the big arch linking the bridge to the rest of the defensive system of fortifications of Castelvecchio. The work was completed on 2 July 1951 *(Plate 26(b))*.

BRIDGE OF SANTA TRINITA AT FLORENCE

Background

A mediaeval bridge was carried away by Arno floods in 1557. Cosimo dei Medici invited Bartolomeo Ammanati to build a modern bridge and this was completed between 1567 and 1569. Until recently the bridge was attributed exclusively to Ammanati. Research by Kriegbaum now indicates that Michelangelo had more or less influenced the architectural design as Ragghianti, Salvini and others have also

a

b

noted. The taut arches seem to vibrate. Offsetting them the heavy parapets seem actually to grip the arches. The enormous, unshakeably solid cutwater piers, and the mass of the nearby palaces present an ideal background—features much more characteristic of Michelangelo than the more superficial designs of Ammanati *(Plate 27(a))*.

This bridge comprises three arches of varying length (26.78, 29.23, and 26.12 metres); they are very low and very taut and of a special form which is a novelty in this period of the history of architecture. The cutwater piers are each 8 metres wide. The bridge spans 98.13 metres and its width from parapet to parapet is 10 metres. It is built in hard Tuscan stone. Like the other Florentine bridges, except the Ponte Vecchio, it was blown up at dawn on 4 August 1944. All that was left were two stumps of the piers, part of the abutments and the debris which filled the bed of the Arno *(Plate 27(b))*.

Proposals

Since certain elements which rarely coexist were found together here (perfection of the architectural line, an indispensable link between the parts of Florence on either bank of the Arno, the qualities of the structures themselves), reconstruction demanded even more particular care than usual.

Every proposal gave rise to controversy, debates and discussions. The technicians argued economy and statics. They wanted to reconstruct the bridge in reinforced concrete and cover it over with stone, mainly in order to cope with the increased weight the bridge would have to bear.

There were also the usual arguments: the need to be authentically modern, to take advantage of technology and not be servile about the past. Since the materials of the bridge would have to be new, what did it matter if the internal structures, i.e. the invisible skeleton, were modern? Examples were quoted of restorations that employed up-to-date techniques, e.g. the reinforced-concrete framework hidden in the masonry used for the reconstruction of the campanile of St. Mark's in Venice; the roof frameworks, also in reinforced concrete, in the Church of San Francesco in Bologna and the Cathedral of Bolzana; the metal framework that supports the small loggias of the palace of Ludovico il Moro at Ferrara; the reinforced-concrete beams used to strengthen the Papal loggia at Viterbo; the injections of grout into the disjointed walls of other monuments; and so on.

It was pointed out in reply that the use of steel or reinforced concrete may be justified to save a work of art and preserve it where it is, or if it offers the only way of saving a monument that threatens to collapse because of age or seismic or war damage. However, a scheduled bridge is a compound of art and technology in which form and material are inseparable: change the material and you most likely also change the form.

Reconstruction

It was finally decided to rebuild the bridge as it had been when destroyed.

Various difficulties had to be faced. Apart from the strictly technical problems, what was to be done about patina and stone-cutting? Scrupulous fidelity based only on drawings was not considered enough; the stone-cutters would need to know all that could be learned from monuments that were contemporaneous with Ammanati's bridge. So the various craftsmen involved studied Santa Croce, the Pitti Palace and Santa Trinita by direct observation, to see how their forbears so successfully 'interpreted' the ideas of the architect.

Once prepared, mounting the material was of crucial importance. To recapture the quality of the destroyed bridge, it was interpretation that was required, not copying. A quarry of hard stone was opened in the Boboli gardens, where the original builders had got their materials, and various experiments were made to test the appearance.

What type of curve had the architect employed in designing the three arches?

Again experiments were made. A parabola was not the original form of the arches (especially at the points corresponding to the imposts); a catenary curve was the closest to what the photographs showed of the original bridge. A solution was thus rapidly found; the curves of the arches were determined for the stone-cutters, who could then work on the stone, block by block, and give it form.

The Santa Trinita bridge was reconstructed according to the best principles of architectural restoration, using no materials that were not used in the original, and duly respecting the structures and lines of the old bridge. The work ended on 4 August 1957, and the inauguration took place on 16 March 1958 *(Plate 27(c))*.

BRIDGE OF LA PIETRA AT VERONA

Background

This Roman bridge, called the bridge of La Pietra since the early Middle Ages, was the oldest in Verona. The first bridge there dated from the end of the Roman Republic. Partial collapse had followed earthquakes or floods many times in the course of the centuries. The reconstruction by the Scaligera of the tower on the right bank and the arch next to it was carried out in 1298, and the two middle arches were rebuilt by the Venetians in 1520. The bridge had five arches with spans varying from 15 to 18 metres. The first two arches on the left were Roman and built of stone; the others, of mixed stone and brick, are of mediaeval construction. The roadway was 4.1 metres wide, the footways 88 centimetres each and the parapets 43 centimetres thick. The total width was thus 6.85 metres. The height from the roadway to water-level was about 13 metres. The Roman piers were each 3 metres wide, and the mediaeval piers 6 metres. In the Roman portions, the blocks of Sant Ambrogio marble were joined by iron cramps set in lead, without cement.

The bridge was destroyed on 25 April 1945 *(Plate 28(a))*. The explosion caused all the arches except the last one on the right, the Scaligera, to collapse, and seriously damaged the piers and foundations. Fortunately, during the last period of the war, the authorities had made detailed drawings and photographs. At the end of hostilities, the blocks and stones which had fallen into the Adige were recovered and numbered one by one, in accordance with a reconstruction plan that had already been worked out on paper down to minor details. To facilitate this classification, the part of the river where the bridge had stood was divided into grids and the squares were numbered (Fig. 31(a)). Each block recovered was given the appropriate square identification number. Recovery and identification were long and difficult.

Reconstruction

The official proposal was to restore the bridge as it had been before its destruction. A counter project, aiming at reconstituting the former Roman bridge (an unconscious return to Viollet-le-Duc), gained support from the recovery of what were possibly the remains of Roman arches that had lain on the river bed for over 1,000 years. It was known that, at the beginning of the twentieth century, some of the old Roman stones of the bridge had been taken from the river for use in wall foundations, so that the bed could contain few usable Roman fragments. Nevertheless, scrupulous archaeological excavations were made.

Only a few blocks were in fact recovered. They were so worn, and so polished by the current that they could never be used. The lack of original materials, the condition of what little had been recovered, the impossibility of finding the original design of the bridge, were cogent arguments against this second proposal. Moreover, it would have

199

Plate 27

The bridge of Santa Trinita, Florence (Italy).
(a) Appearance before the war.
(b) The destroyed bridge.
(c) After reconstruction.
(Photos: Gazzola.)

27b

c

c

Plate 28

The bridge of La Pietra, Verona (Italy).
(a) Appearance after destruction.
(b) Model used in planning the reconstruction.
(c) The reconstructed bridge.

FIG. 31

Bridge of La Pietra, Verona (Italy).
(a) Methods used in consolidating the bridge.
    Left section—recomposition and use of
    cramps; right—the grid system used to
    recover blocks.
(b) Reassembly plans of the two arches. Areas
    outlined in dark ink had survived the
    destruction.

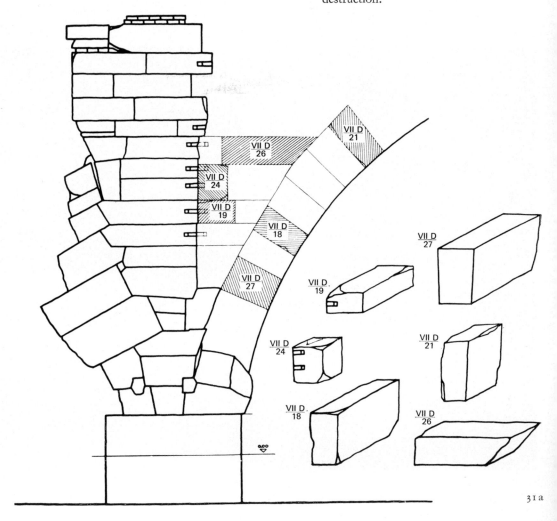

31 a

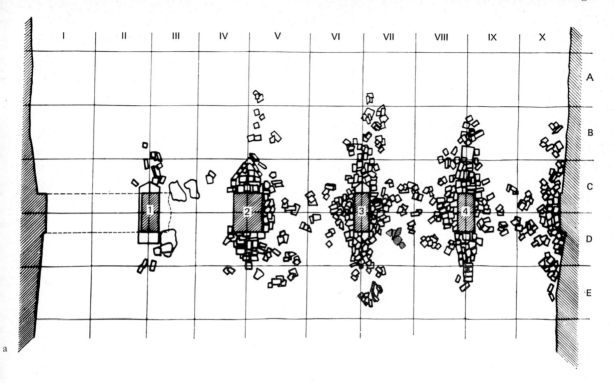

a

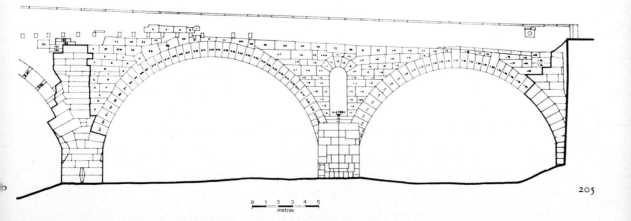

b

0 1 2 3 4 5
metres

been necessary to demolish the remaining mediaeval arch.

For more than five centuries, the pre-war bridge had been a dominant architectural feature of the quarter and of the city, a unique fusion of forms, materials and colours. As much of its constituent material had been recovered, it was decided to reconstruct the bridge as it had been before 1945, identifying the new portions with a conventional sign.

The remaining piers were inspected and consolidated, and the pier that had been destroyed was rebuilt. Soundings to determine the stability of the pier foundations showed that, while the first pier on the left appeared to be in place, a mine had blasted right down to its foundations, displacing the structure. It had to be demolished and rebuilt, the blocks being then linked to one another by iron cramps. The lower portion of the second pier was perfectly stable; it was, however, further consolidated by injections of grout, and iron cramps. The foundations of the third pier had been rebuilt during the Venetian period (Fra Giacondo). It had also been blasted and dislodged. The foundations were consolidated by extracting and resetting the blocks of stone, and by injections of grout at lower pressure (Fig. 31(b), *Plate 28(b)*). The fourth pier was intact.

The first arch was completed well ahead of schedule. The whole job took two winters, as the soffits could be placed only during the short period of low water from December to March. The reconstruction was completed on 8 March 1959 *(Plate 28(c))*.

SUMMARY

Because of their utilitarian purpose and the stresses they must bear, the survival of old bridges is particularly threatened by partisans of technology for its own sake. However, as historic and artistic structures which are intimately associated with the growth of civilization and culture, they merit the same respect and standards of accuracy in their preservation as all other monuments.

Masaru Sekino

The preservation and restoration of wooden monuments in Japan

9

By definition a structure built of organic materials has an average life span much less than one built of stone, brick or other relatively stable inorganic substance. The light, traditional Japanese home is considered to have an average life of forty years under urban conditions. Any such buildings older than 100 years are very scarce. Old farm-houses which used large timbers last longer, and Shinto shrines and Buddhist temples longer still. Nevertheless, with normal maintenance (including periodic re-roofing), a wooden building rarely lasts longer than 250 years; in the temperate zone, under very favourable conditions, 300 years seems to be the maximum.

Biological agents such as bacteria, moulds and insects live off wood. Fire is a constant hazard. Wood also reacts to the presence or absence of moisture—swelling, shrinking and cracking—and other climatic changes. In countries where wooden structures are important to their cultural heritage the necessity for their preservations and restoration have imposed criteria to take these factors into account. Measures thus tend to be more radical than those required for masonry buildings (see *Plates 17, 33, 34*).

In reconstruction the general principle is to use the same kind of wood as found in the original. When some of the wood used, e.g. pine, was not very durable, as it is particularly subject to insect attack or to rot, the trend in the past was to replace it with more resistant species. Today, however, new developments in chemical treatment make this less necessary.

While in principle wood should not be replaced by reinforced concrete, there are exceptions to this rule. In the interest of saving a large beam from the original structure—no longer capable of supporting its load—it may be hollowed, and a stressed concrete beam placed within to preserve the appearance of the original.

In Japan another exception is made in the case of castles built originally of plaster-covered wood which were destroyed through fire or other causes. They have been reconstructed in reinforced concrete (which is cheaper as well as being fire-proof and not subject to biological attack) from measured drawings, photographs and other reliable information, and their external appearance has not been changed. This, of course, results in a sacrifice of authenticity. Several castles classified as historical monuments and destroyed during the Second World War were reconstructed in this way, but this practice has been limited to castles which, in view of their original role as fortresses, have some justification for being rebuilt in concrete. Otherwise, wood has been used in duplicating the original, as was done in the case of the Golden Pavilion in Kyoto (built during the Muromachi period), after its complete destruction by fire.

Four principal methods are used in the case of wooden buildings whose natural life has already expired: (a) dismantling and reassembling, introducing new elements as

29a

Plate 29

The Golden Hall of Chuson-ji Temple,
Hiraizumi (Japan).

(a) After the removal of the early wooden
    shelter, a temporary shelter allowed work
    to continue on the hall itself and on a new
    fire-proof, reinforced-concrete shelter to
    protect it.
(b) Restoration of the gilt and lacquer
    ornamentation—a technician examines a
    fragment detached from the pillar.
(c) The sanctuary after restoration. Traditional
    materials and techniques were used.
(d) The Golden Hall in its present shelter.
(Photos: Sekino.)

29b

29c

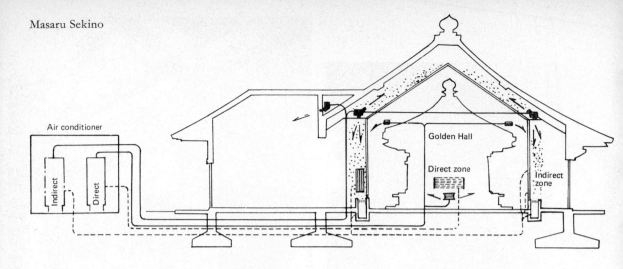

Air conditioner

Indirect

Direct

Golden Hall

Direct zone

Indirect zone

required; (b) sheltering; (c) periodical reconstruction following the original design; (d) construction of a scale model.

DISMANTLING AND REASSEMBLY

The restoration of wooden buildings usually starts by dismantling them completely. Each part is carefully examined, any that are broken or rotten are completely or partly replaced, and the building is reassembled. As much as possible of the old material (especially if decorated) is preserved with care.

A wooden building thus continues to exist at the cost of an inevitable, gradual loss of its original parts—a kind of metabolism through which the old gives place to the new; while preserving its original form, it slowly loses its original material step by step. This is inevitable when restoration takes the form of dismantling and reassembly.

SHELTERING

It is not uncommon for a small building, a model, or a part of a building to be preserved and displayed in a museum. There are also examples of buildings being preserved in fairly good condition on the original site, but sheltered by a later structure. Both are forms of indoor preservation in which the building is treated like a museum

object. Modern technology can provide a large span shelter if it is considered essential to preserve a timber building in perfect condition.

A good example is the Golden Hall of Chuson-ji Temple at Hiraizumi, Japan, built in 1124. This is a small lacquer-covered Buddhist hall. Its interior decoration is a masterpiece, and soon after it was built, a wooden shelter was erected to enclose it. However, the results were unsatisfactory in one respect: the shelter was too small to allow the building to be seen in perspective. The Golden Hall was recently dismantled and restored, and a new, air-conditioned shelter of reinforced concrete was built for it (*Plate 29*, Fig. 32).

PERIODICAL RECONSTRUCTION

The main shrine of Ise (the oldest Shinto shrine of Japan) is preserved on the periodical reconstruction principle, based on religious tradition. For over 1,200 years, an identical new building has been erected every twenty years on one or other of a pair of sites of similar size. The old shrine is destroyed soon after the new one is built. All parts are perfect copies, so that the original design and proportions are always retained. Other shrines were similarly maintained until the Middle Ages, when forests were still abundant in Japan and large timbers were

FIG. 32

Design of the new shelter for the Golden Hall, Chuson-ji Temple, which is air conditioned, fire proof and earthquake-resistant.

available. Since the Momoyama Period (1568–1615), however, periodical reconstruction has gradually ceased, and partial or complete dismantling and reassembly are the principal methods of preservation.

PRACTICAL PROCEDURES

MAINTENANCE

Wooden buildings must be inspected regularly, to guard against damage provoked by wind, earthquake, rain, damp and insects, the major sources of deterioration.

Roof

The roof is the most exposed part, subject to attrition by natural forces, especially rain and wind. Hence roof repairs (or re-roofing) usually head the list of repairs.

Partial dismantling

The edges of eaves, rafter ends, and the roof covering may decay; sometimes even the framework supporting the roof rots. The surrounding veranda and railings may also need repairs. These parts are dealt with by partial dismantling, the main framework of the building being left untouched. If piles have sunken irregularly they arc levelled and the slackened framework is tightened up.

CONSTRUCTION OF A SCALE MODEL

Famous tea-houses have frequently been reproduced as full-scale models, which is fairly common practice among lovers of the tea ceremony. There also exists a scale model of a pagoda which has been preserved in a Buddhist monastery for over 1,200 years; it was built by a master carpenter before the actual pagoda itself. To show all details properly the scale of models should be larger than one-tenth; a one-twentieth or smaller scale model usually has to omit a lot.

Construction or decoration can also be reproduced in models, as documentation to supplement measured drawings and photographs. A model of a coloured pattern or painting, showing its condition before and after restoration, is especially useful.

Complete dismantling

Complete dismantling is necessary if a building is on the verge of ruin. It demands all kinds of repair techniques (see below).

Repainting

If paint is peeling slightly, exfoliation can be prevented by various modern techniques; if advanced, there is no remedy but repainting. Repainting usually accompanies major repairs. Laquerwork is often carried out separately.

DISMANTLING AND REASSEMBLY

Even if maintenance has been carried out properly, sooner or later complete re-roofing will be necessary—usually accompanied by minor repairs elsewhere. A new cycle of maintenance then begins until it is time for a second re-roofing. This is the ideal as well as practical way of maintaining wooden

33a

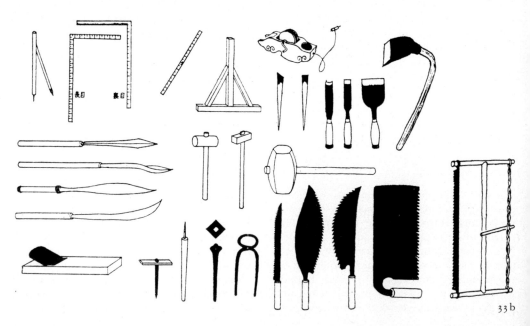

33b

FIG. 33

Traditional Japanese carpentry.
(a) Scene from the scroll of the Matsugasaki-zinja Shrine (thirteenth century) showing carpenters at work building a shrine.
(b) Traditional tools of the Japanese carpenter.
(Photos: Sekino.)

buildings in a condition as close to the original as possible.

However, more frequently than not, maintenance is neglected because of lack of money or proper supervision. Re-roofing always tends to be behind time, and the damage steadily worsens; frequently, it is only after a severe storm or an earthquake that the owner thinks about partial dismantling. But by then, the building may be on the verge of collapse, and the only hope is complete dismantling and restoration.

Temporary roof

A building which requires major repairs or dismantling should be covered entirely by a temporary roof. Large spans of scaffolding are covered with zinc-coated corrugated iron or fibre-glass reinforced sheeting, with tiers of catwalks at vertical intervals of 1–1.5 metres under the eaves. A temporary roof gives protection and allows investigation and repairs under all weather conditions.

Survey and measured drawings

Wood is subject to warping. Drawings of a building in its dilapidated state may be of documentary interest, but for repair purposes, measured drawings are needed of the building as it originally was. Three-dimensional photographic surveys are now feasible also (see Chapter 5); they save time and eliminate the need for scaffolding.

Roofs of ancient buildings in the Far East are characterized by curves. The brackets used to support the curves shrink and become compressed because of drying and the load they bear (particularly at the projecting parts which support the eaves). Rafters are sometimes cut off at the ends through carelessness, and the delicate curved line of the eaves becomes distorted. If that happens, each must be measured and shown on the drawing as it will appear in the restored building.

In other words, the restored roof must be shown on the drawing before work is begun. This demands a thorough knowledge of changes that have occurred in traditional techniques and of the geometric principles involved in the construction of wooden buildings, since the methods used by carpenters to cut lengths and shapes vary over the course of time. The method of sawing wood, the respect for the grain in the curved corner of the projecting eaves, is often regarded as the essence of Japanese carpentry (Fig. 33). The measured drawings to be used by artisans must accordingly be prepared under the supervision of an expert.

The dimensions of house posts and columns, ties, horizontal bands, rafters and their spacing tended to be more and more strictly regulated by *Kiwari*, a system of philosophical principles that defined classical orders and the proportions of the different elements used in buildings towards the beginning of the Meiji Period (1868–1912). These principles must be kept in mind as a check on accuracy in reconstruction.

Photographs, rubbings and the chronological table

Detailed photographs should be taken of the exterior, interior and the various parts of the building. Rubbings should be taken of mouldings and of wooden parts and metal fittings, special care being taken to record the grain of the timber, nail marks and other traces of workmanship. Photographs and rubbings taken before and during dismantling serve both for the reassembling and as technical and historical documents. They should be catalogued, edited for publication and properly preserved, and combined with ancient plans, sketches, drawings, paintings, documents and records of previous repairs in a chronological table to provide a complete record of the building—changes in location, changes in plans and partitions, later additions, and so on.

Dismantling and investigation

A small identification plate is first attached to each element of the building. Dismantling begins with the roof and continues slowly and systematically to the foundation, each element being carefully examined and studied. Traces of older repairs can be distinguished from newer ones by the quality of mortises, notches and nail marks, and they help to document the history of repairs. From many points of view, this resembles an archaeological excavation. Graffiti, ink-marks and scribblings may lead to interesting results. If there is a ridge-pole plate, it will bear the date of the original construction or major repairs and the names of the master carpenters. The types of carpenter's tools and the widths of their blades can be deduced from the marks left.

Not all alterations can properly be called restoration, e.g. earthworks to afford protection against floods or damp; substitutions of copper plate in the roof for the original thatched, shingled or cypress bark for economy and fire-prevention reasons; use of rust-proof steel bolts, plates and bars (where they are not visible); reinforcement of the foundations by concrete blocks or slabs.

Elimination of unwanted alteration

Ancient buildings might be enlarged, be embellished in later periods, be built of second-hand materials taken from other buildings, or even be reduced in size during earlier reconstructions. All these factors have to be taken into account in deciding how to reconstruct.

Reassembling

After the results of the dismantling investigation have been analysed and the proposals for restorations and alterations are approved, reassembling can begin.

The first step is to separate what is serviceable from what cannot be used again. If perfectly sound, serviceable elements can be used without any particular treatment. If partially damaged or rotten they must be replaced or reinforced. Synthetic resins can be used to bind the old and new materials effectively. Carved and painted wood, if fragile, can be strengthened by injecting synthetic resin and filling hollows with a mixture of the resin and saw-dust. Missing decorative details can be replaced by new ones made by copying patterns from the same building, or from another building belonging to the same period and locality. The details should be inscribed (out of sight) on the new parts. New wood introduced is usually dated with a branding iron. Traditional tools are used to give the finishing touches, and sometimes ancient tools are specially restored so that their characteristic marks will be reproduced. However, modern machine tools are often used nowadays to lower the cost of labour, particularly where the wood used is not visible, and the final result accordingly is not impaired. Nevertheless, so far as possible traditional techniques are maintained in the actual reassembly.

It is common practice in Japan to paint new wood to match the colour of the old, but paints easily change colour and the result is often disagreeable. To weather a new section, an alternative is to char the surface slightly with a torch and then scratch it with a wirebrush. The resulting texture and colour are much less liable to change, and the new wood blends in with the old. Inspection, however, will show the difference between naturally and artificially weathered wood.

Once reassembly is complete, the drawings prepared before dismantling should be used to prepare the drawings of the restored building. Photographs are taken, and an inscribed copper plate is affixed inside, describing the restoration, and indicating its cost, initiator, supervisor, contractor, starting and finishing dates. A summary of the investigation, and drawings, specifications and photographs are incorporated into a report that is published and issued to those concerned.

Unused, old wooden elements of value are stored; those which have ancient inscriptions or graffiti are also stored, or displayed in the museum.

CONSTITUENT MATERIALS AND THEIR PRESERVATION

ROOFS

The roofs of most wooden buildings in the Far East tend to be steeply sloped, with wide eaves. Leaks that occur during rain storms should be carefully repaired, to avoid the serious cases of rot that are provoked by the growth of moulds and fungi.[1]

Thatched roofs

Farm houses usually use wheat and rice straw as thatch. It is not very durable. The best thatch in Japan is made from a grass called *kaya* (Miscanthus). When restoring a thatch roof, the wood and bamboo supports for the thatch should be bound firmly to the wooden frame with straw ropes. Layers of *kaya* grass are then attached to horizontal bars of bamboo. Patching is necessary each spring with fresh straw or grass. This kind of roof lasts from fifteen to twenty-five years. If there is an open hearth, smoke from the fire affects the battens and the thatch, and limits rot and insect pests— making an average addition of ten years to the life of the thatch. At the Shrine of Ise, selected *kaya* grass is smoked before it is used, and the result has been very satisfactory.

Shingle roofing

Kokera roofing is a refined type of shingle roofing. Thin plates of split cedar or cypress, each about 27 centimetres long, 9 centimetres wide and 3 millimetres thick, are fixed to the roof with the lower 3–4 centimetres exposed to the weather. The shorter the exposed part and the longer the length of each shingle, the longer the life of the roof, which may last from twenty to thirty years. Shingles should be made by splitting rather than sawing, since the irregular spaces which result between each shingle allow ventilation and prevent water invading through capillary action. Antiseptic treatment to combat fungi, and coating shingles with water-repelling synthetic resin have proved effective. An innovation was the insertion of thin copper plates between shingles at 27 centimetres intervals. The natural corrosion of the copper plate produces blue vitriol (copper sulphate) which spreads over the shingles and helps to control mould and insect damage. It was first applied to

---

1. cf. 'Combating the Moulds which develop on Cultural Property', *The Conservation of Cultural Property*, Paris, Unesco, 1968 (Vol. XI in this series).

Plate 30

Traditional Japanese shingle (*kokera*) roofing.
(Photo: Sekino.)

the roof of Konchi-in of Nanzen-ji, Kyoto, and the roof lasted for forty years *(Plate 30)*.

Bark roofs

Barks are generally waterproof, water-repellant and hard to rot. Cypress bark roofing is typically Japanese. Rectangular sheets of cypress bark are placed in layers (like *kokera* roofing) with only small areas of their lower parts exposed to the weather. Their life span

is a little longer than *kokera* (usually from twenty-five to thirty-five years; exceptionally, as long as sixty years). Cypress bark cannot be treated with antiseptics as it is not absorbent.

Baked-clay tile roofs

Glazed tiles are waterproof, whereas unglazed tiles may absorb considerable amounts of water and do not last long, par-

31a

Plate 31

Tile roofing.
(a) Regular tiles, baked, unglazed; alternate
    courses of convex and concave tiles.
(b) Moulded, ornamental ends of tiles attached
    at the edge of the eaves. (From the pagoda
    of the Horyuji Temple near Nara, *c.* eighth
    century.)
(Photos: Sekino.)

31b

ticularly if fired at a low temperature. However, well-fired unglazed clay tiles are hard, absorb little water and last well *(Plate 31)*.

Two types of tile roofing are used in Japan: regular tile roofing and pantile roofing. The former consists of alternative series of concave and convex tiles; the latter is a composite and simplified version of the former, lighter, and simpler to use. The life span of regular tile roofs is estimated at 100 years, that of pantile roofing at about

217

FIG. 34

Framework of a traditional Japanese building
(posts, beams, ties, etc.)
(a) Side elevation of the Main Hall of the
Daiho-onji Temple in Kyoto (thirteenth
century).
(b) Cross-section of the structural framework.

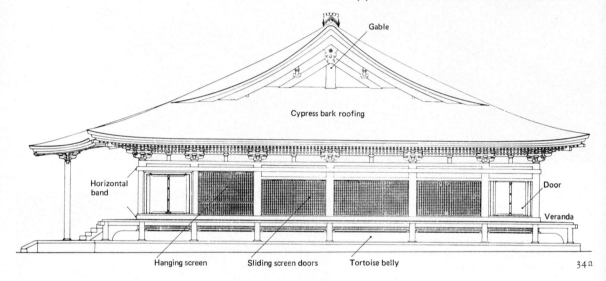

Gable

Cypress bark roofing

Horizontal
band

Door

Veranda

Hanging screen   Sliding screen doors   Tortoise belly

34a

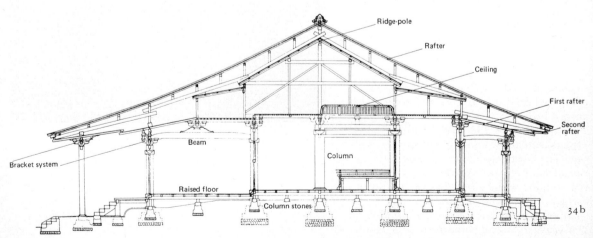

Ridge-pole

Rafter

Ceiling

First rafter

Second
rafter

Beam

Column

Bracket system

Raised floor

Column stones

34b

seventy years. Re-roofing requires replacement by about one-half newly baked tiles (about half being weakened by weathering or breaking during the dismantling). New tiles should be ordered from a factory which makes tiles in the traditional way.

Metal roofs

Japanese roofs are sometimes covered with copper, rarely with lead. Some copper-plate roofs imitate regular tiled roofs, e.g. that of

resistance of copper roofing. Flat copper-plate roofing is usually considered to last about seventy years.

Roof-boards and battens

The usual foundations for roofing are roof-boards or battens which are nailed to rafters. Battens are usually fixed directly to the rafters, but in some buildings of better quality they are placed on roof-boards which are in turn nailed over the rafters. In either

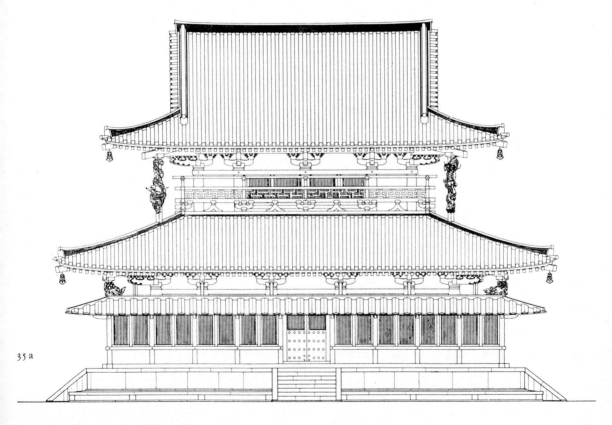

35 a

the Mausoleum at Nikko, which lasted for over 300 years. The flat copper-plate roofs of ancient buildings were usually installed as a substitute for the original *kokera* or cypress bark. In the past, this was done to take advantage of the longevity and fire

case, they should be treated with fungicides and insecticides.

Roof frame

When there is no ceiling, the board of the roof and the roof construction system are exposed, and this is taken into account in the design. If there is a ceiling, the roof frame can be made of roughly finished lumber, and unfinished curved timbers can serve as beams. Since such beams are functional and out of sight, strong timbers like pine and zelkova tree are preferred. Since the Middle Ages, the roof frames of Japanese buildings have usually been hidden by ceilings, and the roof frame became independent from the lower part of the building. Hence dismantling of the roof can be car-

from the walls, openings and verandas, protecting them from damage by rot, frost and dirt. However, of all the parts of a building, the eaves are the most liable to rot. Open-work metal fittings or metal covers nailed to the ends of rafters help to protect them quite effectively from weathering.

FRAMEWORK OF BUILDINGS

Frame

The framework of traditional Japanese

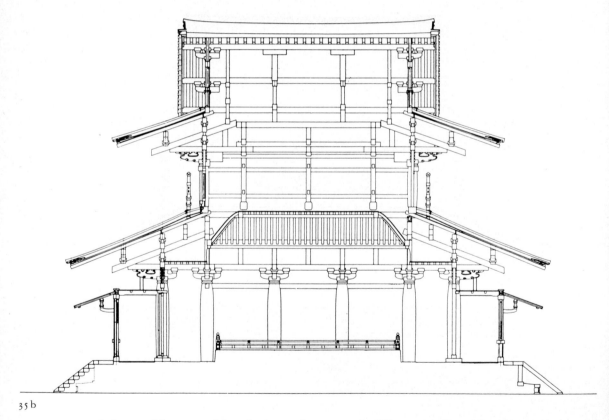

35 b

ried out without touching the lower framework.

Eaves

In much of the Far East, the eaves of a building project a good deal and keep rain

buildings consists of columns or posts, beams, penetrating ties and horizontal bands and a series of interconnected rectangular frames made of horizontal and vertical members (Fig. 34). Walls and openings are made between columns. A system of brackets consisting of square bearing blocks and brackets is placed on the top of the column. This type of support was invented in China before the Han Dynasty and was introduced into Japan during the seventh century. It is an elaborate type of cantilever, supporting the deeply projecting eaves that are widespread in the Far East (Fig. 35).

Sometimes columns are shifted during repairs, e.g. a weathered column in the outer wall may be exchanged for another column that was used inside. Sometimes a

seasoned lumber does to the use of tools. The difference can easily be seen. Mortises and cuts which have become unnecessary may be filled with plugs before reassembly.

Brackets can vary from the simple to the very complicated, in which function becomes secondary to decoration (Fig. 36). Complicated systems involve a number of brackets in which the cumulative slight looseness in each joint which results from shrinkage causes major distortions in shape. Adjustment by inserting wooden wedges

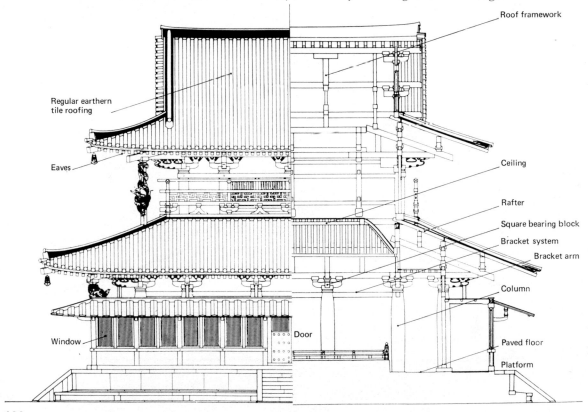

Regular earthern tile roofing

Eaves

Window

Door

Roof framework

Ceiling

Rafter

Square bearing block

Bracket system

Bracket arm

Column

Paved floor

Platform

35c

column is used anew by turning it 45, 90 or 180 degrees in order to turn the unweathered side outwards.

Original cuts tend to be fine and distinct, later ones clumsier, because old wood is often brittle and no longer reacts as fresh,

or lead plates may be necessary when reassembling the bracket system.

The reinforcement of the frame should be minimal and inconspicuous. Reinforcement with galvanized or rust-proof steel bolts, plates and bars is effective and satisfactory.

As the strength of a wooden building lessens year by year because of ageing, degeneration and consequent loss of resiliency in the material, a thorough inspection must be made during the restoration to ensure that the structural strength is adequate.

Outer walls

Walls may be half-timbered or covered, i.e. be divided into sections by the framework, or have the frame covered, and hidden be-

FIG. 35

The Kondo or Golden Hall of the Horyu-ji Monastery, near Nara, founded in 607 A.D. by the Empress Suiko. The architectural style resemble Chinese designs which were current during the sixth century.
(a) Front elevation.
(b), (c) Longitudinal section showing construction features.
(d), (e) End views and cross-section.

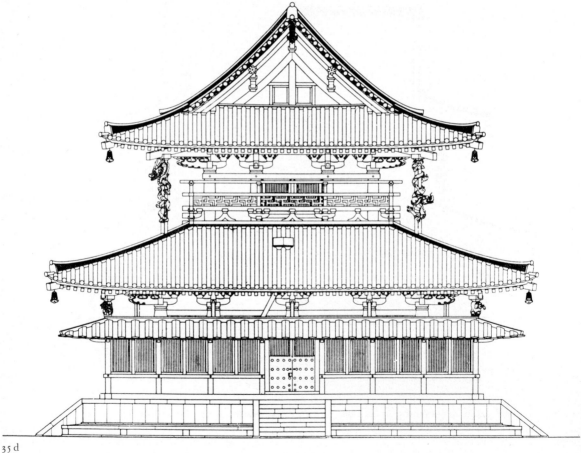

35 d

neath a continuous wall surface. The principal fill or covering used in the Far East is earth or wood. The boarding on half-timbered walls may be vertical or horizontal. Earthen walls consist of bamboo or reed laths, bound and wrapped with straw rope, and covered with mud. This mud wall is then finished off with a coat of plaster. In areas in which extreme weather conditions occur, outer walls are often enclosed with horizontal siding: thin, broad boards are nailed horizontally in lap-streaked design

to columns, and studs and vertical battens are then nailed to these boards at regular intervals.

Store-houses and castles often have the underside of the eaves heavily plastered in order to make them fire-resistant.

The preservation of an earthen wall is comparatively difficult. If an old earthen wall is to be re-used in a restored building, it should be cut whole and preserved—possible only when the wall is small enough (e.g. the wall of a ceremonial tea-house). If

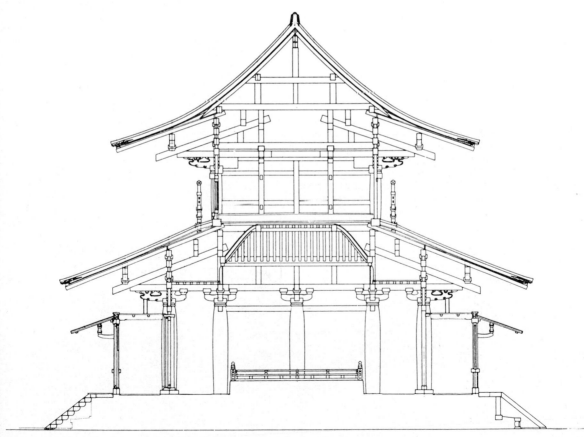

35e

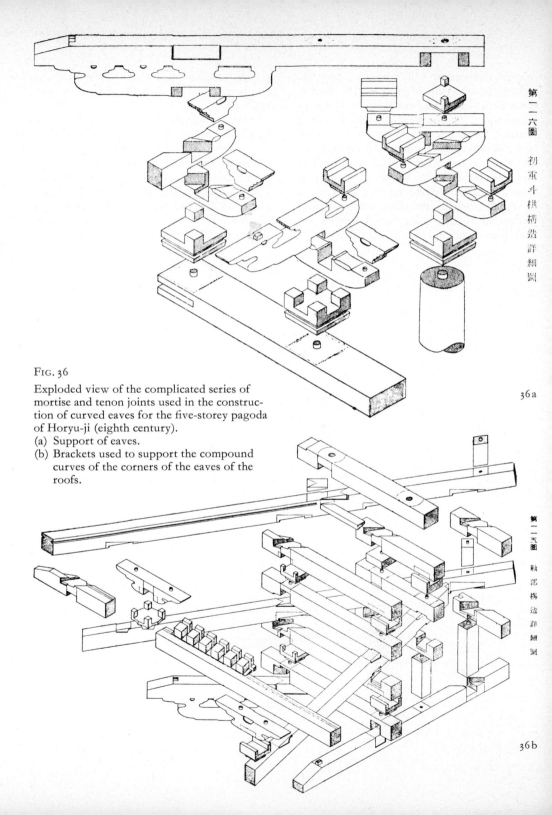

第一一六圖　初重斗栱構造詳細圖

FIG. 36

Exploded view of the complicated series of
mortise and tenon joints used in the construction of curved eaves for the five-storey pagoda
of Horyu-ji (eighth century).

(a) Support of eaves.
(b) Brackets used to support the compound
curves of the corners of the eaves of the
roofs.

36a

第一五圖　軸部構造詳細圖

36b

the earthen wall is large, the only solution is to build it anew, from the laths to the finishing coats. In both cases organic material should be treated with fungicides and insecticides, as materials embedded in earthen walls are liable to rot.

To make earthen walls strong and durable, traditional techniques may be modified and modern materials substituted—water-repellent synthetic resins, for example, have proved very effective.

Doors and screens

In timber-framed buildings, doors, windows and screens seldom last long. Before undertaking restoration, it should be remembered that old door openings may have been walled over, or new doors inserted in old walls. Plank doors and hanging screens are often replaced by sliding doors or a wall. Old fittings are sometimes transferred to the rear part of a building, new ones replacing them in front. These changes should all be retraced. Missing plank doors can be put back on the old pivots or sockets, hanging screens on the hooks on the underside of the horizontal beams, and sliding screens on door tracks or the tracks left on columns or other parts of the house.

FLOORS

Earthen floors and paved floors

Earthen floors may be left unpaved, hardened with lime and sand, plastered, or paved with tiles and stones. Restoration should employ the traditional techniques. Broken tiles or stones are usually replaced; if no similar material is available, they may be consolidated with epoxy resin, blended with powdered material from the original fragments. Replicas may similarly be made if the stones are too fragmentary for repair. After the compound hardens, it can be finished with stonemason's tools.

Raised floors

Raised flooring allows good ventilation and prevents rot (Plate 32). In restoration, floor support posts, joists and the undersides of the floor boards are treated with fungicides and insecticides, the ground also being specially treated in termite areas.[1]

FOUNDATIONS

Podium or platform

The use of a podium or platform probably originated in China and is widespread in house construction in the Far East. The surface soil is removed, and successive layers of earth are compacted by pounding to make a solid platform. The outer edges of the platform are protected with stone walls, and a stair is provided. Rain-water dropping from the eaves runs off in the surrounding ditches. The tops of stones placed on the platform are flattened or tenoned to receive the house supports (posts). Pebbles or small broken fragments are placed in a circle under these stones and pounded; if the supports sink, the joints loosen and distortion of the building follows. Hence, if the podium is poorly built or the ground is too soft to provide a sound foundation, reinforcement with poured concrete becomes necessary. The lower ends of the house supports or posts should be treated with fungicides and insecticides.

'Tortoise belly', sills, direct embedding

Even when floors are raised and covered with boards, a podium-like foundation is sometimes made by building a low, flat mound of earth which is covered with plaster or encircled by a series of hewn stones, and also contains stones to support the

---

1. cf. 'Identification and Control of Insect Pests', *The Conservation of Cultural Property*, op. cit.

Plate 32

Floors of wooden buildings supported on piling.
(a) Wooden columns were based on crossed wooden supports. Site of the Heijokyu Palace, Nara (eighth century).
(b) Typical design and construction of wooden floor supports (floor boards removed).

32 a

32b

house posts. This sort of mound is called a 'tortoise belly' in Japan.

House posts may also be placed on the ground on a support or 'sill' of timber. The sill must be made of the most durable wood (cypress, Japanese cypress or chestnut) and thoroughly treated with fungicides and insecticides. Posts driven directly into the ground cannot last as long as those supported above ground, but can have their life span extended by similar treatment (e.g. application of creosote under pressure to the embedded parts).

PAINTING

External

Most Japanese houses, all of the ceremonial tea-houses and some of the shrine and temple buildings are left unpainted, relying for decoration on the grain of woods, natural materials and the results of fading.

Many of the shrines and temples, however, are painted in bright colours. The traditional paints are mixed with organic glue, which weathering disintegrates. Hence they gradually change colour and flake off. Paint and painted designs should be restored following strictly traditional methods. Synthetic resins help to preserve original paintings.

Lacquer work is typically oriental, but only in Japan are buildings lacquered all over. Lacquers do not resist ultra-violet rays and exterior lacquers do not last long. A section of the original lacquer film is examined microscopically; photographed in colour, this gives the original colour of the lacquer to be restored.

Wall and screen paintings

Mural paintings are sometimes executed directly on plastered earthen walls. They may also be painted on paper pasted to the wall.

Mural paintings may be preserved on earthen walls with synthetic resins: urea res-

ins for the wall itself, acrylic resins to prevent exfoliation of the paints. On wooden walls, they can be preserved by using soluble nylon in the space between the board and the painted surface, or by spreading it over the painting and pressing it with blotting paper. The surplus solution should be removed by a solvent in order to avoid a glossy sheen (synthetic resins which cannot be dissolved after drying must be avoided for this reason).[1]

Paintings on paper are usually mounted on a foundation composed of several layers of paper pasted together. They can be removed and repasted on to a new paper foundation. The work can be easily and beautifully done by a craftsman skilled in traditional paper-hanging techniques.

ROT, INSECT AND FIRE CONTROL

Wet and dry rot

Some bacteria, moulds and fungi only change the colour of the surface of wood or stain it, but saprogenous bacilli attack and destroy the cell-walls of timber. Generally speaking, bacteria grow at temperatures between 0° and 40°C, but they increase remarkably at 20°–30°C with a relative humidity of 80–100 per cent.

Wet rot occurs when there is sufficient moisture to allow the development of lignivorous bacteria and fungi. On the other hand, excessive moisture may save timber from decaying by depriving such organisms of oxygen. Wooden piles, for instance, if driven below the water line, may last for centuries.

The moisture content of wood in a building comes gradually into equilibrium with the surrounding atmosphere. In the main islands of Japan it is 14–15 per cent. Under 20 per cent, wood is not liable to attack, so that wooden buildings on the ground last

---

1. cf. 'The Conservation of Wall Paintings', *The Conservation of Cultural Property*, op.cit.

228

well, provided they are well maintained and the relative humidity is kept within reasonable limits by proper ventilation. When it rises to 70 per cent or more, the moisture content of the wood also rises, and the wood becomes subject to attack by fungi and moulds (dry rot). To prevent rot, timbers should be thoroughly dried before use. The timber's resistance to rot varies. Broad-leaved trees tend to be more durable than conifers.

Care should be taken at every stage. The first consideration should be construction that so far as possible eliminates the possibility of organisms growing which provoke rot; timber should be chosen accordingly and, when necessary, treated with antiseptics.

For this purpose, creosote oil and its emulsions used to be popular, but they tend to stain wood. During the past twenty years, PCP (Pentachlorophenol C_6Cl_5OH) and Na-PCP (Sodium pentachlorophenate C_6Cl_5-ONa), which are colourless, have been widely used. PCP is oleaginous, and is used in a 2–5 per cent solution of light oil or butanol. Na-PCP is water soluble and is used also in a 2–5 per cent solution. Since Na-PCP is not inflammable, it has been applied to the buildings of national importance in Japan. It is sometimes brushed on the surfaces and cut-ends of lumber are dipped in it. Timber treated only with Na-PCP cannot be exposed to rain because it is water soluble. A solution may be prepared by adding aluminium or copper sulphate, which will make it water-resistant. Na-PCP sinks 10 millimetres at the cut end and 0.5 millimetres on the sides of cypress lumber after three days of soaking. Hence it is preferable to have the lumber treated after it is shaped, cut or planed. As a rule PCP does not affect metals and paints, but its effect on art objects and paintings must be investigated before use.

Insect control

Termites are among the pests that are most destructive to structural timber. Dry-wood termites are less dangerous, but subterranean termites which nest in moist ground and attack timber by tunnelling from the ground into wooden buildings rapidly cause tremendous damage. Control measures may include lowering the moisture content of the soil by better drainage, creating chemical (persistant poisons) or physical (metal or concrete) barriers between the insects and the building, and by using termite-resistant or otherwise treated wood.

In the past, arsenic compounds were mainly employed. In the last twenty years, methyl bromide (CH_3Br) has been widely used to preserve historic buildings. It is liquid, and is kept in pressure vessel or bombs. It is applied by first sealing off the space occupied by insect-contaminated wood; filling the space with evaporated methyl bromide (200 grammes per cubic metre) for three hours will kill eggs, grubs and insects. The gas is poisonous, and, as it is non-odorous, should be handled by an expert. At times, a lachrymatory agent is added so that the user is warned of leakages. Vermicidal tanks in which insecticides are applied under low pressure provide an effective means of treatment. However, wood is always liable to renewed attack; it may be coated with a micro-crystalline wax incorporating an insecticide such as lauryl pentachlorophenate.

Fire precautions

The area surrounding an historic building should be designated and publicly posted as a restricted area where smoking and open fires are prohibited. Electric wiring should always be in good condition, with trip breakers to lessen the danger of short-circuits. Lightning conductors must be provided on or near the building.

Detection

The building should be equipped with automatic fire alarms and be regularly inspected

229

by firemen. Automatic fire detection units should be allocated inside and outside the building and especially under the eaves, in the roof frame and beneath the floor. An air-pipe fire detection system which reacts to rising temperatures is preferable to one which reacts to a set temperature. Staples fixing thin copper pipes to the ceilings, walls, roof frame and floor joists should also be of copper, since steel staples damage copper pipe through electrolytic action; otherwise the steel should be coated to prevent electrolysis.

The fire alarm system should be connected to the nearest fire station, or there should be a telephone in the premises with the number of the station prominently displayed. A siren to summon people in the neighbourhood is also desirable.

Fire extinguishing

If a fire is detected early, it may be possible to extinguish it with hand extinguishers. There are many types, and it is important to select those which will not damage cultural property, or spread fires by, for example, their effects on the electric wiring.

If hand extinguishers will not suffice, the fire must be sprayed with a machine pump working from a reservoir or a fire hydrant. If short-handed, the fire fighters can use sprinklers and drenchers.

If the fire shows signs of spreading, the help of professional and voluntary fire brigades must be enlisted.

Fire prevention systems should be planned and equipped by experts with due regard to size, topography, location and surroundings. Regular maintenance and inspection of the equipment is of course essential.

Ernest A. Connally

The conservation of sites and monuments in the New World

Monuments of impressive size and originality were built in North and South America before the coming of the Europeans. The Aztec, Maya and Inca civilizations had large ceremonial centres and planned urban development. The Incas had as highly centralized a form of government as any in the classical civilizations of the Old World.

In the Mississippi Valley and the valleys of its tributaries in what is now the United States of America, large earth mounds that are truncated, conical or made in the form of effigies were found. Most of these are preserved by national or state authorities. In the semi-arid zones of the south-west, Pueblo ruins and the large Hohokam structure known as Casa Grande are preserved by the Park Service.

Apart from pre-Columbian monuments, there are many monumental or historically important buildings, from early colonial times to the present. Early building styles and techniques naturally follow the traditions of the English, French, Spanish, Dutch or other countries of origin. In the course of time new elements were introduced, and eclectic designs, reflecting the interests of architects and clients from widely different periods and places. Their preservation demands research and documentation, and a knowledge of varied building techniques.

UNITED STATES OF AMERICA

Under the federal government, the states, provinces, municipalities and private owners have greater freedom of action than in many more centralized countries.

At the same time, standards and procedures equate to European, and the sheer amount of preservation makes it of international significance. Large historical parks such as Williamsburg in Virginia, and Sturbridge Village in Massachusetts, have had a widespread educational and cultural influence and this is partly responsible for the emphasis in the restoration of an historic building to its original form, for example, in a spirit of strict authenticity that marks a swing away from the grudging attitude prevalent during the late nineteenth century. This fidelity to historical accuracy is now a distinguishing characteristic in America.

By 1969, some 2,000 houses were preserved or had been restored as authentic period pieces, in addition to numerous churches and public buildings, and countless dwellings that are consciously preserved although remaining in normal use. These together represent a wide range in time, place, style, size and quality. They are preserved for one of two basic reasons: historical associations or artistic merit—in some happy instances for both, most notably Thomas Jefferson's *Monticello* in Virginia. Their interest and importance vary from parochial to national. Their owners and sustainers include private citizens, patriotic and preservation societies, churches and other institutions (including business corporations), municipal and state authorities and the federal government. In a few cases private and public agencies work in partnership.

Preservation originated in private initiative. Although some examples date from early in the nineteenth century, when the city of Philadelphia undertook to preserve Independence Hall (the old Pennsylvania State House, where the Declaration of Independence and the Constitution were framed), the first nation-wide movement started in 1853, when the Mount Vernon Ladies' Association was formed to purchase and preserve George Washington's home in Virginia. The nation's most revered historic shrine, Mount Vernon, is still owned and maintained by them.

Later, numerous associations of private individuals enlisted the interest, resources and special abilities of influential men. Many are now sufficiently organized and supported to function with professional competence, and some are able to maintain small staffs. They exist in and for many architecturally rich towns, e.g. Annapolis in Maryland, and Charleston in South Carolina or, on a regional basis, the effective Louisiana Landmarks Association, centred in New Orleans. Outstanding among the regional groups is the Society for the Preservation of New England Antiquities, which owns fifty-six properties, maintains a library and architectural museum, and publishes a quarterly that is noted for its scholarship. There is a tradition of the private gift or purchase of historic buildings for preservation. The most conspicuous philanthropy is the restoration of Williamsburg, Virginia, sponsored by the late John D. Rockefeller, Jr. The heart of the colonial capital has been restored as a historic park, comprising 130 acres with 500 eighteenth-century buildings. From the beginning, in 1927, to 1961, over U.S. $71 million has been spent in this work. American preservation is not exclusively preoccupied with the colonial and revolutionary past, however, and the full range of nineteenth-century architecture is increasingly represented. And just recently, a group of modern architects banded together to promote the preservation of epoch-making buildings by the late Frank Lloyd Wright.

The private effort gradually affected public policy, culminating in the establishment of the National Trust for Historic Preservation, chartered by Act of Congress. The maturity of the movement is also shown by its influence on state legislation relating to the large city-planning and urban-renewal projects undertaken since the Second World War. Beacon Hill, in Boston, and a large area of Providence, Rhode Island, have been declared archaeological districts, with the preservation of private buildings legally controlled as in continental Europe. Municipalities and state governments have long since been concerned with the preservation of important buildings; and in 1935 those historic buildings which had from time to time been acquired by the federal government were assigned to the custody of the National Park Service *(Plate 33)*, heretofore charged primarily with the preservation of natural sites. With historic preservation and increasing responsibility, the service now controls over 800 buildings, ranging from mountaineers' cabins and miners' shacks *(Plate 34)* to public edifices and stately mansions (including the White House), classified as national historic structures.

National legislation

The National Park Service was created in 1916 to promote and regulate the national parks and other designated federal areas in accordance with their 'fundamental purpose ... to conserve the scenery and the natural and historic objects and the wildlife therein and to provide for the enjoyment of the same ... by such means as will leave them unimpaired for the enjoyment of future generations'.

Under subsequent laws, the National Park Service has been given major responsibilities. The Historic Sites Act of 1935 establishes a 'national policy to preserve for public use historic sites, buildings, and objects of national significance for the inspiration and benefit of the people of the United States'. This Act authorizes the National Park Service to conduct surveys; secure and preserve drawings, photographs, and other data on historic buildings; enter into co-operative agreements with states, associations, or individuals; and to develop an educational programme of information concerning historic buildings.

In 1966 the National Historic Preservation Act was passed. Its notable features include: (a) an Advisory Council to advise the President and Congress on administrative and legislative measures to strengthen national programmes, and on issues involving federal constructions projects conflicting with preservation; (b) the expansion of the National Register to include state and local districts, sites, buildings and other objects which are significant in American history, architecture, archaeology and culture. It also allows for a budget to provide matching grants for the conservation of such cultural property. One of the most important provisions of the Act is that which makes provision for co-operation among the various departments. In the past, for example, it was not uncommon to have a scheduled area damaged or destroyed by highway construction. Recently (1969), through co-operative action made possible by the new machinery, the Secretary of Transportation decided against federal support of a proposed highway to cut through New Orleans which would have adversely affected the 'Vieux Carré', the old French quarter of the city. Instead, the government contributed 90 per cent of the costs required for re-routing the express highway around the city (ring-road or beltway).

Three principles are followed in the following order of priority: (a) preservation—the scrupulous retention of surviving work by ordinary maintenance and repair; (b) restoration—recovery of the old form by removing or replacing more recent work; (c) reconstruction—recapturing a form that once existed by means of an entirely new construction.

The criteria can be applied to parts of a building or to entire structures. Preservation is, of course, the most desirable and easiest to accomplish. Reconstruction is the most difficult and least desirable, although occasionally necessary in comprehensive schemes, such as Williamsburg. Restoration is frequently necessary because of the remodellings to which old buildings are peculiarly made subject, and it is usually difficult because of the scantiness or absence of proper records. As a result (especially among the small corps of professionals in the National Park Service), there has gradually been an accumulation of experience and sophisticated techniques to decide how restorations should be carried out, primarily from the internal evidence of buildings themselves, and always with the ideal of achieving the absolute authenticity specific to each case. An acknowledged national standard of physical accuracy has thus been developed. And as more and more structures are restored, each exactly as it was, we begin to have a corrected view of the past, with modified feelings and convictions about it. The insistence on this standard of historical truth for purely cultural and educational reasons is the most challenging, and perhaps ultimately, the most useful aspect of preservation in the United States.

CANADA

The British North America Act (1867) established the Dominion of Canada and instituted a federal form of government. Legislation on property rights was left to the provinces, and this has made the protection of important cultural property difficult. For many years the provinces which protect 'classified' buildings usually permitted classification with the consent of the proprietor. As a result, the federal, and most provincial governments have had to

33 a

33 b

33 c

Plate 33

The Archer House at Yorktown, Virginia, which was built *c.* 1815, containing many architectural features popular in the area some thirty years earlier.

(a) View of the building before restoration.

(b) Examination of deteriorated brick following removal of deteriorated siding. Note old and abandoned doorway to the left of the chimney.

(c) Interior view of the old door frame and restored window.

(d) Archer House restored. Air-conditioning equipment in the restored privy or outhouse. In many such projects fire-fighting equipment may also be kept in privies.

(Photos: United States National Park Service.)

purchase or establish agreements with the proprietors in order to ensure the protection of buildings. During the late nineteenth century, records of many old houses were privately made. A few municipalities also preserved historically important buildings, e.g. Montreal purchased the Chateau de Ramezay (the old Government House) which it then leased to the Antiquarian and Numismatic Society.

buildings and sites, particularly the right to classify or schedule buildings without the consent of the proprietor in order to ensure their protection. Many have established advisory committees with a view not only to establishing priorities and undertaking the restoration of individual buildings, but also to the zoning and protection of entire quarters.

33 d

Legislation

It was not until 1955 that the first federal legislation was introduced. Since then many of the provinces have also introduced legislation to ensure the preservation of historic

Programmes

The first important architectural programme under new legislation was begun by the Department of Northern (now Indian) Affairs in 1958 and 1959, with the restoration

235

of an eighteenth-century house in Quebec City and the reconstruction of two of the framed timber buildings of a British Columbia fur-trading post. Four years later the department started a long-term, $12 million project to rebuild a cross-section of the fortifications and buildings of the early eighteenth-century town of Louisbourg in Nova Scotia, including Chateau St. Louis, originally one of the largest and most elaborate buildings in North America. Sixteen new National Historic Parks and large sites acquired since 1955 include a large early Hudson's Bay Company warehouse on the shores of the bay, two lighthouses, and a turn-of-the-century theatre in the gold rush town of Dawson City, Yukon. Large buildings at several of the parks, some of them architecturally important, are being restored on a basis of structural analysis. The department has also contributed heavily to preserving and restoring nearly twenty other buildings across the country.

Another federal office involved since 1959 is the National Capital Commission, which has gradually acquired twenty-five buildings of architectural or historic value in the National Capital region (i.e. about 50 kilometres around Ottawa). More than half of them are in adjoining blocks in one of the original streets.

A pattern of co-operation has grown up between groups on different levels during the past fifteen years. As early as 1958, the federal government co-operated with the British Columbia Government to finance the restoration of Fort Langley. It also shared the costs of the Maillou House, Quebec City, with the local Chamber of Commerce, which now maintains the building. A 50 per cent contribution (the share has been set by Treasury Board regulation) to the capital costs of acquiring and restoring on condition that the partner or another body will look after maintenance—this has become Department of Indian Affairs practice in some twenty co-operative arrangements with a variety of agencies; the department

is entitled to satisfy itself regarding the quality of restorations, and the buildings must be given to the public.

The many other examples which exist have also contributed to the considerable improvement in standards of restoration in Canada.

MEXICO

Mexico has numerous sites and monuments of importance, from the end of the Pleistocene onwards. Many are monumental in quality and in size. In Teotihuacan, not far from Mexico City, a vast area approximately 5.5 kilometres long and 3 kilometres wide was occupied by a cluster of imposing buildings and pyramid structures built by the Toltecs. The whole area had been paved with plaster many times. The Pyramid of the Sun, the largest, is nearly 230 metres wide at its base and rises in four terraces to a height of nearly 70 metres. Elsewhere in Mexico, Totonac, Mixtec, Olmec, Mayan and other civilizations have left monumental records of their past. The Instituto Nacional de Antropología y Historia (INAH) has national responsibility for research; for the preservation of the major sites; and for early colonial monuments. Later monuments come under the jurisdiction of the Dirección General de Bellas Artes.

Legislation

The first law for the conservation of pre-Hispanic monuments was passed in 1875. In 1896 and 1897, legislation provided for the protection of the cultural heritage, including monuments of the colonial and post-colonial period. The 1934 law is much more explicit than its predecessors. Federal laws apply to the federal district and to scheduled national monuments; some of the states or provinces have also promulgated protection laws.

Plate 34

Early industrial development. Many countries now preserve early examples of industrial development.

(a) Remains of an eighteenth century iron furnace in Hopewell, Pennsylvania. At the right note the framing for a long-missing moulding shed.

(b) Reconstructed iron-furnace complex. In the rear are the furnace and bridge house, in the foreground the reconstructed moulding shed.

34a

b

Training

Mexico requires a lot of trained staff because of the varied nature and large number of its sites and monuments. The INAH employs architect-restorers, many of whom receive training abroad. With Unesco aid, a training laboratory has been established in Churubusco, a suburb of Mexico City. Unesco has provided international lecturers on various subjects (preservation of mural paintings, of objects made of wood, stone, metal, and so on). The laboratory accepts students from other Latin American countries.

The federal district authorities are running a programme of direct aid with legal measures to control development, in order to preserve the heart of the city and safeguard its quality and socio-economic role.

PERU

Peru has had national legislation to protect its archaeological heritage since 1929. New legislation was prepared in 1969. Pre-Hispanic monuments are administered by the National Archaeology Association, while colonial monuments come under the Council for the Conservation and Restoration of Artistic and Historic Monuments.

The Inca civilization has no peer in the New World except in Mexico. Along the coast and in the highland areas many civilizations developed. The largest structure found along the coast, the Mochican monument known as the 'Huaca del Sol', consists of a terraced pyramid, the base of which measures 228 by 136 metres, composed of a solid mass of rectangular adobe (earthen) bricks built in a series of high and thick juxtaposed walls and columns. Chan-Chan, another important site, is a city built during the late Chimu period, covering approximately 18 square kilometres and consisting of at least ten large walled units.

When the Spaniards came, Inca civilization was in full development. The empire included what is today southern Ecuador, Peru, and parts of Bolivia and Chile. The most important Inca sites are centred about Cuzco, the ancient capital of the empire. Sacsahuaman, the fortified retreat of the Inca Emperor, was part of the site of Upper Cuzco extending over the plains and dominating the city. It has been carefully excavated and measures have been taken to ensure its conservation. Nearby is the spectacular site of Machu Picchu, located on a high ridge overlooking the Urubamba River.

The Cuzco-Machu Picchu zone is now to be developed as a tourist attraction which will justify the budget required for the conservation of the Inca monuments. In colonial times, it was an administrative centre, and many monuments of importance date from this period. The government is planning a major project for Cuzco, involving urban development, the renovation of the historically important quarters, and the restoration of some of the buildings such as the Palacio des Almirantes, the Casa de los Cuatro Bustos, and so on, which have deteriorated badly. When the work is finally complete, the city will be adequately preserved, and will offer a vivid display to the people of Peru and to foreign visitors.

BRAZIL

Practically all monuments of importance in Brazil are of European inspiration. The Constitution enables classified cultural property to be protected by the federal government; the appropriate department classifies immovable cultural property and maintains records, and details of conservation, repairs or restoration.

Legislation

Under existing legislation, private owners of mobile or immovable cultural property deemed to be of exceptional value are notified that the property is to be classified, and that classification will exclude destruction, mutilation or interference without prior approval. However, the owner may submit, within a fortnight of the receipt of the official notice, a formal protest stating his grounds for opposing the administrative measure. This is heard by a council composed of ten experts and the directors of Brazil's museums of art and history. If the owner's claims are considered groundless, classification takes place compulsorily; he may however appeal to the President of the Republic.

Principles

1. The original elements and features of monuments should be maintained or restored.
2. The setting of monuments should be safeguarded by preventing the erection of unsuitable new buildings or the destruction of others which would alter the setting.
3. The use of modern materials should be limited to those necessary for essential repairs.

The mostly tropical climate is a major source of conservation problems in Brazil. Most historic buildings derive from Portuguese architecture, adapted to local conditions. There is little influence from aboriginal cultures since, by and large, the Indians of Brazil were hunters and gatherers, or at the most practised horticulture. Churches, chapels, convents and some military and civilian architecture form the bulk, most early monuments (from the seventeenth century) being found in cities and rural areas in Bahia and Pernambuco and in the highlands of São Paulo. However, the great majority of buildings date from the eighteenth century, the period of expansion during the colonial era. A number of small historic cities are being preserved as entities.

Ouro Preto

The city of Ouro Preto was the former capital of the State of Minas Gerais. It is laid out on a steep hillside and bears the mark of its history, a period of wealth when the gold mines were first discovered, a period of rapid development and a century and a half of administrative power. Its progressive decline, loss of status and general impoverishment has led, paradoxically, to the preservation of its many fine churches and public buildings. It was classified as a national monument in 1933, and since then various programmes have been adopted to ensure its preservation.

Until recently a national highway traversed the old city, and the constant procession of heavy lorries has endangered the old structures. A ring road has been built to permit traffic to by-pass the city.

Many of the churches were designed and decorated by Aleijadihno, the outstanding Baroque sculptor of Brazil. Today Ouro Preto is gradually becoming an important tourist centre. It has, incidentally, provided a good training ground for conservation specialists in the government service.

San Salvador de Bahia

Salvador is the capital of Bahia. Its economic development was based on the export of sugar and the import of slaves from Africa. By the end of the eighteenth century 100 churches graced the city (Plate 35); official buildings and the homes of the wealthy produced a city of baroque magnificence. A period of decline followed. With the recent discovery of off-shore oil and the building of refineries, the historic city has experienced a sudden prosperity—with a simultaneous threat to its historic quarters. During the period of economic decline many of the older buildings had suffered and have since been replaced with modern structures. However, there are now plans to save the central quarter, the Pelourinho, and others such as Soledade (Plate 36).

As in many other cities, the preservation of the historically and artistically interesting quarters of San Salvador involved social and economic problems; multiple ownership due

Plate 35

Brazil. The Church of St. Francis was built
during the early eighteenth century in typical
Brazilian Baroque style. Ecclesiastical structures
of this type and those built during the following
century throughout Latin America derive from
contemporary Baroque in the Iberian Peninsula.
(Photo: *Unesco Courier*, June 1968.)

Plate 36

A historic quarter in the city of San Salvador de
Bahia, covered in a Government of Brazil
restoration project which has social, cultural
and economic aspects.
(Photo: *Unesco Courier*, June 1968.)

to inheritance patterns, and social and economic ways of life which may have to be modified if the quarter is to be renovated, adding to the complications. It is anticipated, however, that part of the budget required for the improvement of the old quarters will be met through increased tourist revenue.

The government has similar projects to protect old squares and streets lined with historic buildings in cities such as Rio de Janeiro, and smaller towns such as Vassouras.

GENERAL

Unlike Europe and Asia, a sharp division exists in the countries of the New World between the cultures which developed locally, and those which followed the arrival and progressive penetration of Europeans from the sixteenth to the nineteenth century. All are vividly aware of their responsibility for preserving this heritage.

The ecclesiastical and official buildings of the colonial periods in Latin America were largely based on baroque designs derived from Spain and Portugal. To the north, however, other influences prevailed, and the difference is fairly marked. In the early history of the United States and during its colonial period, great forests yielded first-class timber in quantity and inexpensively. Much preservation is perforce devoted to the conservation of wooden buildings. Structures in brick and stone are to be found, but in much smaller proportions than, for example, in Europe.

In many cases in Latin America, the documentation on religious structures is in archives in Europe. The plans and cost estimates of official buildings sent back home also furnish data. Such documentation usually needs to be verified, as there may be considerable differences between official plans and actual buildings. Furthermore, brick sizes, types of nails, details of carpentry work, and so on, were usually not recorded, and excavation, or detailed analysis of parts of buildings under repair, are necessary. Domestic architecture, and early buildings dating from access to political independence in many of the American states, may have had few or no records. Thus, for example, the restoration of the Saugus Iron Works in Massachusetts was based on research which revealed the size of the operations, the techniques employed, the tools used, and so on, during the eighteenth and early nineteenth centuries. Needless to say, the restoration of indigenous (pre-Columbian) monuments calls for a good deal of archaeological excavation.

In view of the many common problems, various regional programmes are planned, e.g. the Andean Route project, involving Bolivia, Chile, Colombia, Ecuador and Peru. These countries plan to carry out a programme for the conservation and development of their sites and monuments (pre-Columbian and colonial); to establish common standards; and to develop a regional cultural tourist industry. On a larger scale, the Organization of American States has launched a series of conferences to bring leading experts from the different countries of the Western hemisphere together to review progress and discuss principles and techniques. Many countries have national committees of the International Council of Monuments and Sites which allow them opportunities to take part in international meetings and take advantage of the Unesco programme.

Interest is thus being developed rapidly, and standards among the various countries concerned are constantly rising.

BIBLIOGRAPHY

ANON. *Recording and preservation of buildings of architectural or historic value in Canada*. Ottawa, Department of Indian Affairs and Northern Development, National and Historic Parks Branch, 1967.

GURMENDI, Victor P. La Restauración de monumentos en el Perú. *The preservation of monuments*. Washington, D.C., OAS Cultural Relations Division, 1966.

MARINI, Carlos F. La restauración de monumentos coloniales en México. *The preservation of monuments*. Washington, D.C., OAS Cultural Relations Division, 1966.

MEDALLIN, Jorge L. *The preservation of the historic monuments of Mexico City*. Paper presented at a conference given in the Museum of the City of Mexico, 1967.

PARENT, M. *Brésil, protection et mise en valeur du patrimoine culturel dans le cadre du développement touristique et économique*. Unesco, Paris, 1968.

SANTISTEBAN, Fernando S. Problems of the conservation and restoration of historic monuments in Peru. *The preservation of monuments*. Washington, D.C., OAS Cultural Relations Division, 1967.

SOEIRO, Renato. Conservation of historic monuments in Brazil. *The preservation of monuments*. Washington, D.C., OAS Cultural Relations Division, 1967.

The conservation and restoration of historic quarters and cities

It is not uncommon in many communities to see a well-preserved or carefully restored monument which has lost all of its historical associations and perspective because of the modern structures which surround it. The proper safeguarding of a monument and its surroundings involves problems that are complex because they likewise affect the social and economic life of the community.

For some time now, the design of buildings has been based on using mass-produced elements, accepting the advantages and disadvantages of mechanization. The result is that modern neighbourhoods tend to look alike. Urban growth and urban renewal patterns which destroy and replace older areas with contemporary buildings are gradually removing from the townscape much of its individuality. Insufficient attention is being paid to the import of these replacements which have erased entire chapters of history.

The destruction of old quarters is not inevitable. Rather is it the result of widespread ignorance and indifference, common even in educated circles, so far as the city and its architecture are concerned. The cultural significance of this problem must be made clear. A city is not something static. It is a focal point of life, and life in a sense which exceeds the span of individual existence. It is a manifestation of human activities which resists time. A city absorbs the technological achievements which give it life, and little by little there appear road networks, sea and river ports, railways, air-ports. But these, too, undergo changes (e.g. the vanishing tramways) and are therefore conditioned by the city.

These aspects, striking but transient, make up a city precisely because of the continuity of culture it offers to its inhabitants. The uncontrolled destruction of historical buildings and their associations has resulted from economic considerations which have overridden less tangible needs, and prevails where the basis of critical judgement is largely utilitarian. Every town now wants to become a metropolis or be absorbed by a neighbouring city. Each is all too ready to turn its back on the past, believing that in the city, economic, social, educational and cultural opportunities are richer. But in the process it exchanges its certitudes for a none too certain future.

Of whatever size, each town has a personality of its own, to lose which is always an impoverishment.

Historical awareness is always essential to us. The same is true of cities. If the authorities in Boston, Rome, London, Warsaw or Venice lacked this perception, they would be unfit to govern their cities. With time, cities, towns, and even villages assume a character which reflects their history and is often the explanation of their survival. Their past can be read from the form they have taken, the way streets and squares are laid out, their shape and size, their place in the natural landscape, their position in relation to rivers, to coastal outlines, and so on.

What is said here in a few words is

the subject of whole disciplines, from archaeology to town planning, from sociology to civil and political history. There is a legal background to every urban form that sometimes even affects the form of the landscape, and it offers rich ground for anyone interested in studying the shaping of cities. It behoves us, in most cases, not to destroy or alter the character of places and cities. This is a duty we owe to ourselves, for here, as in a common language, we find the old as well as the more recent bonds of custom, and the explanation of the personalities of our cities. If we compare our human personalities with those of certain places, we can immediately see the parallel. The destruction of one jeopardizes the other. It is not easy, or necessary here, to decide which features are the most important. What matters is that in the examination of a particular case, the general criteria set forth here shall be given due consideration.

On what main elements should our appreciation be based? There are various kinds, valid even in isolation, and even more so in combination. First, there is the age of a city. The further it dates back, the more interest it has for us today. Then its form—the grouping of its buildings, streets and squares, rivers and bridges, sea coasts and ports; the events which have marked its history, making of it a powerfully evocative pageant that is still relevant to our lives; the traditions attaching to squares, streets and palaces, the accumulation of works and records piling up over the years; the beauty of individual buildings, great or small. Many forms of life connected with the old city are still alive and in a sense contemporary. They stem from traditions and mark a culture—associations with places, civic buildings, libraries, theatres, art galleries, meeting rooms, palaces, places of worship, universities, all are connected with activities that need a setting in which to develop—it is for this basically associative reason that cities come into being. It is our duty to see that these places are preserved, not necessarily unchanged, but time should move more slowly there than in purely commercial areas.

Except in such exceptional cases as Brasilia or Chandigar, cities develop slowly, period by period. Apart from fortified cities like Constantinople, whose walls, rivers or other natural barriers are real boundaries, traces of the change from one period to another usually remain. Of course, what stands or stood outside city boundaries may also be of historical interest—outside the confines of Treviso, Barcelona or Baghdad for example, which have been variously traced at different periods. But for practical purposes we must draw the line at something that can be clearly, though not too strictly, located and defined. It may be difficult to locate the old centre of a city exactly, but it is easy to find a number of areas which should then be protected and preserved.

The limits of such areas should be officially defined; they need not coincide with streets, but should go through blocks of buildings if necessary, to avoid such anomalies as having opposite sides of a street coming under different regulations (*Plate 36*).

CO-ORDINATION AND TOWN PLANNING

At the identification stage, liaison should be maintained with town-planning authorities. In most countries responsibility for the protection of monuments and for town planning is divided between the ministry of education and the ministry of public works; in the case of old cities, however (and landscapes which, unfortunately, are rarely protected by legislation), close collaboration between all concerned and unanimity of approach are essential. Cities cannot really be regarded in isolation from their surroundings. Nothing is less static than an urban fringe, even at a fair distance from the city; the expanding city gradually encroaches on the landscape and transforms it into an urban area. Planning should aim at preserving both city and landscape.

When old buildings are occupied, the relations between town planning and conservation are complex. It is difficult to work out a plan for the preservation, let alone the restoration, of the oldest part of a city by the usual town-planning methods. The area may have a misleadingly squalid appearance, defaced by changes occurring during its use over the centuries. The services of an experienced architect-restorer, well acquainted with administrative procedures and the law, are necessary if regrettable demolitions are to be avoided. The poor state of repair of individual buildings or of a built-up area should never be allowed to justify hasty changes—it is precisely in such cases that recovery can often be most successful and effective.

Before a decision is taken to preserve, preliminary research is necessary. But it must stop at a certain point, either on the score of time or because it cannot, by definition, become practically operational. Hence the need to have documentation on the history and the present condition of the area available that is as complete as possible. This means changing over to more flexible planning procedures which would allow the administrators to deal with exceptional cases on their merits. Plans should not be hard and fast (which would make them cumbersome, inoperative and possibly injurious), but amenable to modification if necessary, even after having been officially adopted. Plans should be made for four, five or ten years at the most, so that they can be kept up to date and employed more effectively. This entails having administrators who will direct them with insight and authority, an adequate budget, and a professional staff aware of new developments, of independent judgement, legally well informed, who can take decisions without having to base them on second- or third-hand opinions, as often happens. Some such solution is urgently needed in densely populated countries, and even in countries which are large but have expanding populations, and are relying on recent solutions to contemporary town and landscape problems.

SCHEDULING

Towns can be grouped into three main categories.

First, there are those whose role has changed as a result of political or commercial decay: abandoned or largely destroyed cities and those which, after an illustrious past, live a different, more humble life. The past of these cities is perpetuated by their monuments. They may even live largely on tourists—Venice, Nara and Bourges are famous examples. Single buildings or groups can similarly be turned to account (cf. the Acropolis in Athens).

Second, there are towns which have never decayed or been abandoned, which are as alive and active as ever, having passed through the successive phases of a way of life that has developed but continued over the centuries and sometimes over thousands of years. These are the cities which need some protection against unthinking renovation, levelling for building purposes, encroachment on squares, gardens and outlying green belts, degradation of buildings, and so on. The old centre or other notable centres should be delimited or zoned. Zones should be based not on their relative richness in monumental buildings but on the homogeneity of particular groups of blocks and streets. It is not only the presence of buildings of great historical or architectural interest which counts, but the homogeneous character of an area, even though consisting in the main of minor buildings and private houses.

Third, there are young cities with only a recent history. The concept of conservation applies now to towns less than 100 years old, where there is no really old centre, but there may be individual buildings or small homogeneous groups of buildings of architectural interest. These, too, deserve protection. Chicago, for instance, protects buildings by Sullivan and Wright that date from the end of the nineteenth century.

LEGISLATION

So far we have been speaking of precautionary measures and the more or less passive defence of the urban and natural landscape. Such measures can be made mandatory, and can then be used to suspend any change for some time. This may be necessary to preserve certain buildings (and even these may have to install electricity, lifts, central heating, and so on). But the approach to conservation should be dynamic, not negative and static; no one holds a brief for immobility in conservation.

Legislation must be extremely practical if it is to be able to cope with the economic problems. It varies greatly from one country to another. Financially, buildings generally must be turned to the best account; comfort and appearance must also be considered. Regulations should aim at simplifying procedures, and not complicating them with red tape; they should be constructive, with as little coercion or, still worse, punitive action, as possible—the rigours of the law being reserved for recognizably serious abuses. Inexpensive loans and tax concessions clearly offer one of the best solutions. There should be uniform scheduling procedures, and due recognition if an extra burden is borne by owners of buildings which enhance a city.

If entire blocks are to be conserved, it could take a very long time if all owners have to be given formal notice separately. Moreover, the account is not on individual buildings, but the group as a whole. If feasible, collective notice can be given by the appropriate authority. Once notice is given, the owner or responsible agency is, as a rule, obliged to submit the plans to the competent authority for prior approval. The object should be to regulate, not to prevent, the execution of works that will ensure the conservation and use of the building. Prior notification may lower rent or sale values, but this may be counterbalanced by tax concessions. In due course, moreover, the value of the property should rise. The restoration of a block may be opposed by one or more of the owners. However, many relatively small towns of great architectural and historical interest have been scheduled in their entirety. Parks and gardens can of course be included when notice is given. Border zones have to be observed around buildings or sites of particular interest when their protection is in one way or another necessary to that of adjacent buildings or sites.

If they are to be effective, regulations must be simple, readily understood, justified by the facts and they must meet a real need.

SOCIOLOGICAL ELEMENTS

A thorough analysis, leading to a better understanding of the life of an area or city, provides a good basis for a dynamic conservation policy. One of the worst dangers to old cities is that of having a way of life forced on them for which they are totally unfit. As a practical result of conservation, accordingly, a type of life should be reintroduced in keeping with the local environment.

In many old cities, the ground floor overlooking the street was not always residential. In the Mediterranean area homes opened on to gardens or inner courtyards, and people lived on the upper floors. This has changed and, for various reasons, the now residential ground floors of many of these buildings have become dark and unhealthy. Their original accessory purpose must be restored, or they can be made available for small businesses or workshops. If these grow into large commercial concerns, they should be transferred elsewhere, since they consort ill with private houses, and the streets of an old city are seldom fitted to cope with heavy traffic and parked vehicles.

SCHEDULING AND REGISTRATION

The occupations that can be retained in the different parts of an old city must be based upon the scheduling of individual buildings.

The index cards used in scheduling should be designed to include all the relevant details (e.g. see Fig. 1): a photograph, street and number, type of building (residential, commercial, administrative, workshop, etc.), electricity, bathrooms, water supply, lifts, stairs, general state of repair, original elements, disfiguring additions, stability of building, number of occupants, their occupations, rent and estimated fluctuations, if any, as a result of scheduling, and so on.

The card should be easy to consult. The data on all cards should be comparable, so that plans can be drafted for the different floors of buildings, block by block, in addition to surveys of their street frontage, important parts of the interiors, courtyards and gardens, and any other data which will make up the architectural register.

Making up a survey from general location plans is a laborious task, but essential, because on it subsequent projects for restoration and conservation will be based. A scale of at least 1:100 should be used. The sheets should not be too large. For a street front of 100 metres it is customary to have a plan 1 metre wide. Transparent copies should be made of the different floor levels, and care should be taken to ensure that plans can be superimposed for immediate comparison.

Many attempts have been made to standardize hatching and other conventional signs for such items as original and added structures, utilization of premises, nature of materials, and so on, but so far without success. However, the signs can easily be explained in tabular form on the plan, and varied as required without detriment to the lucidity of the plans. It is only in the same set of plans, or research, that it is important to standardize the signs used to represent ground plans or elevations.

Much use has been made of colour for the identification of types and zones, and it is convenient for rapid consultation. However, colour is hard to reproduce in ordinary copies, unless topographical systems are employed (as they are for town-planning schemes); it is preferable to use a system of lines or squares on drawings or tracing paper from which further copies can then be obtained.

In addition to the schedule and the general location plans of the buildings in individual blocks, complete photographic documentation is required to record the appearance of all the buildings, inside and outside. Aerial photographs, too, are useful. Reduced to the same scale as the drawings, they can be used for comparison and for ascertaining particulars such as the form and nature of roofs (sometimes difficult to discern otherwise). Photographs are usually black and white, but now colour is feasible (slides or prints), though the cost is still high.

A recent development is architectural photogrammetry, by which exact measures can be taken of a building by the use of photographs (see Chapter 5). Measured drawings (scale drawings based on actual measurements) provide the more traditional means of recording historical monuments. They must be carefully done to show proportions and, beside the exterior façade, include floor plans, interior architectural features, cross-sections, and so on, with notes on colours, materials, and other pertinent information.

DEVELOPMENT PROGRAMMES

When these studies are complete, an analysis can be made and a programme established for the development of the area, whether it be a single block or a vast network of blocks and streets. The adequacy of the road network must be assessed in relation to the traffic and the parking requirements. Parking facilities must be provided both for residents and for those who work in the quarter, but

249

should not adversely affect the building or area to be conserved. Hence the argument for controlling the nature and purpose of the quarter (residential, commercial, artisan, tourist, recreation, etc.) so as to keep traffic within the limits imposed by the capacities of streets and squares. By-passes should be encouraged, so that motorists need not traverse the quarter, especially if it has narrow or crooked streets, as is often the case. Underground car parks may be considered if they can be suitably sited and do not encroach on unexplored ground that may be of archeological interest (sometimes, indeed, their construction may open up opportunities for archaeological research). Frequently they can be built unobtrusively beneath public gardens or parks. Consideration should be given to the possibility of arranging pedestrian passages through blocks, either to facilitate circulation or to allow for arcaded shopping centres.

In individual blocks, the main concern should be to demolish successive accretions in courtyards and gardens. The narrowness of the streets in old centres very often contrasts with the size of courtyards and gardens. The additions, sometimes quite large, often permanently deteriorate the main building. Clearing the spaces inside blocks has proved the best solution. The losses and gains must of course be accurately estimated before demolition, due account being taken of the recovery and rejuvenation of valuable buildings. As the individual buildings are renovated and regain their aesthetic and historic values, so do their surroundings; footpaths, small squares and gardens for the pleasure and convenience of the passer-by may impart an even greater vitality than the quarter had originally.

Sometimes what are really workmen's houses can be of exceptional documentary and aesthetic interest, even if built of clay or other cheap materials and primitive techniques. Once these houses have been renovated—the stability of a wall, a balcony or a roof ensured—no structural alterations should be introduced which might affect the general appearance of the streets or individual buildings. This holds good even at street level. Valuable features such as ornamental string-course and stone inlays should be conserved. Today there is a regrettable readiness to spread asphalt over such features, hiding, impairing or destroying them.

The removal of unsuitable businesses needs prior arrangement as part of a general town-planning scheme. On the other hand, others regarded as suitable should be attracted or encouraged to stay, since the rejuvenation of the quarter depends to some extent on their presence. They should be selected mainly according to the nature of the quarter, without prejudice to its basic purpose, which is residential.

There is sometimes a temptation to try to resurrect the past and embroider on typical local themes. This is a danger to be avoided—even harmless imitation, if conservation is to serve its purpose. An unsound building may have to be demolished and the gap may have to be filled in order to complete a square or a group. Should the new building copy the old? It is generally held that something in the same style will not disturb the harmony, but the opposite may also be true; and a building in contemporary style can be more acceptable if the architect ensures that the materials and volumes tone in with the surroundings.

STANDARDS

What standards, whether compulsory or not, should be observed in restoration or conservation? The standards referred to early in this chapter are those which are in honour binding on the restorer. Each period, each style has had its own methods, but the results have not always been happy. The present more critical approach to restoration may beguile us into thinking that an optimum has been reached, but this may well prove fallacious. It is easy to cast doubt on the validity of norms which are merely recommendations, leaving the restorer free to contest the underlying principles. Yet these norms are of value precisely because they embody statements of principle and are not mandatory. Today the efficacy of norms in general is called in question—and particularly building and health regulations that are out of date before they are issued, mainly because arbitrary formal and technological hypotheses tend to be incorporated in administrative measures, and coercion is often applied by short-sighted bureaucrats.

If architecture is an art, any restriction on architects is absurd; it is like prescribing a style, materials and dimensions for painters and sculptors. If architecture is not an art, a mandatory norm is still dangerous when it consists of rules which bureaucrats regard as inviolable. Yet we cannot do away with all building regulations. They have an ancient lineage, although it is only in recent times that they have become so detailed that the builder has no choice but to base the style and dimensions of his building upon blind observance of them.

This problem of norms obviously looms large in town development and conservation. In relation to old centres it needs to be entirely reviewed; the norms should be limited to general principles which do not impose restrictions as to dimensions and style on these restorers who have a long experience of this type of work. The restoration of an area is a matter of synthesis, and more than the restoration of each of its buildings individually. Any regulations enforced must have this synthesis in view, and should take the form of general principles that do not restrict freedom of action and of choice. Results will be best if there is full confidence in the restorer and in his professional knowledge, experience and conscience. When a building site becomes vacant in an old area, it is possible: (a) to leave the site vacant for public or private use; (b) to take advantage of it in order to extend an existing building; (c) to use it for the reconstruction of a former building whose basic elements remain; and (d) to use it for a new building.

The insertion of a contemporary building in an old setting may be permissible. In each case dimensional and technological norms must be observed, so that the new building, while not imitating its neighbours, at least harmonizes with them. The aesthetic quality of the new structure is the essential consideration. This principle has always obtained and, irrespective of the merits of individual buildings, has proved the best means of avoiding irreconcilable contrasts.

It may be all right to leave the site empty if it harmonizes with the rest and does not create a gap, reveal ugly aspects of adjacent buildings or upset the general balance.

It is also possible to join a new building to an existing one; it may differ in style, or even in materials, as long as dimensions and volumes are respected.

Reconstructing from architectural remains is a difficult and delicate operation, to be attempted only with remains which are of outstanding interest or importance.

Piero Gazzola

Training architect-restorers 12

The current confusion and uncertainty all over the world regarding university education makes it particularly difficult to survey trends in the teaching of the historical disciplines in faculties of architecture.

Originally, the training of architects consisted mainly in learning how to make architectural drawings. It was not until later, in 'schools', that the study of the history or architecture was added to the syllabus—at the beginning of the Renaissance, when the history of the architecture of the past began to be considered as a subject for study. In addition to studying architectural drawing, architects from all over Italy and, above all those from Florence, began to make detailed examinations of classical edifices revealed by the excavations being carried out in Rome. Another, quite different source of information was provided by notebooks from the Middle Ages, containing details of the dimensions of classical buildings but characterized by the empirical mediaeval approach that offered so marked a contrast to the methodical, scientific research of the early Renaissance surveys.

From the seventeenth century onwards, with the progress in printing methods and the development of the art of engraving, architectural surveys, or the graphic representation of monuments, became more realistic and more conventional: instead of being merely factual notes, they became elaborate drawings.

The craze for the excavation of ancient monuments during the first half of the eighteenth century, and the subsequent analysis of classical monuments gave rise to two different schools: the romantic-naturalist school, which found its champion in Goethe and later developed into analytical positivism; and the classical, historical school represented by the work of Winkelmann and Milizia. Those of the first school, interested in nature mainly as the environment of man, concentrated on the prehistorical and mediaeval epochs, and regarded monuments as a part of the environment, important for their emotional and picturesque element rather than their artistic value. The classical school, on the contrary, was concerned mainly with the acquisition of knowledge and with the study of Greek and Roman architecture: its most mature and striking productions are to be found among the monumental works of Canina.

With the development of engineering and historiographical studies, the contrast between classical and romantic became less acute; eventually the clash between romanticism and classicism, intuition and logic produced the eclectic style of architecture characteristic of the second half of the nineteenth century. But whether the architecture was neo-classical or historico-eclectic, surveying combined with archaeology was a vital element in training. With the introduction of draughtsmanship, axonometry, perspective and the theory of shadow, architectural drawing also developed.

At the same time, the 'individualist' approach to monuments, the tendency to abstract them from their surroundings and concentrate on theoretical research and restoration, culminating in the work of Viollet-le-Duc, affected architectural research during the first decades of the twentieth century.

The final general acceptance of modern schools of architecture as part of the university system occurred between the end of the nineteenth and the early part of the twentieth century.

SYLLABUS

The syllabus of architectural studies has always represented an uneasy compromise between what might be called the fine-arts approach and the polytechnical approach, although neither has ever disputed the importance of studying the history of architecture, or of having a knowledge of the past as the best basis on which to build the future.

From 1920 onwards, nevertheless, the first doubts about the validity of architectural surveys began to be expressed. By 1938, students were finding the subject irksome, questioning its educational value, and regarding it solely as part of the background to the restoration of monuments, and nothing more. In the architectural faculty in Rome, it was dropped from the syllabus in 1935 and reinstated only in 1949. At the same time, there were proposals to include surveying in the architectural restoration course—an implicit recognition of its importance for restoration work.

Early in the twentieth century, independently minded architects began to assert their right to originality, challenging the validity of historical research which, they contended, stifled creative activity. This marked the beginning of the reaction against the imitation of historical styles; eclecticism was discredited, and the need to keep architectural designing and historical research apart proclaimed. The schools were, however, slow to follow, even in cases where *avant-garde* elements were most vociferous; and it was not until the first decades of the twentieth century that the teaching ceased to be based on a slavish imitation of historical styles.

Nevertheless, the two elements, artistic and technical, continued to be kept artificially apart and regarded as separate factors, regardless of the fact that the two combine to form an architectural unit. Hence the critical attitude that tends to belittle contemporary trends, going only so far as to record them as facts of modern development. This accounts for the stand taken by the founders of modern architecture, Gropius and Le Corbusier, who denied the importance of the history of architecture and art criticism and set out, with the assistance of the politicians, to make creative activity part and parcel of everyday life.

This attempt to reject the culture of the past and build a new culture, though frequently successful as regards individual creative activity, takes no account of the kind of historical perspective that can see every new development as a link in the unbroken chain extending from the past to the future. But since the importance of history cannot be dismissed completely, there has developed a school of historiography, concentrating solely on the phenomena of the past fifty years; and this, constituting the only source of inspiration, has produced a new type of eclecticism, based on imitation rather than original inspiration and no less stultifying, artistically, than the eclecticism of the nineteenth century.

The rejection of the past, combined with the relaxation of standards due to the new wave of eclecticism, has had disastrous results for the conservation of monuments and sites, and more especially as regards what has replaced buildings that have been demolished in towns.

NEW IDEAS ABOUT CONSERVATION

In the nineteenth century there were two main schools of thought on the subject of conservation. The English was an offshoot of the romantic movement, and embodied sociological and moralistic conceptions. Ruskin was the main influence on the school which turned from industrial civilization to take refuge in archaeology in the narrowest sense but eventually produced the great English and German archaeologists.

France and Italy, on the contrary, on the basis of the research carried out by Viollet-le-Duc, which extended the study of the classical and mediaeval world, treated ancient monuments as something divorced from their environment, worthy of conservation for their intrinsic artistic value. This was responsible for the urban reconstruction of a kind that has done so much damage to the structure of our ancient cities, such as—to quote the supreme example—Haussmann's reconstruction of Paris.

From these two schools developed two different theories of restoration: the archaeological theory, scientifically based on analysis and philological research; and the interpretative theory, based on a subjective artistic approach and frequently involving the construction of additional parts.

Architects took no part in this cultural dispute, feeling that restoration was being taken over increasingly by specialists. They therefore left it to the art historians, the critics, the archaeologists and the architect-restorers to decide whether and how monuments should be restored.

From 1930 onwards, a new emphasis on architecture as a whole and on the relation between monuments and domestic building led the specialists to take a wider view of conservation, which now became a part of town planning, with the general idea of enhancing the whole environment. This inevitably entailed a new recognition of the importance of historical research. However, when this was limited to a perfunctory study of a limited period, i.e. examples of recent building, it led, for example, to a revival of the ornamental details of the Liberty style, used purely formally in a mistaken attempt at modernization. None of these developments could be said to amount to the founding of a new school. The return to history is necessary when it corresponds to a deeply felt creative need to apply the values of the past, but not when it is made only for purposes of form and convenience.

The idea that the study of history has a direct formative value is now coming into its own again. The history of architecture should be treated not as an aspect of the history of art but rather as a study of the organization of the world in relation to the needs of man.[1] This implies rewriting the history of architecture so as to trace, civilization by civilization, century by century, all the human activities which went into the making of townscapes and suburbs. What interests us is not the work of the individual architect but architectural *ensembles*, the character of the towns in which a man can live, rediscover his real roots and assert his individuality.

The word 'rediscover' is not inapt, since something has disappeared which we must find again if man is to recover the equilibrium which, for some decades past, he has lost and to which he anxiously continues to aspire.

The appearance, in any civilization, of a rift between the artist and the critic, the culture of the past and of the present, is invariably symptomatic of a certain lack of sanity, inimical both to creative activity and to a proper understanding of the past. Such a rift has unfortunately existed for the past fifty years, despite all the praiseworthy efforts made by certain outstanding people to heal it.

---

1. cf. the definition given by Morris in 1881: the sum total of the changes and modifications made to the surface of the earth in accordance with human needs.

THE EDUCATION OF THE ARCHITECT

It is clear from recent history that one of the chief dangers stems from nationalism in art.

Splitting history up according to geographical divisions fails to take account of the links which have always existed between civilizations, and creates the false impression of a series of isolated, mysteriously labyrinthine worlds, an impression which does not stand up to critical examination.

The history of architecture cannot be divorced from art criticism, any more than authentic culture can be divorced from life: in fact no phenomena can be considered in isolation.

Similarly, the new study of the history of architecture must cover the monuments of the past as well as those of today.

We need to evolve a new method of interdisciplinary research, giving due prominence to certain features of special importance for town planning, and indicating how the methods used in ancient times for the distribution of limited architectural space can be applied in planning urban agglomerations in the modern world. We need, further, to revive our awareness of the aesthetic values of fabrics, of the architectural arrangement of space, of materials and colours. And this entails taking fresh stock of the whole subject.

History should be taught as follows in faculties of architecture:

History of architecture, combined with a study of art criticism and general art history without forgetting poetry and music, and concentrating on the artist as a product of a specific period and civilization.

The purpose is to give future architects a keener appreciation of the beauty of forms, shapes, dimensions and colours.

Historical development of architecture including political background, town planning, and a detailed study of specific periods.

Co-operation with other disciplines will inevitably alter history teaching which, instead of concentrating on facts, kings and wars, will survey the structure of society and the development of thought, social conditions, production, human relations, the law and contemporary ideals.

The purpose of architecture is to impose order on man's surroundings, and provide him with a suitable setting. This involves certain cultural, technological and spiritual options, and certain modifications to the landscape.

History of architectural techniques: basic principles of architecture, surveying of monuments, social and economic aspects, town planning.

Surveying and drawing are related, both involving skills to be learned and providing opportunities for architectural composition.

In relation to town planning, architectural surveying has a slightly different purpose; for a precise knowledge of the general layout of cities, based on an imaginative reconstruction of individual monuments, is essential in any restoration of historical sites.

The teaching of architecture must be reorganized accordingly. This is the only way to meet the demand now being made on schools of architecture: to improve the quality of teaching and turn out more architects qualified to work on town planning, and urban and rural building projects.

There is a steady increase in the number of young people, all over the world, who are selecting architecture as a career, but it would be no solution to turn out large numbers of mediocre architects, who are unable to solve the problems of today, let alone those of the world of tomorrow.

In addition to their strictly professional training, architects should be acquainted with the multifarious aspects of human life, and the eternal sources of human hopes and suffering. They are called upon to add to man's artistic heritage, and the sum of human knowledge and understanding.

We should take as a warning the words of one of the great masters of modern architecture, Louis Sullivan:

'...If, as I believe, true culture is of the utmost utility, in that it implies the possession and application of the finest powers of thought, imagination and sympathy, then the works of a cultured man should reflect his culture in a way that proves that he has used it for his people, and not for his own ends alone: for the welfare and enlightenment of the people as a whole, and not for the enrichment of a single class.

'The work of a man of culture should, in short, prove (and it is incumbent on him to produce the proof) that he is a citizen, not a slave; a true exponent of democracy.... There can, in a democracy, be only one question to which the citizen is required to reply: how do you use the capacities you possess, for the people or against them?'

It is to this 'true culture' that we should aspire. And, for this, we must not be afraid to turn to history: far from being an obstacle or an impediment, it can render an immense service to those who are capable of using it as a means of widening their horizons and increasing their understanding; those who are able to discern, in day-to-day happenings, the eternal pattern linking present and past; those who have learnt from history not to be afraid of looking far ahead, and understood that history is the only means to commanding a broader vision, a wider view, thinking with dignity and acting with courage: the only path, in fact, that leads to hope.

Training of architect-restorers

Arrangements for the post-graduate training of architects intending to specialize in restoration were, until a few years ago, highly unsatisfactory in all countries.

Regional schools may be important, but they are less so than the development of a small group of really first-class schools, so placed geographically as to be able to cater for the world's needs. Rationally this would mean having one such school in each of the following: Far East, Middle East, Near East, Latin America, North America.

International facilities

The Faculty of Architecture of the University of Rome has offered graduate courses in restoration for several years. But it was not until 1965 when a co-operative arrangement was worked out with the Rome Centre[1] that the courses assumed an international character. The centre supervises the programme of studies of the foreign students; lectures are given by members of the faculty and other specialists from Italy and abroad.

Courses are held in Italian, French and English, and written summaries are provided. Simultaneous interpretation was begun in 1970.

The syllabus is in five parts as follows.

Theory and methods of conservation and restoration
1. Introduction.
    (a) Historical survey of the restoration of monuments in different civilizations.
    (b) Ethical value of historical monuments in modern civilization.
2. Methodical study of edifices from the historical, artistic and technical viewpoint.
3. General principles for the conservation and restoration of works of art.
4. Theory and methodology of the conservation of monuments; special theory of restoration.

Urban and rural architectural units, including sites and monuments, with an introduction to the conception of active conservation measures
1. Historical centres and town planning.
    (a) Introduction to methodology.

1. The International Centre for the Restoration and Preservation of Cultural Property, familiarly known as 'The Rome Centre', was established by Unesco and the Government of Italy in 1959 and ten years later had about fifty member States.

(b) Saving and reconstituting historical centres; social, legal and administrative problems.

(c) Making methodological analyses of and assembling documentation on historical centres.

(d) Cleaning up historical centres.

2. Historical and natural landscapes.

(a) Protection of landscapes and natural settings.

(b) Presentation of archaeological and pre-historic sites.

(c) Upkeep and reconstitution of gardens.

3. Monuments.

(a) Conservation and restoration of monuments.

(b) Utilization of ancient edifices.

(c) Setting up museums inside historical monuments; museology.

Technical aspects of conservation and restoration, technological research, documentation and scientific research

1. Causes of the deterioration of monuments.

2. Stability of monuments and means for consolidating them.

3. Ancient and modern technology of structures and building materials.

(a) Mediterranean region.

(b) Central and northern Europe.

(c) Tropical countries.

(d) Middle East.

(e) Far East.

4. Diseases of building materials and care of these materials.

(a) Stone.

(b) Baked clay, mortar and plaster.

(c) Wood.

(d) Metals.

5. Laboratory techniques.

6. Special practical problems and techniques.

(a) Ground and foundations.

(b) Humidity in buildings and methods for remedying it.

(c) Protection against vibrations.

(d) Protection against biological agents (vegetation, insects).

(e) Protection against fire.

7. Archaeological research.

(a) Excavation methods.

(b) Methods for taking soundings and borings.

8. Technique of topographical and architectural surveys.

9. Photogrammetry.

(a) Theory.

(b) Exercises and practical applications.

10. Use of aerial photography in archaeology and the study of monuments.

11. Methods of conservation and restoration of mural paintings, stained-glass windows and articles of furniture.

(a) Mural paintings.

(b) Stained-glass windows and articles of furniture.

Legislation covering conservation and restoration operations, international activities and administrative organization

1. Principles of legal protection and comparative law.

2. Administrative principles.

3. International regulations governing artistic heritage.

4. Drafting specifications and organization of work.

Practical work

1. Study a monument and prepare a survey of it.

2. Assist in making borings and carrying out excavations, under the supervision of a specialist.

3. Visit monuments and restoration workshops, under the supervision of professors or assistants.

4. Spend periods doing practical work in a restoration workshop.

There can be no doubt that the establishment of this school responds to a real deeply felt need in all countries for people qualified to deal with problems arising in connexion with the care of monuments. The extension of the Rome facilities and regional schools would be a logical development under Unesco's universal mandate for the protection of cultural property and would, at the same time, help to meet a responsibility which our civilization owes to the future.

RECOMMENDATIONS OF A COMMITTEE OF EXPERTS

The lack of qualified personnel and the need to establish standards for training to meet the requirements of today resulted in Unesco convening a meeting of experts in Pistoia (Italy), from 9 to 12 September 1968. The meeting included representatives from many countries and from many of the leading institutions where architectural restoration is taught. Its Chairman was Professor de Angelis d'Ossat of Rome. It made a number of recommendations:

1. The tendency to drop architectural history should be reversed. Courses should give due attention to the social and historical changes which accompanied architectural changes in design.
2. Town-planning courses should cover the historical development of urbanization and problems of integrating new and old buildings in town-planning schemes.
3. Courses should include not only techniques of conserving old buildings, but analyses of actual projects for the preservation and adaptation of historic quarters to meet contemporary social and economic conditions.

It was considered desirable to have specialized degrees for architect-restorers, who should not only be familiar with contemporary building techniques and materials, and historical methods, but a proper understanding of urban problems. Apprenticeship under an experienced architect-restorer was necessary in view of the multiple problems which a single monument might involve before a satisfactory solution could be found.

The committee further emphasized the continual need for skilled artisans. Craftsmen were gradually becoming rare, as modern building techniques tended to demand less manual skill. Several countries had had to train special teams who would be permanently available for restoration work.

The following resolutions were adopted.[1]

1. Training of architects and town planners in general

Considering that historic monuments and sites are to a large extent, and in most countries of the world, part and parcel of the living architectural background of the inhabitants,
Considering that the preservation and development of that background, including the landscape, are mainly the responsibility of architects and town planners,
Recommends that training in architecture and town planning include the teaching of history and the humanities, whereby all architects and town planners may learn to appreciate the importance of preserving the heritage of monuments and landscapes and to recognize the value of their specific features,
Recommends that the curriculum of all schools of architecture include a thorough education in the preservation of historic sites and monuments, the history of art, the history of architecture and architectural techniques, and the history of town planning and of the development of landscapes and gardens.

2. Training of specialized architects

Considering that the preservation, restoration and presentation of monuments and of historic gardens and sites form a separate discipline,
Recommends
(1) That the preservation, restoration and presentation of historic sites and monuments be entrusted exclusively to specially trained

---

1. The full report was published by Unesco under the title: *Final Report of the Meeting of Experts to Study the Problems Involved in the Training of Architects and Technicians Responsible for the Preservation of Monuments and Sites* (Unesco doc. SHC/MD/2 of 24 January 1969).

experts, so as to guarantee that work on monuments will in no way impair their value;

(2) That closer collaboration be developed between architects and specialists in other university disciplines concerned with preserving the heritage of monuments, such as: town planners, art historians, archaeologists, engineers, chemists, physicists, etc., by directing or supplementing their training to meet preservation requirements;

(3) That specialized courses of a post-graduate type be extended or introduced at national or regional level and at the international level.

3. Training of craftsmen and foremen

Considering that the training of specialized architects would lose something of its effectiveness without the existence of a number of craftsmen capable of interpreting the architects' directives correctly,

Considering that the existing trend of architectural techniques is leading to the gradual disappearance of most of the traditional building crafts,

Recommends the training, both theoretical and practical, of site foremen and craftsmen belonging to the various disciplines of traditional architecture.

4. Arrangements for financing and for exchanges of teachers, architects and technicians

Expresses the hope that Member States, with a view to ensuring the implementation of the proposals set forth in the foregoing paragraphs, will make adequate financial means available to appropriate institutions and individuals for the creation of study and travel grants and for exchanges of teachers, architects and technicians.

5. Preparing public opinion

Considering that the preservation, in all its forms, of a nation's heritage of monuments depends mainly on the interest taken in it by the population,

Recommends that Member States have recourse to such forms of publicity as are needed to make the public aware of the importance of preserving and enhancing its heritage of monuments.

It may be noted that the meeting did not anticipate any slackening in the demand for qualified personnel. On the contrary, social and economic changes are taking place so rapidly that, provided programmes are undertaken to ensure that the cultural heritage will be preserved, the need for staff will continue at least at the same level in the foreseeable future.

Hiroshi Daifuku

Summary and discussion 13

Historically and artistically important buildings have been disappearing at an ever-increasing rate during the twentieth century. In part such destruction or wear is due to natural process in which stone is converted to gravel, sands, clays and earth; timber to humus; metals to oxides and salts. Geological and climatological factors, bacteria, fungi and the higher plants degrade such materials in their natural state as well as when they are found in buildings. Moreover, industrial wastes, in which acids, salts, and many organic compounds are introduced into the atmosphere and water supplies, attack monuments as much as they affect the biosphere adversely.

Objects in museums can be kept and shown under optimal conditions in which temperature, humidity and light conditions are stable. Very fragile objects can be further isolated in hermetically sealed containers, filled with an inert gas to replace the comparatively corrosive gases of the atmosphere. It is impractical to utilize such methods for larger cultural property such as historic buildings or monuments. On the other hand, technical advances for the conservation of cultural property have been developed over the years. Methods and standards have been steadily developing.

Cataclysms have taken their toll. Floods, earthquakes, volcanic eruptions, violent storms have levelled or destroyed many important structures in the long history of human civilization. Nevertheless, the most serious threat is man. Wars, the action of vandals, even neglect, have razed countless monuments; and economic and social factors pose the biggest challenge to the conservation of our material cultural heritage.

The rising price of desirable urban real estate, the cost of paying skilled craftsmen to carry out conservation or restoration work on buildings made before power tools existed, means that it is frequently less expensive to destroy groups of historically or artistically important buildings and replace them with ones of contemporary design, than to restore or adapt them to meet acceptable standards of lighting, sanitation, and so on. Thus it happens that a scheduled monument remains, but bereft of the buildings which were historically associated with it, and surrounded and dwarfed by high buildings.

ADMINISTRATION AND LEGISLATION

To be successful, conservation programmes must be planned on a broad scale and involve both the public and the private sectors. This may need enabling legislation. In many countries the required laws and budgets have been adopted. An excellent source for such legislation is provided by the International Recommendation for the Preservation of Cultural Property Endangered by Public and Private Works, adopted by the Unesco General Conference in November 1968.

Zoning laws help to ensure the preservation of historically interesting buildings and control the types of new construction that may be permitted. Positive measures must also be taken to encourage proprietors, whether private, institutional or municipal, e.g. tax concessions; long-term interest loans (or even grants); technical advice at nominal cost or free of charge, to ensure that the highest possible standards are maintained.

Many countries have national services and quasi-governmental agencies such as national trusts or associations which, frequently, can be called upon for aid and advice.

In countries undergoing rapid development, over-population, the need to improve agricultural production, or adapt industrial technology to meet their own requirements, and so on, constitute additional factors to be considered, and mean that conservation has to produce economic justification to a much higher degree than elsewhere. One solution is to consider monuments and sites as part of the investment required for tourist development—a solution also favoured in many of the more advanced countries.

RESTORATION PRINCIPLES

It is gradually becoming an agreed principle that buildings and monuments, just as much as paintings and sculpture, should no longer be restored in such a way that all traces of age and of the work of original artists disappear.

Discreet methods are used to enable an observer to distinguish between the original and the restored areas; increasing use is made of laboratory analysis and of new chemical products. Even in presentation, just as museums try to set outstanding works of art on exhibition against a suitable background, the architect responsible for restoration today no longer concentrates exclusively on a monument, but also pays attention to environment; he tries to preserve its surroundings, so that old associations are maintained and the scale of the monument is preserved.

Nevertheless, there are striking differences between the conservation of art and the conservation of monuments.

Most buildings, whether or not classified, are something more and something less than a work of art. They were constructed to be used. A cathedral, for example, may have had to be enlarged and may have undergone repairs and additions in different styles; if these are harmonious they may well be preserved. In contrast, in restoring Leonardo da Vinci's *Last Supper*, for example, an attempt was made to remove all accretions and the effects of earlier restorations, so as to expose as much as possible of the artist's original work; restoration was limited to careful insertions to make up the lacunae which would have destroyed the composition. This principle (with few exceptions) is followed in restoring smaller works of art.

As indicated above, even when it has been decided which parts of a monument will be preserved, the sheer mass of a large structure imposes many more compromises than does a physically smaller object. Thus conservation frequently represents a less rigorous process for monuments than for smaller objects, although ideally, this should not be so.

As a building has to serve practical needs, electricity, running water, central heating, sanitary facilities, air conditioning, and so on, may have to be installed—no one, for example, expects to see liveried footmen in an historic monument pushing about portable sanitary facilities as they would have done in Versailles under Louis XIV. If a palace is converted into a museum, government offices, a library, a hotel, or put to some other use, the necessary alterations again represent a deviation from the original plan of the structure. This sort of problem does not of course arise in the case of a work of art.

Budget problems, social prejudices, variations in taste and so on all complicate the task of the agencies or experts who must persuade public authorities and owners that restoration has to respect the historical and aesthetic values a monument acquires through the passage of time.

However, the restorer can now call upon a growing body of scientific data on building materials, and very useful products are available to him. There are various publications to inform him of new discoveries and development, and to report on the work of specialized national and international organizations. Accordingly, when he has to incorporate modifications in an old building, he no longer has to rely on intuition or guesswork, but can study the technical details of solutions which have stood the test of time.

Of course, there are really no hard and fast rules in this work, and there can be considerable variations in the manner and degree of restoration. Hence a possible dichotomy: the architect considers himself free to alter or remove anything he finds anachronistic or displeasing, and to add whatever he considers appropriate;[1] or he keeps strictly to historical accuracy and makes no attempt to adapt the monument in order to fit it for new practical uses.

Such extreme positions still exist. In practice, however, historically interesting buildings which are not classified and can be adapted for contemporary use can be restored under less intransigent conditions and still respect the intentions and designs of the original builders. Run-down residential quarters whose formerly pleasant homes have degenerated into grubby tenements, shops, ateliers and bars, are now often purchased and imaginatively restored. A marked change occurs in the whole socio-economic environment.

Restoration can easily be overdone in the case of archaeological monuments whose only function is to bear witness to a past civilization or culture. Modern surveying instruments used in the reconstruction of a mound or temple impose strict geometric controls on the craftsmen doing the work— and the resultant structure then gives a false impression of the knowledge of geometric principles and of the level of techniques used by the original builders, and

the visitor gets the impression that he is visiting a monument built yesterday. A stupa which has survived in brick and stone with fragmentary remnants of plaster can be simply consolidated; or it can have a thick layer of lime plaster added, so that little is left to the imagination of the visitor and, again, any impression of age is eradicated. It would be preferable, in many such instances, just to consolidate the ruins; in a nearby museum, models, charts and diagrams could be used to illustrate the archaeological history of the site and display items recovered during excavations.

In many countries, religious property is not controlled by the State or subject to regulations governing the preservation of restoration of historic structures. Thus, even when a church or temple is historically or artistically important, or is a key element in the architectural composition of a square or of a group of buildings, the religious or lay authorities may decide to demolish it in favour of a new modern structure, or carry out radical alterations which affect the basic elements of the building and change its appearance. Similar results may follow when a local population, exposed to the cheapest products of modern industry, 'modernize' an old historic religious structure, using plastic paints, linoleum, aluminium, neon lighting, and so on, producing a tawdry and vulgar degradation of what had once been charming and interesting. When people later become more sophisticated, it is necessarily more complicated and expensive to remove such accretions and restore the 'modernized' areas.

VARIATIONS ON A THEME

The partial or total destruction of a group of historically important buildings and monuments by fire, earthquake, vandalism or war

1. cf. the 'free though imitative elaborations on a theme' referred to by P. Gazzola in speaking of Viollet-le-Duc.

263

poses problems of a different nature. Decisions taken differ widely and social, historical or political factors may enter in, in addition to the question of cost.

The Soviet Union had a long-term programme for the restoration of monuments damaged during the Second World War. To restore the Summer Palace near Leningrad, to take one example, workmen had to be specially trained in parquetry, damask weaving, and other forgotten skills.

The complete destruction of the Stare Miasto, the old town of Warsaw, posed other problems. The individual buildings were not in themselves outstanding, but the complex as such warranted monumental status and classification. Alternatives were considered, such as completing the demolition and constructing new buildings of contemporary design. However, the final decision was to restore. Architectural drawings had been made for decades by students from the architectural school as experience in the preparation of line drawings—in addition to the Canaletto paintings —which served as a guide in reconstructing Warsaw as it appeared in the eighteenth century.

A different decision was taken in the case of Coventry cathedral in England. Except for the steeple, the building was destroyed by bombing. After considering various alternatives, the final decision was to retain the steeple as a memorial, set in a garden, and to put up a new contemporary building to one side of the garden.

The Kinkaku (Golden) pavilion of the Rokuon-ji Temple in Kyoto (Japan), posed another type of problem. It was burned to the ground by an act of vandalism. It stood in a garden overlooking a pond, surrounded by carefully selected rocks and trees, and the pavilion and its setting was considered to be one of the masterpieces of Japanese architecture and landscape gardening. Complete and detailed records existed, and it was decided to build a replica in its place. Today the pavilion stands as the original did, in the fourteenth century, the interior resplendent in its coat of gold leaf, bright and airy, the culminating expression of Japanese architecture during the Muromachi period. Yet, there was a good deal of controversy before it was rebuilt. The original structure, its wooden elements silver-grey with age, just bearing traces of gold leaf which gave it its name, belonged to the setting in an association which had lasted for centuries. The new is imposed—although without it, the composition of the carefully planned whole, following aesthetic principles which are still valid today, would have lost its central feature.

COMMON PROBLEMS

Insufficient budgets and a shortage of qualified personnel are among the most common problems. Increasing attention is now being given to these questions (see table 1).

Conservation measures are not always successful. For example, measures are frequently taken to lower the moisture content in an old building in order to inhibit the growth of bacteria, moulds, lichens, termites and other pests and prevent the introduction of salts through capillarity in a stone or masonry structure. But the resulting change in the micro-climate may cause shrinkage (see *Plate 37*) and warping in wooden structures; dried-out foundations may cause settling and result in the splitting of stone or brick walls.

Products which seem very promising under laboratory conditions may prove harmful in use. An outstanding example was the early use of silicones as a consolidant and water-proofing agent for masonry. The impermeable film created on the surface retained moisture within the stone or brick and, in due course, the considerable pressure that developed caused spalling, so that the surface of the brick or stone was much more damaged than if it had not been treated at all.

Thus, a word of caution is necessary. The rapid and urgently required expansion of

TABLE 1. Comparison of financial appropriations for conservation

Country	1963		1968	
	Amount in local currency	Equivalent in $U.S.[1]	Amount in local currency	Equivalent in $U.S.[2]
Austria	8 300 000 schillings	321 331.78	17 350 000 schillings	671 699.50
Bulgaria	1 000 000 leva	854 700.85	2 400 000 leva	1 200 000.00
Czechoslovakia	75 000 000 Czech crowns	10 416 666.66	135 000 000 Czech crowns	9 401 114.20
Denmark	220 000 kroner	31 851.74	1 625 000 kroner	216 666.67
Finland	1 067 949 Finnish marks	333 734.06	1 405 376 Finnish marks	334 613.33
France	60 000 000 francs	12 244 897.95	70 000 000 francs	14 285 714.28
Federal Republic of Germany	22 806 905 German marks	5 701 726.25	20 313 471 German marks	5 078 367.75
Ghana	7750 new cedis	10 851.30	27 399 new cedis	26 861.76
Hungary	41 157 000 forints	1 752 853.40	57 000 000 forints	1 900 000.00
Italy	607 000 000 lire	977 455.71	5 631 491 000 lire	9 010 385.60
Netherlands	17 300 000 florins	4 779 005.50	32 200 000 florins	8 944 444.44
Sweden	325 000 Swedish kronor	62 826.21	555 000 Swedish kronor	107 558.14
Turkey	22 330 000 Turkish pounds	2 481 111.11	31 700 000 Turkish pounds	3 522 222.22

1. As at 1963.
2. As at 1968.

conservation programmes at a time when skilled personnel with long experience are in short supply poses severe problems which, unfortunately, it will take time to solve.

SHOWING MONUMENTS

Son et lumière (light and sound) techniques are now widely used to give visitors an impressionistic description of the cultural life and the historical personages associated with particular monuments. Tape recordings of texts and music are used with spotlighting and flood-lights. The first such programme was made for the Château de Chambord in France. It has had many successors—the Château de Versailles, Château de Vincennes, the Red Fort in Delhi, and so on.

Changing social conditions may demand a special kind of presentation. For example, most Americans are not descended from the original settlers, but from those who came during a series of immigrations during the nineteenth century. The clothing, manner of life and customs of the early settlers are thus completely foreign to the average American. To give them an understanding of the culture of the seventeenth and eighteenth centuries in certain historic show-places, guides are dressed in period costumes, taverns and restaurants are reconstituted in which the food and drinks are based on early recipes, re-built smithies produce souvenirs and so on—so that the centre is a cross between a 'historic quarter' and an open-air museum. It may be that, as regional and folk traditions break down, similar methods will be necessary in Europe and in Asia within a generation or two.

In any case, public support is essential. The day is long past when the appreciation of the beauty of a monument—bridge, aqueduct, temple platform, building—and of its historical role and associations, was the monopoly of a few. Educational programmes are necessary, apart from what can be achieved by television, press, films and books. Whether a monument serves as a backdrop to a pageant, or is the featured object in a *son et lumière* programme, the interest and support of an enlightened public is the surest guarantee of the continued survival of our material cultural heritage.

SOCIAL ENVIRONMENT

As urban change, provoked by demographic and economic pressures, accelerates, viable neighbourhoods are increasingly threatened by development projects, by new zoning regulations that encourage commercial and industrial undertakings, and so on. In many cities, they were formerly communities that had existed as independent social organisms for many generations. Patterns of mutual responsibility and of social obligations existed. Their removal and replacement by high buildings may have resulted in a more 'efficient' use of valuable urban real estate. On the other hand, all too frequently, the changes have not produced a new viable social unit to replace the old. Indifference and social disorganization follow, and the end result is a loss to the society as a whole.

Unfortunately, not nearly enough is known about the social and psychological consequences of radical changes in the urban environment. Greater prudence is called for. While many groups of old buildings which are dilapidated or unhealthy might be destroyed, those which are basically sound or which in addition have historic interest, could more profitably be improved and brought up to contemporary standards. A large city could have many such neighbourhoods that would provide transitional zones and a large measure of social and cultural stability.

Finally, the increasing standardization which results from mass-production techniques means that new developments everywhere tend to resemble one another. High buildings and mass housing develop-

Plate 37

Changes in the micro-climate of a structure may
also result in damage. A modern heating system
installed in an eighteenth-century wooden
building separated dove-tailed joints and some
had nearly reached the point of total failure.
It was necessary to expose the joints, pull the
structure together and refasten them
(Photos: United States National Park Service.)

ments are found everywhere, so that the
modern sections of Tokyo, London, New
York, New Delhi, resemble each other more
than they do in the older quarters within
their respective boundaries. Traditional
architectural patterns developed over the
course of generations in relative isolation
have produced marked differences between
one place and another. Preservation programmes should help to perpetuate urban
variety and maintain continuity between
the present and past generations.